Evolutionary Language Understanding

COMMUNICATION IN ARTIFICIAL INTELLIGENCE SERIES

Artificial Intelligence (AI) is a central aspect of Fifth Generation computing, and it is now increasingly recognized that a particularly important element of AI is communication. This series addresses current issues, emphasizing generation as well as comprehension in the AI communication. It covers communication of three types: at the human–computer interface; in computer–computer communication that simulates human interaction; and in the use of computers for machine translation to assist human–human communication. The series also gives a place to research that extends beyond language to consider other systems of communication that humans employ such as pointing, and even in due course, facial expression, body posture, etc.

Communication in Artificial Intelligence Series Editors:
Robin P. Fawcett, Computational Linguistics Unit, University of Wales College of Cardiff
Erich H. Steiner, IAI EUROTRA-D and University of the Saarland

From Syntax to Semantics: Insights from Machine Translation, eds: Erich Steiner, Paul Schmidt and Cornelia Zelinsky-Wibbelt

Advances in Natural Language Generation: An Interdisciplinary Perspective, 2 vols, eds: Michael Zock and Gerard Sabah

Text Generation and Systemic-Functional Linguistics: Experiences from English and Japanese, Christian M.I.M. Matthiessen and John A. Bateman

Expressibility and the Problem of Efficient Text Planning, Marie W. Meteer

Linguistic Issues in Machie Translation, ed.: Frank Van Eynde

New Concepts in Natural Language Generation: Planning, Realization and Systems, eds: Helmut Horacek and Michael Zock

User Modelling in Text Generation, Cecile L. Paris

Text Knowledge and Object Knowledge, Annely Rothkegel

Evolutionary Language Understanding, Geoffrey Sampson

Evolutionary Language Understanding

Geoffrey Sampson

CASSELL

Cassell
Wellington House, 125 Strand, London WC2R 0BB
215 Park Avenue South, New York, NY 10003

© Geoffrey Sampson 1996

All rights reserved. No part of this publication may be reproduced or transmitted in any form or by any means, electronic or mechanical, including photocopying, recording or any information storage or retrieval system, without permission in writing from the publishers.

British Library Cataloguing in Publication Data
A catalogue record for this book is available from the British Library

ISBN 0 304 33650 5

Library of Congress Cataloging-in-Publication Data
Sampson, Geoffrey.
    Evolutionary language understanding / Geoffrey Sampson.
      p. cm. – (Communication in artificial intelligence series)
    Includes bibliographical references and index.
    ISBN 0-304-33650-5
    1. English language – Data processing. I. Title. II. Series: Communication in artificial intelligence.
PE 1074.5.S364   1996
006.3'5–dc20   95-41537
                                                                     CIP

Printed and bound in Great Britain by Biddles Limited, Guildford and King's Lynn

Contents

Acknowledgements		vii
1	Prologue	1
2	The Origin of the Task	4
3	Simulating Evolution	30
4	An Early System	53
5	The Current System: Goals and Standards	84
6	The Current System: Front End and Parsing Algorithms	102
7	The Current System: Language Model	129
8	Parallel Tree Optimization	157
9	Epilogue	182
References		186
Index		193

Acknowledgements

My first debt of gratitude is to John Bridle (now of Dragon Systems UK) and Roger Moore (of DRA Malvern), who saw the research reported here as worthy of support at a time when few others shared that view.

The fact that we have come as far as we have in eight years is due to the hard work and ability of my current researchers, Miles Dennis and Alan Wallington, and of their predecessors. Among the latter I must mention by name Robin Haigh, who has put more man-years of thought and effort into parsing by simulated annealing than any other individual to date. I am deeply grateful to all those who have participated in the project at different periods.

Sometimes the research has benefited greatly from people not formally attached to the project who have been willing to share their time with us out of the kindness of their heart. We would particularly like to thank Gareth Richards and Chris Booth, and Malcolm McIlhagga, for much advice and help with the transputer/Occam environment, and C and the Sussex computing environment, respectively.

I am grateful to Paul Gregory and David Bounds for inviting me to spend several months with the Research Initiative in Pattern Recognition; to the various agencies, identified in the book, who have supported the research financially; and to the University of Sussex for granting the leave which has allowed this book to be written.

Material from the journal *Literary and Linguistic Computing* is reprinted by permission of Oxford University Press, and material from the *Journal of Experimental and Theoretical Artificial Intelligence* is reprinted by permission of Taylor & Francis.

Geoffrey Sampson
Heathfield, Sussex
December 1995

1 Prologue

In early 1986, I was living in a converted barn high on a hillside above the hidden Yorkshire valley of Lothersdale; from my study I looked across to the house on the far slope where Charlotte Brontë's work as a governess had led to the writing of *Jane Eyre*. That winter was bitterly cold; much of my electronic data was destroyed, the magnetic patterns literally frozen out of the floppy disks. But my current project was progressing despite such setbacks. One January evening, the software coding complete, I set up my computer to begin a first trial run before leaving to drive my family to a New Year party in the village: I knew that, if the machine achieved anything, it would need hours to do it. Very late that night, bed beckoning, I looked in on the computer to shut it down. Sheet after sheet of intermediate results trailed on fanfold paper from the printer, and there at the end was the final output I had hoped to see. For the first time ever, a machine had been set to understand human language by a radically novel technique – to evolve an analysis by the method of random mutation and selection of fitter alternatives that Nature uses to evolve new species; and the technique had worked.

This book is about the programme of research which has grown out of that piece of beginner's luck in 1986. What began as a project done by one university teacher on a home micro in his spare time is now a research programme sponsored for hundreds of thousands of pounds by bodies such as the UK Engineering and Physical Sciences Research Council and the Ministry of Defence; at various stages it has employed a total of about a dozen researchers, working with a network of state-of-the-art computing equipment. Furthermore, while our approach was initially seen by most of the rest of the research community as too self-evidently misguided to take seriously, quite quickly views have changed: a few years later, academics who were among our most outspoken critics began to announce changes of heart and to take up positions not too far from ours. Evolutionary language understanding is beginning to look like a technology with a bright future.

The discipline within which the work described here is situated has come to be known, perhaps more frequently in Europe than in North America, as *language engineering*. The implications of the word 'engineering' are significant. The study of computing machinery and its uses is normally called 'computer science', but a better phrase might be 'computer engineering', since it is concerned with techniques for managing and deploying resources of known properties to achieve practical results. Not much of 'computer science' is about discovering laws of Nature.

In the past, computational approaches to 'natural language' – human languages such as English, German, Japanese – have often been seen as an exception. Language is obviously a leading manifestation of the distinctively intellectual nature of our species, and researchers have seen the development of computational models of natural language as a technique for studying the nature of human cognition. The programme of work reported in the following chapters has not been conducted in that spirit. It may be located at the 'researchy', intellectually innovative end of the language engineering spectrum, but it is intended as an engineering exercise, aiming to develop reliable systems for executing practically useful functions related to natural language. In so far as humans can be said to execute the same functions, there is no suggestion that they do it in the same way.

The idea that studying the behaviour of the glorified calculating machines we call computers can explain the cognitive life of creatures endowed with the divine spark of creativity tends to be most persuasive to people whose direct experience of computers is fairly limited. At an early stage of my career I imagined it might be true myself. Some decades later, I no longer believe the two topics have much to do with one another; but this does not matter – it is clear that computers can be successfully harnessed to execute various economically useful language processing tasks, without our needing to enquire how people process language.

The pages that follow describe the internal structure and some of the intermediate results of a developing system of natural language processing (NLP) software. In describing these things and how they have developed, I have found it unnatural to exclude all mention of contingent features of the research situation which happened to lead the work in one direction rather than another, or of intellectual errors on my own part which sometimes retarded progress or even put it temporarily into reverse. Like Imre Lakatos (e.g. 1976: 142–3 n. 2), I believe the habit of suppressing allusions to such matters in academic writing is misleading, in that it lends an air of unchallengeable authority to activities that in reality are fallible. It appears to place the academic author in the role of judge; but the individual author can only act as witness and as advocate – the roles of judge and jury necessarily belong, collectively, to the readers.

I hope that occasional references to our external circumstances and internal errors may not only help readers to understand why we did what we did, but may also make the book more readable. If some readers care to penetrate deeper below the surface of our intellectual activities, they can. It happens that the research programme to be described here caught the attention of a sociologist of science, Greg Myers, who with our permission decided to use it as a case study of interpersonal and communicative relationships within a successful computational research project. I personally have found it an intriguing experience to contemplate the texture of my own working life through an outsider's eyes, and I commend Myers' article (Myers 1991) to others who may be interested.

Readers who would like to know more about the background to the work described here may care to visit the author's World Wide Web site at http://www.cogs.susx.ac.uk/users/geoffs.

2 The Origin of the Task

The Need for Parsing

Getting computers to 'understand' natural languages such as English – whatever it could mean for a machine to understand – is a dream as old as computing itself. The first successful operation of a stored-program electronic computer took place, at the University of Manchester, in June 1948. Within weeks Alan Turing, the mathematician who had as good a claim as anyone to be regarded as the computer's inventor, was drawing up a list of potential uses for his brainchild: the second and third items were 'learning of languages' and 'translation of languages'.

It is not clear what application Turing had in mind when he wrote of computers 'learning languages' – and indeed Turing was probably thinking about tasks designed to explore the abstract concept of computer as man-made intellect, rather than about practical, economically valuable applications of the new machine. But many highly valuable applications involving the processing of natural language have subsequently opened up. Machine translation between natural languages, for instance, has been a routine reality at least in limited contexts since the late 1970s, when the Canadian government began using it as the normal way of translating public weather forecasts into French. Weather forecasts are an unusually favourable case for automatic translation (their vocabulary and grammar are both quite restricted), and although machine translation is nowadays used in a much wider range of commercial and government settings, its performance to date leaves a lot to be desired: commonly computers are used to produce first-draft translations which are then edited into acceptable form by humans. But even this level of success is proving profitable, since it makes the human translator's productivity much greater than in an all-human translation situation; and the level of demand for translation in the modern world is so massive that any contribution by the computer is to be welcomed. (On machine translation – 'MT' – see Hutchins & Somers 1992.)

MT was the first application of automatic natural language processing to become a commercial reality, but by the 1990s many other applications have begun to make the transition from pure research into systems doing economically useful work. Examples would include:

- *database interfaces*, allowing users to put questions to computer systems in plain English and get answers in the same form – either via keyboard and screen, as with systems such as AICorp's 'Intellect', or, even more valuable when it can be achieved, via the spoken medium: the experimental 'Vodis' system sponsored by British Telecom and Logica answers telephone enquiries about train timetables, for instance;
- *speech-to-text* systems, sometimes called 'talkwriters' – Dragon Systems' 'DragonDictate' is a leading current example – which, most basically, enable written documentation to be created automatically through spoken input; companies such as Shakespeare SpeechWriter are embedding the technology in larger software systems to permit a wide range of office-management functions (file retrieval, for instance) to be executed automatically under voice control;
- *message understanding* and *report generation*, whereby a computer will extract usable information from natural language documentation, and arrange information held in a machine-oriented format into a coherent, readable written report;
- *announcement systems*, allowing machines to produce natural-sounding announcements over public-address equipment or the telephone – if the range of announcements is limited enough this is a trivial problem that can be solved with prerecorded human utterances, but if the nature of the application requires speech to be synthesized mechanically at the time of the announcement, current technology is not yet able to make it sound natural rather than stilted and robot-like.

All of these applications are at present in a fairly primitive state of development; natural language processing is an exceedingly difficult technology. But all of them, and others not mentioned here, are already finding markets: there is no lack of demand for the technology, the problems lie with supply. Human beings have an overwhelming preference for spoken and written natural language as their medium for exchanging, storing and processing information, and any technology that enables computer systems to satisfy that preference more fully is unlikely to go short of customers. (For authoritative surveys of the recent scene and likely future prospects in commercial NLP, see Johnson 1985, Engelien & McBryde 1991, or successive issues of the magazine *Language Industry Monitor*.)

Indeed, one kind of 'natural language processing' is easily the most important current application for computers: namely, word processing (WP). The way that word processing has come to overtake all other applications of computers (which were earlier seen as machines primarily for scientific and engineering uses), since they became cheap enough to install in ordinary offices in the early 1980s, perhaps confirms the point that natural language processing is potentially one of the most significant areas of information technology ('IT'). Language is all-important in most aspects of human life, so it is little wonder that it should offer a large scope for exploiting what are inherently general-purpose machines. But word processing is in a different category from all the other NLP applications mentioned above, which explains why it is already a successful going concern whereas the other applications still hover on the margin between research and implementation. Word processing does not require the computer to 'understand' the text in any sense at all. Indeed, for word processing it is unnecessary for the machine even to know what language a text is written in; typical WP operations such as word-wrap at the end of lines, moving or deletion of paragraphs, page numbering, and so on depend on surface properties of texts, such as placement of spaces and carriage-return characters, which are above the level at which one natural language differs from another.

All the applications listed earlier, by contrast, depend on the computer analysing language so as to extract at least some of the internal structural organization which a human listener or reader relies on to understand an utterance or text. In the case of machine translation this is rather obvious. The fundamental problem of machine translation is that a given form in a source language – a word, a grammatical construction, an idiom – typically corresponds to a range of alternative, non-equivalent forms in a target language, and choosing between the alternatives requires the computer to work out how the form fits into its context in the source text. To take a simple example: the English word *round* is a preposition in *He walked round the bush*, a noun in *It's my round next*, an adverb in *Don't try to get straight through, go round*, a verb in *We expect to round the Cape by evening*. Each instance of *round* would correspond to a different translation in French, but to determine which use of *round* a particular instance corresponds to requires one to look at the grammatical properties of the neighbouring words; to resolve all the ambiguities relevant to determining the appropriate translation of a sentence commonly requires one to analyse its grammar – to *parse* it – more or less completely.

But structural analysis turns out to be needed even for applications where its relevance is less apparent. Take the case of text-to-speech systems, where a machine is made to generate spoken announcements from messages in something more similar to their ordinary written form. The unpleasant, robotic monotone flavour of synthesized speech at the present day derives largely from the fact that although the 'segmental' aspects of speech (the vowel and consonant sounds) are produced rather successfully, the systems do not get the variation of pitch and loudness that we call 'intonation' right. Natural intonation is extremely important for an utterance to be acceptable to a human hearer; but intonation patterns are governed by the grammar and semantics of a text, so if a computer cannot handle these aspects of linguistic analysis it cannot hope to produce human-like speech.

Or consider automatic speech recognition, whereby an acoustic speech signal is converted into a sequence of specific words. It might seem that 'understanding' is irrelevant here because all that is needed is to compare the properties of successive segments of the acoustic waveform with the properties specified for the pronunciations of words in an electronic dictionary. But the truth is that the information physically present in a segment of a speech signal representing a word is scarcely ever enough to eliminate all of the vocabulary other than the one word which was actually spoken. Even if one knows where words begin and end in the signal, the most that can be expected from acoustic analysis is to narrow down the possibilities to a small number of similar-sounding words; and, since in practice word-boundaries are themselves not often physically marked, what one usually gets is a lattice of alternative word-hypotheses, with many alternative paths from beginning to end which differ in terms of the number as well as the identity of the words on the respective paths. A human hearer works out the intended words by understanding the utterance, and unconsciously reasoning that if words A, B, C, and D are each compatible with the physical signal at a given point, then C must be the word spoken because A, B, and D are each for one reason or another inappropriate in that context – they would make the utterance ungrammatical, or nonsensical. He 'hears' all the sounds of the word, but what he hears is partly supplied by his knowledge – it comes only partly from the physical signal.

Even word processing, as it becomes more sophisticated, is starting to involve language understanding. Classic WP software allowed a writer to create and modify a document efficiently, and to view and print it in various formats, without contributing anything to the task of composing the text; but at an early stage spelling checkers were added to help people avoid misspellings. These involve no linguistic analysis at all – they just check each text word against an electronic dictionary and flag any word not found. But, recently, this concept of automatic text editing has begun to be extended to the areas of style and grammatical usage, in systems such as Reference Software's 'Grammatik' and Houghton Mifflin's 'CorrecText', and here automatic analysis is clearly necessary. A machine cannot tell that a text contains a grammatical error unless it is capable of achieving at least a limited amount of parsing, although the limitations on the performance of current parsing routines mean that the categories of error handled by the grammar checkers now on the market are themselves quite limited.

Understanding natural language, then, is by common consent a key discipline for the future of information technology, one of the most important frontiers which computer science must somehow transcend if the contribution that computers can make to the work of the world is to become significantly greater than it is at present. Let us not be sidetracked here by the anthropomorphic overtones of the word 'understand'. Computers are only machines, and I am emphatically not one of those who believe that one day, when hardware is sufficiently complex and rapid and software sufficiently sophisticated, the point will come when machines can appropriately be said to possess minds or intelligence in the same sense as humans. The phrase 'artificial intelligence' is to my mind a questionable and potentially misleading one. What we are talking about here is the automatic extraction by a mindless machine, from ordinary speech and written language, of various of the grammatical, semantic, and pragmatic properties by virtue of which humans can understand the language – the kinds of linguistic property which are not relevant for ordinary word processing but are needed for the more sophisticated language processing applications surveyed above. 'Automatic language understanding' is a phrase that has become current for this research domain; in coining terminology for different areas of information technology it is almost unavoidable in practice to borrow words that originally refer to an intelligent human activity that is to some extent analogous. It would be cumbersome and artificial to avoid using the phrase 'language understanding' in connection with the topic of this book, and I shall use it freely; but, to repeat, I know perfectly well that what computers might be made to do with natural language is not at all the same as what humans do.

Central to automatic language understanding is parsing: the automatic assignment, to an example of natural language, of a grammatical analysis, normally in the form of a labelled tree structure showing how the words group into phrase and clause tagmas of various categories.[1] Discovering the grammatical structure of an input is not the only desirable achievement for an automatic language understanding system: for many applications it will also be necessary to decide the meaning in context of ambiguous lexical items, and to establish the pragmatic role played by an utterance in the dynamic relationship between speaker and hearer. But some applications need little more than parsing; and furthermore, many researchers feel that parsing is a precondition for successful automatic analysis at other levels: if a computer cannot get the grammar right it may be unlikely that it could get the pragmatics right. According to K. K. Obermeier (1989: 69), automatic parsing is widely recognized as '[t]he central problem' in virtually all NLP applications.

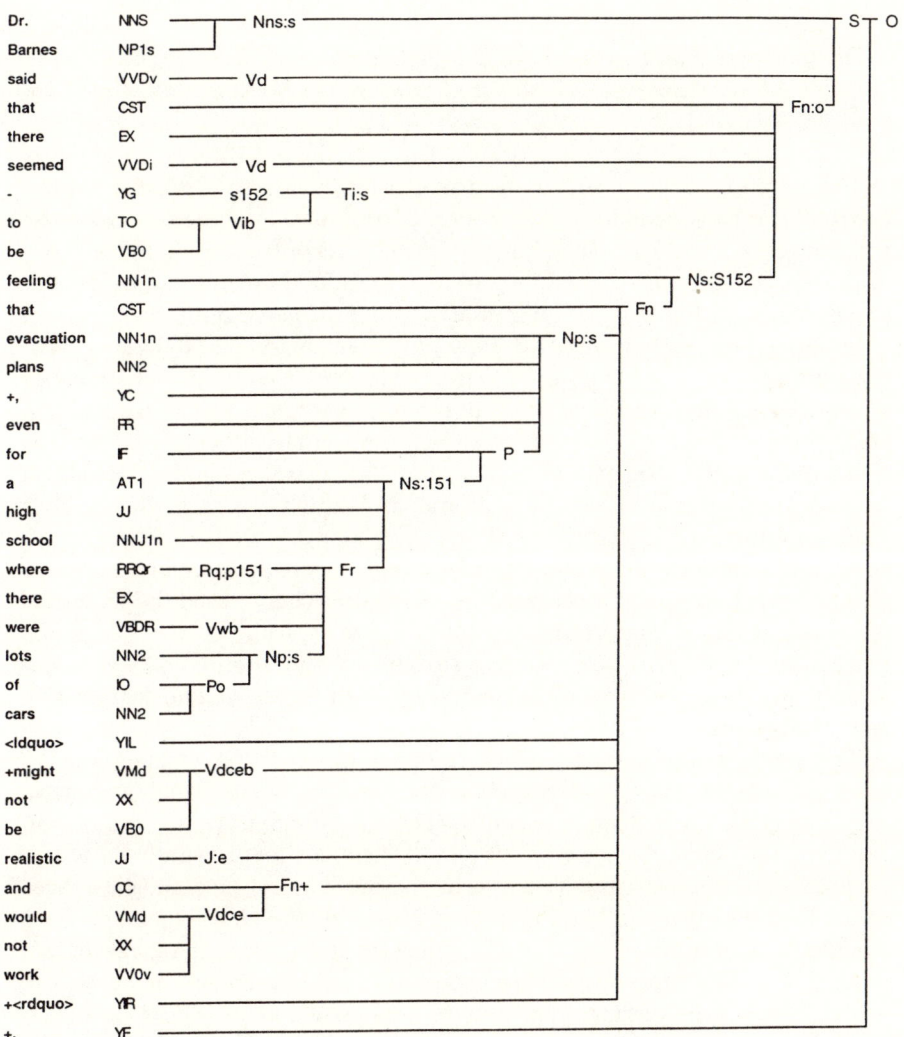

Figure 2.1 A sample English parsetree

As an example, Fig. 2.1 shows a parsetree (extracted from the SUSANNE Corpus discussed in ch. 5 below) for the following sentence, taken from a news item in *The Oregonian* newspaper:

Dr. Barnes said that there seemed to be feeling that evacuation plans, even for a high school where there were lots of cars "might not be realistic and would not work".

The goal of work on automatic parsing systems is to achieve software capable of receiving as inputs examples of a natural language, such as the English sentence just displayed, and producing as outputs analyses of those examples which indicate the kinds of information about the examples that are indicated in Fig. 2.1 (not necessarily using the same notation).

Language researchers usually draw parsetrees with the analysed examples written out horizontally in the ordinary way, and constituency structure indicated by slant lines above the examples. For typographical convenience I have used a different (but notationally equivalent) convention which displays the example vertically, with a parsable unit (normally a word or punctuation mark) on each line, and which 'squares off' the lines indicating the constituency.

To the right of the column of words in Fig. 2.1 are their *wordtags* – codes for grammatically distinct classes of word; in the scheme used, NNS stands for an abbreviated 'noun of style or title' which typically occurs as a prefix in a proper name, NP1s represents a surname in the singular, VVDv represents the past-tense form of a verb having both transitive and intransitive uses, and so on.

The labels within the tree structure to the right of the wordtag column are *tagmatags* – labels for units such as phrases and clauses which in general may comprise more than one word. The entire example is a paragraph (indicated by 'O' at the top right of Fig. 2.1) consisting of a single sentence, S, followed by a full stop (American 'period'). The sentence has three immediate constituents. The tagmatag Nns:s, for *Dr. Barnes,* stands for a singular proper noun phrase functioning as both surface and logical subject of its clause. Vd represents a 'verb group' marked as being in the past tense – a verb group in English can include a sequence of auxiliary verbs and other items as well as a main verb, as in the case *might not be* later in the example, but *said* functions as a one-word verb group. All the rest of the wording, from *that* onwards, is a nominal clause, Fn, functioning as both surface and logical direct object (:o) of *said.*

Within this nominal clause there is a case where logic and surface grammar diverge. The material from *feeling* onwards is a singular noun phrase (Ns) which in surface grammar is functioning as subject of *seemed.*

Logically, though, the long *feeling* phrase is the subject of *to be*, and the *be* clause is the logical subject of *seemed* – what Dr Barnes asserted was an appearance of something, and that something was the existence of a feeling. The index number 152 is used to make this divergence explicit: it shows that the *feeling* phrase, marked ':S' as surface subject of its clause, also has a role as logical subject (s) within the *to be* clause, though it has no physical manifestation in that clause. (For full details on the meanings of the various wordtag and tagmatag elements, see Sampson 1995.)

Not only is parsing as a task central to most NLP applications, it is more clearly defined than other analytic goals: there is a good deal of agreement among researchers about what the correct grammatical analysis of a given sentence ought to look like, but people feel much less certain about how one should appropriately represent lexical meaning or pragmatic force. (Even in the area of grammar there is plenty of disagreement, but often the differences are largely a matter of different notations to represent more or less the same facts; in areas such as lexical semantics or pragmatics, few researchers feel at all confident about what the facts are.) In sum, if we want the benefits of automatic language understanding we have to get automatic parsing right; and for many years now automatic natural language parsing has been the focus of intensive research efforts by many groups throughout the Western world – sometimes in the context of specific applications that depend on the ability to parse text, but often as a freestanding research problem potentially relevant to diverse applications. (For surveys of the topic, see e.g. Reyle & Rohrer 1988, Grune & Jacobs 1990.)

The Compilation Metaphor

These efforts have been dominated by one very powerful intellectual paradigm or metaphor: the *compilation metaphor*. Parsing a natural language like English was seen as a task fundamentally no different from that of compiling a formal computer language. Let me explain. People who program computers use a variety of artificial, formal languages – Fortran, Basic, Pascal, C, Lisp are some of the better known. None of these are the 'native language' of any computer. The 'native language' of a computer – the language to which it responds appropriately by virtue of its physical construction – is its *machine code*; different computers have different machine codes, but normally these are not the same as or even similar to the *high-level languages* used for programming. (I ignore some special cases for ease of exposition.) Here is a short sample of IBM 7090 machine code,[2] for instance (or, more precisely, a symbolic equivalent, *assembly code*, which uses mnemonic letter-groups – e.g. CLA for 'clear and add' – to stand for the arbitrary numerical symbols used in machine code proper):

12 Evolutionary Language Understanding

YA	ZET	R
YB	TRA	YF
YC	CLA	X
YD	STO	Z
YE	TRA	YH
YF	CLA	Y
YG	STO	Z

This sequence, input to a 7090 computer, has the same effect that could be achieved in the high-level language C by writing:

```
if (r == 0)
        z = x;
else
        z = y;
```

What both these four lines of C and the seven lines of assembly code are in effect saying is 'Assign to the variable z the value x if r has the value 0, and the value y otherwise' (though the assembly-code version is more explicit about the concrete activities within the computer by which this is to be achieved). But the C commands cannot be directly input as instructions to a 7090 or any other computer. Instead, using a high-level language is normally a two-stage process: first, the high-level program is translated into an equivalent machine-code program (by a translation program which can itself be understood by the computer because it is written in machine code); then the resulting machine-code program, which the computer can now understand, is run.

The process of translating a high-level program into a machine-code equivalent is called *compilation*: and the central problem in the design of a compiler program which does this translation for a particular high-level language is how the machine is to break the statements of that language down into a structure of meaningful units – how to parse them. Machine code itself has a very regular structure: note how my example consisted of a series of lines each containing just three code elements, and this corresponds symbolically to the fact that in real numerical machine code a program will be a sequence of digit sequences with exactly the same number of digits in each sequence. But in a high-level language there is far more diversity of structure. High-level programming languages are designed to be easier for humans to work with than machine code, and they achieve this by adopting some aspects of the recursive, clause-within-clause grammatical structure of natural languages. Note the *if* . . . *else* . . . structure in my C example, for instance. In machine code each line instructs the computer to perform one elementary action; but in a high-level programming language, as in a natural language, some 'sentences' may be very simple and others highly complex. The C statement:

```
r = 0;
```

represents a simple instruction which might require only a single line for its translation into machine code; but the C statement:

```
z = ! r ? x : y;
```

is a one-line paraphrase of the four-line example shown earlier, and is again equivalent to the seven machine-code lines. The logical structure of this last statement is far from obvious on its face: to understand it correctly, you have to know (for instance) that by the grammatical rules of the C language the exclamation mark (meaning 'not') forms a unit with the following symbol r, because the exclamation mark has a higher 'precedence' than the question mark which occurs on the other side of the r; if the precedence of the exclamation mark were lower than that of the question mark, the statement would have a very different meaning.

Thus, the design of automatic routines (preferably, efficient automatic routines) for 'understanding' examples of language by deducing their grammatical structure is a familiar and important topic to computer scientists. It quite often happens that a novel programming language is invented for some special purpose, or extensions are added to an existing language, and a compiler program is needed to translate examples of the new formal language into machine code. Compilers are not normally created from scratch by hand in this situation; that would be laborious and difficult to achieve. Instead, there exist general-purpose programs called *compiler-compilers* or *parser-generators*, which take as input a definition of the language to be compiled, and return a compiler for the language. The inventor of the novel language will normally have given it a rigorous formal definition; provided this definition conforms to certain standard formats that a parser-generator is capable of dealing with, an automatic parser for the language can be derived from this definition without further human effort.

The upshot is that, to someone approaching natural language processing from a computer science background, it seems self-evident that the route towards an automatic parser for a language must lie via a rigorous formal *definition* of the language: a specification, in mathematically precise terms, of just which sequences of symbols count as valid examples of the language and which do not. A computer scientist will expect such a definition to be expressed in the form of a *production system*: a set of rules showing how the various legal symbol-sequences can be built up, which simultaneously enumerates the range of legal sequences and also specifies the logical structure of each such sequence. In books on formal programming languages it is common to find an appendix displaying a definition of the language in terms of a production system, although the body of the book will probably describe the language in more informal, intuitive terms. Here, for instance, is part of a production system defining the IPL-V language (Higman 1967: 99):

```
<programme> ::= <controls><mainpart><endline>
<controls>  ::= <9-line>|<controls><region control line>
<mainpart>  ::= <block>|<block><mainpart>
```

The term `<programme>` (in recent British English normally spelled 'program' in this sense) is the *initial symbol*, from which any particular legal program can be derived. The sign '::=' can be glossed 'consists of': thus the first line says that any IPL-V program consists at the highest level of three elements, belonging to the respective categories `<controls>`, `<mainpart>`, and `<endline>`. The vertical bar means 'or', so that the second line defines alternative ways in which the category `<controls>` can be instantiated. The full production system will have many further lines, some of which will have individual characters to the right of the '::=' symbol; so that any legal IPL-V program will consist of an array of characters associated with successive leaf nodes of a tree structure in which each nonterminal node is licensed by one of the productions (for instance a node labelled `<controls>` and dominating two nodes labelled `<controls>` and `<region control line>` respectively is legal), and in which the root node is labelled `<programme>`.

When computer scientists and linguistics researchers began to collaborate in order to create natural language processing systems, the computer specialists were the ones with experience of automatic parsing (which had not previously been an interesting issue within linguistics); but the linguists were the ones who knew about natural languages, which are clearly phenomena far more complicated than any computer-programming language. One might have expected a certain tension in their joint development of techniques for automatically parsing natural languages, as a consequence of contrasting assumptions inherited from the different intellectual backgrounds. In some areas of computational linguistics there probably have been such tensions, but with respect to the subject under discussion there were none. It happened that dominant intellectual trends in linguistics contained elements which dovetailed closely with the assumptions of computer scientists, so that on the question of how to parse natural language the separate disciplines reinforced one another rather than clashing.

Linguistics as an academic subject is a house with many mansions. Different members of university linguistics departments are interested in topics as diverse as children's acquisition of their mother tongue, the common origin of the Indo-European language family, the role of language in maintaining social or political relationships, the ways in which authors use language to achieve literary effects, efficient classroom techniques for language teaching, and many others. But it happens that for many years from about 1965 onwards, one specific area of linguistics came to be seen as centrally important in the discipline, and other branches of the subject to a large extent tended to define their own work in terms of that 'core' subfield. The area allotted this special status was grammar, and specifically the theories of *generative grammar* elaborated by the American linguist Noam Chomsky.

Chomsky posed a novel set of questions about the grammars of natural languages, and argued that the answers to those questions held vital and unexpected implications for our understanding of the nature of Man and the human mind. He conducted these arguments with such brilliance and rhetorical skill, and was (and is) a man of such remarkable personal charisma (at a period when the human sciences were otherwise not well supplied with impressive individuals), that the subject almost inevitably reoriented itself in terms of his interests. Indeed, many people came to linguistics as a by-product of their interest in Chomsky as a public figure – he was a leading exponent of radical left-wing politics, at a period when such politics were very fashionable; naturally, when students decided to sample the wares of linguistics departments because they were curious about the professional work of an individual whose politics they admired, they expected to be taught Chomsky's type of linguistics.

For Chomsky, the central question of linguistics was how to formulate a rigorous definition, or 'generative grammar', specifying the range of legal sentences for a natural language. He began his first book (*Syntactic Structures*, 1957) by writing 'The fundamental aim in the linguistic analysis of a language L is to separate the *grammatical* sequences which are the sentences of L from the *ungrammatical* sequences which are not sentences of L . . . ' (Chomsky 1957: 13). In the context of Chomsky's thought, the reason for treating this aim as fundamental was an issue quite separate from automatic parsing (which was not a topic that concerned him). Chomsky argued that if one constructs grammars which succeed in generating 'all and only' the grammatical sentences of different natural languages, one finds that these grammars have various highly specific and quite unexpected formal properties, which do not differ from one natural language to another, and that these universals of natural grammar are a pointer to the fact that (as he later put it) 'we do not really learn language; rather, grammar grows in the mind'

(Chomsky 1980: 134) – and that, more generally, an adult's mental world is not the result of his individual intellectual inventiveness responding to his environment, but rather, like his anatomy, is predetermined in much of its detail by his genetic inheritance.

This idea of Chomsky's, that linguistic structure shows our cognitive life to be controlled by our genes, seems when the arguments are examined carefully to be quite mistaken (cf. Sampson 1980a, 1989b), though it was influential for many years. (It has recently been popularized in an uncritical book by Steven Pinker (Pinker 1994).) For our present purposes, though, the motives for Chomsky's emphasis on generative grammars are beside the point. What matters is that, when linguists and computer scientists began talking to each other (which happened on a wide scale from about 1980 onwards), the linguists agreed with the computer scientists that the important thing to do with a natural language was to design a production system for it. What linguists call 'generative grammars' are what computer scientists call 'production systems'. (Indeed, these two concepts were not independent developments: the early work of Chomsky and some of his collaborators, such as M. P. Schützenberger, lay at the root of formal language theory within computer science, as well as of linguistic theory. But few of the linguists who became convinced in the 1960s and 1970s that generative grammars were central to the study of natural language had any awareness of the role that this concept played in computer science.) Here is the beginning of the specimen generative grammar for English given in Chomsky's *Syntactic Structures*:

$$\text{Sentence} \rightarrow \text{NP} + \text{VP}$$
$$\text{VP} \rightarrow \text{Verb} + \text{NP}$$
$$\text{NP} \rightarrow \left\{ \begin{matrix} \text{NP}_{sing} \\ \text{NP}_{pl} \end{matrix} \right\}$$

In a computing book, it would look like this:

```
Sentence ::= NP VP
VP ::= Verb NP
NP ::= NP.sing | NP.pl
```

but this is a mere cosmetic difference of notational traditions. Both versions – the linguistic version using arrows, and linking alternatives by curly brackets, and the computer-science version which contains ': : =' in place of the arrow and vertical bars instead of curly brackets or commas – exemplify the type of production system called *context-free phrase structure grammar* (Chomsky 1963). A context-free phrase structure grammar (or *context-free grammar*, for short) consists of a finite set of rules, each rewriting an individual symbol as some sequence of one or more symbols, with one particular symbol ('Sentence', in this example) picked out as the initial symbol from which rewriting begins. The class of context-free grammars has special importance in computer science and in linguistics, for several different reasons; one reason is that a language defined by a context-free grammar can be parsed particularly efficiently.

I do not mean to say that Chomskyan theoretical linguistics taught that the generative grammars of natural languages contained the same sorts of rule that were needed for the definition of formal programming languages. Not so: it was a central tenet of Chomskyan linguistics that the formal definition of natural languages required, in addition to context-free rules, some much more powerful kinds of rule (so-called *transformational rules*) which would not normally be found in the definition of a programming language. Programming languages are artificial constructs designed to be convenient in use; it would be surprising if anyone created a programming language whose definition required the use of transformational rules, since the best algorithms for parsing such languages are much less efficient than the algorithms available for context-free languages, and efficiency of parsing is a key desideratum for a programming language. For the same reason, one might have expected that natural languages, although not consciously planned, would have evolved as context-free languages; but Chomsky argued that this is in fact observably false. (Nowadays, incidentally, many linguistic theorists argue that Chomsky was mistaken about this, and that natural languages either are context-free, or at worst belong to a class which is only fairly trivially wider than the class of context-free languages; see e.g. Pullum 1991: ch. 17, Gazdar & Mellish 1989: 146–7.)

But that is not the point. What matters here is that linguists and computer scientists both took for granted that natural language processing required the development of formal language definitions. The linguists gave the computer scientists the bad news that these definitions would require formalisms going beyond the familiar and convenient context-free level, and this was perfectly understandable to computer scientists – they knew there were other kinds of formal rule and that parsing was more difficult when these occurred, and they realized that they could not expect natural language to have properties as convenient as those designed in to artificial languages; this just meant that parsing natural language was not going to be an easy nut to crack, but it was not a reason to query the relevance of formal grammars to parsing.

The Messiness of Real-Life Language

However, the compilation paradigm makes a crucial assumption about the nature of language – an assumption which is certainly true for formal programming languages, but which is at least not so obviously true for natural languages. The paradigm assumes that a language can be rigorously delimited by some fixed set of grammatical rules or principles, so that it always makes sense to ask, "Is this sequence in the language or outside it? – 'grammatical' or 'ungrammatical'?" Books and articles on theoretical linguistics commonly revolved round series of example sentences, some of which were preceded by asterisks, indicating that they are not grammatical, while others had no asterisk, meaning that they are grammatical. With programming languages a given sequence of characters either is a valid program or it is not, and it is a very common experience to find one's attempt at writing a program rejected by the compiler with the message 'Syntax error'. Computational linguists felt that the definition of a natural language would comprise a much larger set of rules than are needed for the definition of a programming language, since programming languages are designed to be simple whereas natural languages are products of long historical evolution, full of irregularities and redundant accretions; and, as we have seen, they held that the rules of natural languages might be of a different formal type from those of programming languages. But they did not question the idea that some set of rules could be framed to capture the grammatical facts of a natural language.

Yet, on the face of things, human languages seem to be less rigorously rule-governed than formal programming languages. Of course we have grammatical rules, and much of the time we obey them; but anarchy keeps breaking in. The compilation paradigm seems to assume that the rules of English grammar are akin to the laws of physics, which can never be deviated from in the least particular. One might alternatively feel that the grammar rules of English are like the laws of England, which we all accept as important guidelines but we are physically free to break and do break on occasion (has the reader never driven at 35 m.p.h. in a built-up area?), and which furthermore have plenty of grey areas where it is not clear whether an action is legal or not. The example sentence used on p. 1 to illustrate the parsetree concept struck me as odd when I encountered it – if I had written it myself I would have felt bound to insert *a* before *feeling*; but it was printed in the form shown, and minor oddities of this kind are all-pervasive in real-life usage.

One way I like to put this is to say that, if a believer in rigorous rules of grammar nominates an English rule which he believes to be reliable, I would expect sooner or later to be able to find some example drawn from authentic usage where the rule is violated, yet the example 'works' – the violation yields an utterance which succeeds in context in furthering the speaker's or writer's communicative purposes in a form acceptable to other

English-speaking hearers or readers. To reuse an example I have used elsewhere: English grammarians normally hold that it is a definite rule that reflexive pronouns (*himself, myself,* etc.) occur only when the same entity is referred to earlier in the same clause. This implies that a reflexive pronoun cannot be the subject of its clause. Yet a *New Statesman* article about nuclear war by Bertrand Russell contained the sentence:

> *Each side proceeds on the assumption that itself loves peace, but the other side consists of warmongers.*

Itself is the subject of the subordinate nominal clause: a clear violation of the rule, but one can see why Russell chose to word his statement this way – he wanted to contrast a State's perception of *itself* with its perception of rival States. Obeying the grammar rule would have interfered with Russell's point without helping his readers in any way, so quite naturally he ignored it. It is that kind of status, as flexible guidelines rather than rigid requirements, that grammar rules have in practice in natural languages.

But this creates a major problem for the compilation approach to automatic parsing, because a parser created by a compiler-compiler will work only if the language samples input to it do conform to whatever set of rules the parser was generated from. If a parser is generated from a set of rules that are really just flexible guidelines, then whenever an input deviates from the guidelines the parser will reject that input as grammatically deviant, without identifying its structure. On the face of it this does not look like a promising route towards practical natural language processing applications. Attempts were made to extend compiler-like parsers to handle 'deviant' inputs (see for instance the July–December 1983 special issue of the *American Journal of Computational Linguistics*), but while these attempts were not without some successes they seemed to run against the grain of the compilation paradigm.

For me it was difficult to overlook the contradictions between an approach to automatic natural language analysis that relied on language being rigidly rule-governed, and the anarchic flexibility of language as it is actually used, because I had been fortunate enough to spend most of my career at the University of Lancaster, which is one of the main centres internationally of what is called *corpus linguistics*. As computers began to be applied to the study of natural language, a major need was for large 'fair samples' of language in machine-readable form that would enable linguists to make statements about usage based on systematic logging of examples, rather than on cases encountered by chance in conversation or reading, or on impressionistic feelings about what one 'would say' or 'wouldn't say'. The first standard computerized corpus of British English, the million-word 'LOB (Lancaster-Oslo/Bergen) Corpus', was produced by the founder of my Lancaster department, Geoffrey Leech, together with Norwegian collaborators: it was published in 1978. All of us who became involved in research based on the LOB Corpus quickly had our noses rubbed in the endless diversity and unpredictability of authentic English usage (the Russell example quoted above was from the LOB Corpus, for instance).

But in the 1980s it was not yet usual for computational linguists, or indeed linguists in general, to work with corpus data. The academic literature on grammatical theory had for many years standardly used as examples sentences which the theorist himself had invented and put forward as legal or illegal by virtue of his authority as a native speaker of the language. Some linguists (notably the sociolinguist William Labov, e.g. Labov 1975) had questioned the scientific respectability of this procedure, but Labov's doubts were not widely shared.

This willingness of linguists to rely on data derived from introspection did not rest merely on the fact that corpus data were unavailable: it had a theoretical basis. One of the central principles of the dominant paradigm of linguistic research was that speakers' observable linguistic 'performance' is a poor guide to their underlying 'competence' (the terms were introduced by Chomsky (1965: 4)): people make slips of the tongue, their speech is interrupted by hesitations and memory lapses and degraded by extraneous factors such as colds in the head, and in order to gain insight into language as a psychological system which a speaker has internalized it is more efficient to ask him directly to say what is in the language and what is not than to make indirect inferences about the system by observing the performance resulting from interactions between the speaker's mastery of his language and other irrelevant factors. In fact corpus data for American English had been available for many years. Geoffrey Leech created the LOB Corpus as a British counterpart of the 'Brown Corpus' of American English, which was published by Nelson Francis and Henry Kučera of Brown University, Rhode Island, as long ago as 1964. But American linguists (who were more thoroughly convinced by the Chomskyan paradigm than their British counterparts) made very little use of this resource; they preferred to study linguistic competence via introspection rather than linguistic performance via electronic corpora (cf. Aarts & van den Heuvel 1985: 303–5). Although linguistics, like many academic disciplines, is dominated numerically by American scholars, corpus linguistics developed as a European speciality, practised mainly in Britain, the Netherlands, and Scandinavia. Only very recently have Americans begun to participate in corpus-based research in significant numbers.

The fact that so many linguists were used to relying on introspective rather than empirical data to check the facts about English gave the compilation paradigm in NLP a much fairer wind than it might otherwise have received. It is a very normal human trait to believe that one's behaviour is more regular and rational than it really is; a linguist might well feel confident in starring the Russell sentence as not possible in English, even if he himself might on another occasion produce just such a sentence. And if a linguist noticed cases where real-life usage is messier than the compilation paradigm requires, that in a way looked like an objection not to the compilation paradigm but to real-life usage – it went to show how degraded 'performance' is by comparison with the theoretically more interesting competence.

Meanwhile, if linguists were coming to computational linguistics with assumptions about natural languages being rigorously definable grammatical systems, their collaborators whose backgrounds lay in computer science clearly were not going to call this into question: they needed natural languages to be like that in order to apply the parser-generating techniques they were familiar with, and they had no professional experience of the messiness associated with authentic usage. In consequence, as computational linguistics developed, it became one of the understood assumptions of the discipline that automatic natural language analysis systems were worked out by reference to invented language examples. One did not test a natural language parser by submitting samples of real-life language to it; and one did not criticize other researchers' systems on the ground that they would fail such a test. Reports of research progress at computational linguistics conferences focused on dapper little sentences which were fine in themselves but were not representative of the endless quirkiness of authentic usage. Consider, for instance, the following characteristic examples from papers read at the Inaugural Meeting of the European Chapter of the Association for Computational Linguistics in 1983:

Whatever is linguistic is interesting.
A ticket was bought by every man.
The man with the telescope and the umbrella kicked the ball.
Hans bekommt von dieser Frau ein Buch.

Compiler-like parsers performed badly on real-life examples; and they still do perform badly. Black *et al.* (1993: 2ff.) discuss the results of recent objective tests of a number of contemporary parsers; they conclude: 'It is only recently that many creators of major parsing systems, by beginning to test their systems on previously unseen, general-English text, have themselves become aware of the dismal state of the art in parsing English.'

Black *et al.*'s comment perhaps exaggerates NLP researchers' naivety. I believe many of them were fully aware that systems worked out for examples as neat as those quoted in the previous paragraph would quickly fall over if tested on real-life material. But they believed that the route towards the ultimate goal of NLP systems that could cope with the full complexity of realistic language lay through systems designed to deal with neat invented examples – just as theoretical linguists believed that eventual theories adequately explaining people's complex linguistic behaviour would be produced by starting with theories of people's underlying linguistic competence, and adding on extra bits to explain the distortions that arise in practical performance (cf. Chomsky 1965: 9, 15).

Yet, even if it is true that a natural language as it is organized within the mind of one of its speakers has the same rigorously rule-governed quality as a formal programming language, there are at least two reasons why linguists might have hesitated before allowing the preoccupation of pure theoretical linguistics with rigorous generative grammars to be inherited by computational linguistics, which is an applied discipline aiming to achieve practical results. One point is that, although pure theoretical linguistics can reasonably treat the organization of language in a speaker's mind as a more significant subject of study than the manifestations of that psychological ability on paper or in speech, computational linguistics cannot. If computational linguistics research hopes to produce the practically usable software systems which justify the considerable resources spent on it, then it must obviously deal with language as it actually occurs, rather than language in an idealized form. It would be just silly for the developers of a voice-driven typewriter, say, to claim that their machine works fine – but only provided users always conform perfectly to the rules of English grammatical competence, despite the fact that in practice speakers do not do this. Agreed, it *might* be that starting with systems which cope with simple, idealized versions of the language is a good strategy for moving step by step towards systems that cope with the complexity of realistic language; but this is just one possible strategy, not self-evidently the correct one, and it would only be justified if it did eventually lead to the realistic systems.

Theoretical linguists concentrate on competence rather than performance not just because of the belief that competence theories are a necessary prerequisite for performance theories, but because in many cases they are not interested in performance anyway. Computational linguists *must* be interested in real-life usage.

And the second point is that the kind of fact about language which the generative grammar approach is best able to deal with is a type of fact that is largely irrelevant to most of the practical applications that computational linguistics aims to serve. Generative grammar is fundamentally about distinguishing things that people do say from things they do not say. It would seem a highly appropriate paradigm in the context of some IT application where the first thing one wanted the system to do with a natural language input was to say whether or not it was grammatical. In the context of formal language compilation, this *is* the first thing one wants the system to do. If a user attempts to write a program but makes a mistake in the syntax, it is important that the compiler should reject it forthwith; if the compiler tolerated syntax errors, it would produce object code whose properties would be highly unpredictable. In the context of natural language, on the other hand, deciding whether an utterance is or is not an example of the language is almost never a relevant procedure. One wants an NLP system to succeed in dealing appropriately with linguistic inputs that users do produce; normally one does not specifically want the systems to detect the oddity of inputs that users do not produce – if human users of a language never say or write certain things, presumably those things will never occur as inputs. (There are exceptions: notably, grammar-checker systems as discussed on p. 7 above clearly do need the ability to detect users' deviations from standard grammatical norms. But this is only one application among many, and not such a central one as to require that the fundamental strategy of NLP should be geared to it.)

Human beings do not commonly operate as grammaticality detectors when they hear or read language. If I listen to a young child or a foreigner whose language is grammatically distorted, I impose sense on it as best I can – if the language is severely distorted, my understanding will probably diverge to some extent from the speaker's intention. I do not believe that a human hearer typically finds himself thinking, 'This input is grammatically imperfect, so the issue of interpreting it does not arise'. Surely it is the other way round: first one interprets an utterance as best one can, and only as a secondary issue does one sometimes observe that the utterance is grammatically imperfect (if the imperfection is slight, it will often fail to be consciously noticed). I would not want to suggest that the aim of computational linguistics should be to produce software which mimics every aspect of human beings' linguistic behaviour. But when, as in this case, there seems to be a systematic contradiction between the way humans deal with natural language and the way that orthodox computational systems deal with it, one might feel that it is at least worth considering an alternative computational strategy.

Probabilistic Approaches

At Lancaster, we believed that techniques capable of dealing with the messy anarchy of corpus data would have to deal in statistics and probabilities. Techniques based on rigid logical rules would always be too fragile to cope with our material. In fact the Lancaster team (before I became involved with it) had scored a notable success using a probabilistic approach to one particular natural language analysis task: the task of automatic *word-tagging*, i.e. identifying the grammatical roles of the words of a text.

In English, many word-forms taken out of context are ambiguous between several grammatical roles (cf. the example of *round* discussed above, p. 6). Research on the structures of a language using a machine-readable corpus is greatly helped if each word-token in the corpus is equipped with a tag codifying the grammatical role it is playing in its context, so once the LOB Corpus was complete the Lancaster group undertook to produce a tagged version. With a million word-tokens to deal with, it was desirable for as much as possible of this work to be achieved automatically; and they succeeded in developing an automatic word-tagger, 'CLAWS', that worked extremely well, correctly tagging between 96% and 97% of word-tokens (depending on text type), so that only an acceptably small level of postediting was needed. CLAWS used an algorithm based on tag-transition probabilities: that is, the kind of knowledge about English incorporated in the system – apart from knowledge about what tags were candidates for a word out of context – was knowledge of the relative frequencies with which different pairs of tags (say, preposition and past participle, or definite article and adjective) are found adjacent to one another in English texts. Given a string of words, each associated with a set of one or more candidate tags, CLAWS chose that path through the candidates for successive words which maximized probability, measured as the product of the probabilities for successive transitions between pairs of adjacent wordtags on the path. (The CLAWS system is described in detail in Marshall 1987.)

Word-tagging is a limited form of natural language analysis, and in itself perhaps not one with many direct practical applications. But the significant thing about CLAWS was that it worked well, despite flying in the face of prevailing linguistic orthodoxies. I myself would have predicted, before CLAWS was operational, that a system based on transition probabilities could not yield useful results. I had read my Chomsky, and knew that 'one's ability to produce and recognize grammatical utterances is not based on notions of statistical approximation and the like', and that 'the approach to the analysis of grammaticalness . . . in terms of a finite state Markov process that produces sentences from left to right, appears to lead to a dead end' (Chomsky 1957: 16, 24). (A *Markov process* (Cox & Miller 1965) is a process that emits a sequence of symbols in such a way that the probability of emitting a given symbol at any point depends exclusively on the identities of the last n symbols emitted, for some fixed finite n; thus the tag-transition probabilities of CLAWS would be the fundamental data for a system which used a Markov process with $n = 1$ in order to generate English-like sequences of words.)

What Chomsky actually says in the remarks just quoted is perfectly acceptable and compatible with the success of CLAWS: namely, that *if* one's focus is on the question of how to distinguish grammatical from ungrammatical sequences of words, then probabilistic techniques are not the way to go about it. But, because Chomsky had been so successful in influencing the discipline to make this question its central focus, we wrongly took the point to be a wider one: that probabilities could not help in achieving any grammar-related task. The task of word-tagging is not connected with the question of grammaticality. The creators of CLAWS were not aiming to produce a system which correctly tagged sequences of words that do occur in English, while failing to generate tags for ungrammatical sequences. If a sequence is ungrammatical because of some specific local error – say, a verb failing to agree with its subject – then the creators of CLAWS hoped that the sequence would have its words correctly tagged, because such sentences do often occur in practice. That is, in this case it is positively desirable for the system to ignore the issue of grammaticality. If on the other hand one means by 'ungrammatical sequence' a random, meaningless jumble of words, then the creators of CLAWS did not care what their system would do with such an input; giving CLAWS an input of this sort would serve no purpose.

Perhaps we should not have been surprised, then, that CLAWS was a success. But the idea that one might work on *grammar* without concerning oneself with *grammaticality* was entirely novel, and it was easy to overlook the fact that setting the issue of grammaticality aside meant setting aside the arguments against using probabilities. So it did come as a shock that CLAWS worked; and this air of success through heresy which surrounded the CLAWS project made all of us at Lancaster alert to the idea that statistical techniques might be usable for broader NLP tasks. Specifically, we wanted to use statistics in order to parse.

Parsing, as we have seen, means fitting a labelled tree structure to an input word-sequence. A parser designed in accordance with the orthodox compilation paradigm uses a generative grammar to define a class of legal labelled trees, and contains routines which systematically construct the legal tree whose successive leaf nodes are labelled with the input words, if there is such a tree; if the input is ungrammatical, there is no legal tree for its leaf-sequence.[3] If we give up the idea that some labelled tree structures are grammatically 'legal' and others 'illegal', the orthodox algorithm has no application. But it still makes sense to think of a specific class of labelled tree structures that are well-formed in a much broader sense: that is, structurally they are indeed trees, with a single root node dominating all other nodes and with nodes branching only away from, not towards, the root, and the label on each nonterminal node is always drawn from some agreed vocabulary of grammatical symbols. Once we fix the label vocabulary, the set of alternative tree structures in this sense that can be drawn over a particular string is perfectly well-defined, though most of its members will be linguistically quite absurd. Provided singular branching is forbidden – that is, so long as each mother node has at least two daughters – then the class of distinct labelled trees over a given input will contain only finitely many members.[4]

Our idea was that we should find some quantitative way of estimating the plausibility of labelled trees, by comparing the properties of an individual tree with the statistics of a large sample of correct parses of authentic language material; and then, faced with an input sentence to be parsed, rather than moving directly to the unique 'legal' parse, the system would evaluate the plausibility of each possible labelled tree over the input and select the most plausible. This might be a time-consuming approach by comparison with the orthodox compilation technique; but it should be far more robust, because it does not depend in any way on the input actually being a grammatically perfect sentence. Provided the function which assigns figures of merit to labelled trees is defined for *all* trees which are well-formed in the broad sense that they are topologically tree structures and have nonterminal labels drawn exclusively from the agreed vocabulary, then a garbled, bizarrely ungrammatical input can be parsed in just the same fashion as a polished example of textbook prose. In each case, the system will simply find the most plausible analysis among the class of labelled trees over the respective input; in the case of the grammatical input the plausibility of the best analysis will be greater than in the case of the garbled input, but the algorithm does not care about absolute plausibility values – only about relative values of different analyses for a given input.

We began work along these lines in 1983. One of the requirements for this approach was a database of manually parsed material, analysed in terms of a range of grammatical categories that was sufficiently comprehensive and well defined to offer a predictable, consistent analysis for anything that cropped up in our data, to act as a source of grammatical statistics; producing this 'Treebank' was my own particular responsibility within the project.[5] In consultation with my colleagues I developed a formal annotation scheme for the Treebank which later evolved into the 'SUSANNE' scheme of Fig. 2.1 (though the Treebank scheme was considerably simpler). Others worked on the tree-evaluation function, and on the software for locating the best-valued analysis for an input. But there was an unsolved problem.

For any finitely long input string, provided we allow no singular branching, then the class of distinct labelled trees over that string has a finite number of members; but, if the string is more than three or four words long, combinatorial explosion means that the number of distinct labelled trees will be extremely large. The number $d_{v,n}$ of distinct unlabelled tree structures having v leaves and n nonterminal nodes can be calculated recursively from the formulae:[6]

$$d_{v,1} = 1 \text{ (for any } v\text{)}$$

$$d_{v,n} + d_{v,n-1} = \frac{(v + n - 2)!}{(v - n)!n!(n - 1)!}$$

With a vocabulary of H nonterminal labels, the number of distinct labelled trees having v leaves and n nonterminals is $H^n d_{v,n}$. The total number of distinct trees over v leaves can thus be calculated by summing $H^n d_{v,n}$ over values of n from 1 to $v - 1$. (Without singulary branching, the number of nonterminal nodes must always be at least one fewer than the number of leaves.)

To put this in perspective, if v, the number of leaf nodes, is 22 (which is the average sentence-length in our material), and H, the number of alternative nonterminal labels, is 14 (corresponding to the crude vocabulary of nonterminal categories used in the 'toy' system to be described in ch. 3, which was smaller than the nonterminal vocabulary used in the Lancaster parsing work), then the number of distinct trees without singulary branching is about 3.4×10^{35}. To call a number of this order 'astronomical' is something of an understatement. Certainly there is no possibility of having a computer systematically evaluate each possible analysis in turn and choose the best, if there are this many analyses; if a million alternatives could be examined each second, running through all the possibilities would take something like a trillion (10^{12}) times the estimated age of the universe. There are so-called *dynamic programming* techniques which would cut the task down to a more manageable size if we could assume that the evaluation function had certain convenient properties. In dynamic programming, one would consider all possible ways of drawing a structure over the first few input words, and select the highest-valued; then, keeping this part of the structure constant, one would consider all possible ways of linking it into a larger structure with the next few words, and select the best again; and so on. This greatly reduces the total number of alternatives to be considered, when it is applicable; but it involves assumptions about the nature of the evaluation function which I was reluctant to make (I return to this point in ch. 4 below).

My colleagues attacked this problem using a technique (described in Garside & Leech 1987) which represented a compromise between the probability-based and logic-based approaches to analysis. In essence, since there were far too many possible trees for each to be evaluated, they used absolute rules about legal and illegal substructures in trees in order greatly to reduce the number of alternatives to be considered, and then applied the evaluation function just to the smaller set of trees permitted by the absolute rules. Some success was achieved in this way, but there were also problems – the absolute rules did not always cut out a high enough proportion of the *a priori* alternatives for the remaining set to be evaluated in a reasonable time, particularly in the case of longer sentences; and, conversely, at least occasionally it happened that the absolute rules eliminated what was in fact the desired output analysis.

This is the type of problem which inevitably crops up in the early stages of a novel computational technique, of course, and often it can be overcome through modifications of detail. Perhaps the absolute rules were not as well chosen as they might be, and tweaking these and other aspects of the system would solve the difficulties. But my instincts urged me in a different direction. I did not like the hybridity of a system which used both absolute logical rules and probabilities in order to choose an analysis. Our reasons for abandoning the orthodox, logic-based compilation paradigm and adopting a statistical approach were good reasons, it seemed to me; I wanted a parser to use statistics exclusively, and not to include any absolute rules about grammatically well-formed tree structures – even though some rules might be violated far less often than others, the anarchy of real-life language ensured, it seemed to me, that no such rules would be genuinely absolute. Yet, if the system was to be purely statistical, how could one get over the problem of those more-than-astronomical numbers of trees?

And then, in the opening days of 1985, just after I had moved from my Lancaster post to the Chair of Linguistics at Leeds – although the term had not begun, and I had yet to meet my Leeds students – I went down to London for a one-day conference at which Geoffrey Hinton, a visiting speaker from America, and others spoke about the novel concept of the *Boltzmann machine*. The main topic of the conference turned out to be less relevant to my work than I had initially thought it might be (Boltzmann machines – see e.g. Hinton & Sejnowski 1983 – are artificial-intelligence systems which simulate certain aspects of learning, whereas I wanted to make the computer achieve some of the tasks carried out by a mature user of a language, ignoring the question of how an individual becomes a mature language-user); but the exposition of the Boltzmann machine concept involved the notion of stochastic optimization (that is, optimization via a random process), and specifically the newly invented stochastic optimization technique of *simulated annealing*. Simulated annealing was the tool I had been searching for.

Notes

1. I use the term *tagma* for any unit of grammatical analysis larger than the individual word; a tagma has *constituents* which may themselves be tagmas, or may be words. On the need for this piece of terminology, cf. Sampson (1995: 44).
2. The IBM 7090 is obsolete; but it happened to be the machine on which I learned machine-code programming, and is described in a textbook (Leeds & Weinberg 1961) that was widely distributed at a period when people concerned with IT applications learned more about computer hardware than is usual today. The point in the text would not be affected by substituting a newer example machine.
3. An input may be structurally ambiguous; a well-known example is *The old men and women went ashore*. This corresponds to the existence of two or more distinct legal labelled trees, all dominating the same word-sequence. Within the compilation paradigm, parsing algorithms differ as to whether they return one legal analysis, or all possible legal analyses, in response to a structurally ambiguous input.
4. The parsing scheme exemplified in Fig. 2.1 above, and most other schemes for representing English grammatical structure, do make some use of singulary-branching nodes – cf. the Vd node over *said* in Fig. 2.1, for instance. We shall see below that various special devices are adopted in our research to deal with the implications of singulary branching.
5. I believe our group at Lancaster was the first to coin the term 'Treebank' for a collection of grammatically analysed language samples, but it has since come into use more generally. The resource described above is called the *Lancaster-Leeds Treebank* in contexts where confusion might arise (but I shall often write simply 'the Treebank'); it is described in Garside *et al.* (1987: 83ff.).
6. I am indebted to Professor Graeme Segal FRS of St John's College, Cambridge, for working out these formulae.

3 Simulating Evolution

Stochastic Optimization

If you had studied at the University of Cambridge in the nineteenth century, one of the books you would have been required to read was William Paley's *Natural Theology* (published in 1802). Paley's was the most influential statement of the longstanding 'argument from design', according to which we can infer the existence of God from the nature of Nature. 'In crossing a heath,' Paley begins, 'suppose I pitched my foot against a *stone*, and were asked how the stone came to be there: I might possibly answer, that, for anything I knew to the contrary, it had lain there for ever . . . But suppose I had found a *watch* upon the ground, and it should be enquired how the watch happened to be in that place: I should hardly think of the answer which I had before given,– that, for any thing I knew, the watch might have always been there.' The subtlety with which the watch is designed to be fit for a purpose shows that it must have had a designer; and likewise, Paley argues, the subtle complexity of the organs which serve the needs of living creatures show that we too must have had an intelligent Creator.

Nowadays – specifically, since Darwin – we see that Paley got it precisely wrong. An animal's complex, efficient anatomical structure is not the product of intelligent design at all: it has emerged from the operation, over immense periods of time, of repeated random mutation with selection of favourable alternatives. This idea is not an easy one to accept. Anyone who thinks about the question seriously must surely find an explanation along Paley's lines intuitively much more credible than an account which takes one from the amoeba to a sparrowhawk's eye and wing via pure dice-throwing and the struggle for survival. Yet the evidence for the Darwinian account is sufficiently compelling to have become the accepted scientific consensus despite its intuitive implausibility.

Indeed, it is only because a watch is not so very complicated that it can be designed successfully. The more we have learned about biology, the more unimaginably complex and subtle the machinery of life-forms has turned out to be – Paley, and indeed Darwin, did not know the half of it, and nor, probably, do we; whereas full information about the structure of a particular model of watch can be set out in a manual of modest size. Part of what the theory of evolution is saying is that random mutation with natural selection, given long enough, can not merely simulate the output of a creative intelligence but can create products whose intricacy and efficiency far surpass anything that could be designed through diligent effort by an intelligent mind.

Stochastic optimization is a computing technique which exploits this insight. If random mutation with natural selection can produce such good results, where a computing problem is too hard to solve systematically it may be better to get the machine to generate a solution through random mutation with artificial selection for favourable alternatives. The obvious difficulty about modelling an artificial process used for human purposes on the natural process of evolution is the time required by the latter; but computers work fast. If an evolutionary process can be simulated in a fashion which reduces the length of a 'generation' to microseconds or nanoseconds, then worthwhile results may be attainable within periods that humans can cope with.

Several stochastic optimization techniques emerged during the 1980s (see e.g. Bounds 1987, Davis 1987). Some of them are relatively specialized, in the sense that they apply only to problems whose solutions are guaranteed to have certain specific formal characteristics – for instance, *genetic algorithms* (Holland 1992) deal with problems whose solutions can be represented as character-strings, normally strings of a fixed length. This is not a natural way to represent solutions to parsing problems (it is certainly possible to represent a parsetree linearly as a labelled bracketing, but alternative trees for a given input will not in general be the same length when expressed as labelled bracketings, and the requirement for brackets to balance imposes limitations on which strings count as potential solutions that could not easily be reconciled with the genetic-algorithm approach). Simulated annealing is more general than other stochastic optimization techniques, and one well suited to the domain of natural language parsing.

Many researchers used simulated annealing as a tool for optimizing *neural network* models of human cognition (Boltzmann machines, mentioned on p. 28, are one variety of neural network model). Some impressive results were achieved with neural network models for certain aspects of natural language (Rumelhart *et al.* 1986). But, again, for the parsing task neural network techniques seemed insufficiently general: alternative structural analyses of word-strings are not naturally representable as alternative patterns of excitation in a network of fixed structure (Sampson 1987c: 884–5). I wanted to optimize the data structures that actually counted as target outputs for a parser directly – rather than to optimize structures chosen primarily for their resemblance to the physical machinery of the brain, and which might be used to encode parsetrees indirectly. The great generality of the simulated annealing technique makes it neutral between alternative types of data structure.

Optimization by Simulated Annealing

At an intuitive level, optimization by simulated annealing can be explained through a metaphor. Suppose we are dealing with a large area of mountainous terrain, and we wish to locate the lowest point in it. (In practice, real mountain ranges are surrounded on all sides by lower-lying land or sea, but for the sake of the metaphor imagine that low places are found only inside the territory, which is surrounded by walls rising to the sky.) Mountains are jumbled together in irregular patterns, so one cannot go straight to the low point by a neat logical rule – even if the boundaries of the terrain are regular, there is no reason to expect its lowest point to coincide with its geometrical centre, for instance. How might we go about finding that lowest point?

One 'naive' method would be to fly over the territory and drop a cannonball somewhere at random. After hitting the ground the cannonball would roll downhill, until it reached a place where all adjacent points are higher: and we might hope that that place was the lowest point. But I called this technique 'naive', because of course this hope would almost always be in vain: the fact that the *immediate neighbours* of a point are all higher than it does not imply that *all other points* are higher. Commonly, the cannonball would get stuck in a pothole or cup of land that might be high on a hillside: the ball would find a *local minimum*, but not the *global minimum*.

But there is a way we might solve this difficulty. We could (within the metaphor) pick up the terrain and shake it, enabling the cannonball to bounce over obstructions. We would begin by shaking vigorously enough that the ball could bounce over the highest mountains; and then gradually reduce the strength of shaking, so that the ball approximates increasingly closely to its normal, downhill-only mode of behaviour. At the same time the shaking would contain a horizontal component pushing the cannonball randomly this way and that, in so far as it was not blocked by hillsides.

As this process continued, the ball would seek out low areas: at first in gross terms – it would tend to move out of Himalaya-like and into Dead-Sea-like areas – and then in terms of progressively finer detail, so that with gentle shaking it would tend to move off pavements and into gutters. With gentler and gentler shaking the cannonball would eventually stop moving relative to the landscape; we could declare the process terminated after some specified period had elapsed without movement by the cannonball, and it might then be reasonable to predict that the place where it ended up was indeed the lowest point.

Let us translate the metaphor into a concrete algorithm. And, to make the algorithm clear, let us illustrate it by reference to a specific problem that it can be used to solve. Parsing natural language is far too complicated a problem to make a suitable first illustration; instead, like everyone else who writes about simulated annealing, I shall use the *travelling salesman problem* to illustrate it. This problem is very easily stated (though very hard to solve).

Suppose someone has to visit each of a set of towns, moving in a straight line between any pair of towns and ending where he started. Which ordering of the towns will yield the shortest route over all? It is obvious that some orderings will make the route far longer than it need be (if two of the towns are Edinburgh and Glasgow, it is unlikely to be a good idea to place London between them in the sequence); but there does not seem to be any efficient method of finding the minimal route deterministically, if there are a large number of towns. Yet it is quite desirable to be able to solve complex instances of the travelling salesman problem in some efficient fashion: problems of this type crop up in many practical situations.

To do the job by simulated annealing, we consider the set of all possible solutions, or *solution space* – in the travelling salesman case, this will be the set of all distinct sequences containing each town exactly once. We specify an *evaluation metric* that associates each point in the solution space with a number that tells us how 'good' or 'bad' a solution it is. For the travelling salesman problem, this is straightforward: the cost of a route is its length, the shorter the better. And we choose some method of *transforming solutions into other solutions*, allowing us to execute a random walk through the solution space. For instance, we might say that a route is transformed by reversing some subsequence within it, so that (if there are eight towns represented by letters a to h) a single transformation could change the solution $a\ b\ c\ d\ e\ f\ g\ h$ into, say, the solution $a\ d\ c\ b\ e\ f\ g\ h$ or into the solution $a\ b\ h\ g\ f\ e\ d\ c$, but not into $a\ c\ b\ d\ g\ f\ e\ h$. It is essential that the chosen method of transformation always changes solutions into solutions (we would not want to use a transformation defined as 'Change the second town to h', because this rule would change, say, $a\ b\ c\ d\ e\ f\ g\ h$ into $a\ h\ c\ d\ e\ f\ g\ h$, which is not a solution: b is not visited, and h is visited twice). And it is also essential that the transformations always provide some way of getting, perhaps via a long series of moves, from any solution to any other solution – the move-set must be *closed* (Cox & Miller 1965: 100). (This property of the move-set provably applies in the case of subsequence-reversals.)

The method of transformation chosen defines a *neighbourhood relationship* on the solution space: for any particular solution, certain solutions can be reached from it by a single move, others cannot. And the neighbourhood relationship and the evaluation metric between them give the solution space a geometry – they produce the mountainous terrain of the metaphor.

The neighbourhood relationship specifies which points in the solution space are adjacent horizontally, and the evaluation metric defines the altitude of each point. (The 'mountain' metaphor has limitations, of course: the points of a solution space are discretely separate rather than continuous like a real land surface, and although one can say how far apart two points are, in terms of the minimum number of moves needed to get from one to the other, one cannot describe a point as having an absolute position in terms of Cartesian co-ordinates or the like.)

One way to look for the best solution is to begin with a randomly chosen solution and to generate a random series of transformations, accepting each move that reduces (or leaves unchanged) the cost of the current solution, and rejecting each cost-increasing move, until a solution is reached which is better than each of its neighbours. This is like dropping the cannonball without shaking. To introduce 'shaking' into the calculations, in order to avoid getting trapped in local minima, we complicate the rule for accepting or rejecting moves by making it depend on the current value of a variable T (which we can think of as representing the strength of shaking). At the outset of a run, when we choose the first random solution, we set T to some large positive real number. As the run proceeds, with changes to the current solution being generated successively, we make T decline steadily towards zero. Whenever a candidate move is generated, we calculate the increase in cost, d, that would result by adopting the move. If d is negative or zero (that is, the new solution is better than or has the same value as the current solution) then we make the move, as before; but if d is positive, we do not reject the move out of hand. Instead, we choose whether to accept or reject it by (as it were) tossing a coin, except that we set the probability of acceptance not at one-half (as in the case of coin-tossing), but at the value $\exp\left(\frac{-d}{T}\right)$. (The notation 'exp x' is another way of writing e^x, where e is the base of natural logarithms, approximately 2.7.) If d and T are both positive finite numbers, as they will be whenever this formula is used, then $\exp\left(\frac{-d}{T}\right)$ is bound to be a real number between 0 and 1 – hence meaningful as a probability. The acceptance probability is relatively low if d is large (moves that would take the cannonball steeply uphill tend to be rejected); it is relatively high if T is large (almost any move tends to be accepted when the shaking is strong enough). But, even when d is large and T close to zero, there is a small finite probability of acceptance, and conversely there is a small finite probability of rejection even when d is near zero and T is large.

The act of 'tossing a coin' is executed on the computer by using a random-number generating routine to produce a random real number between 0 and 1. If this number is less than the current value of $\exp\left(\frac{-d}{T}\right)$, the move is accepted; otherwise it is rejected.

To complete the definition of the algorithm, it only remains to specify a criterion for terminating the random walk through the solution space. There are various ways of doing this, but they all depend on the fact that, as T approaches zero, fewer and fewer of the moves generated are accepted, until eventually the current solution remains unchanged for long periods while candidate moves are generated in vain – the cannonball comes to rest. A simple way to specify the termination criterion is to fix some large positive integer f at the outset and say that the process terminates once f consecutive generated moves have been rejected.

If individual solutions have many neighbours, then there is a possibility, even after many random moves have been rejected, that some neighbour might exist which is better than the current solution but happens never to have been proposed by the move-generator. To guard against this possibility, one refinement of the technique (see e.g. Lundy & Mees 1986: 122, Huang et al. 1987: 383) adds a deterministic search phase at the end of a run. After f consecutive rejections, each neighbour of the current solution is systematically checked; if any are found that are better than the current solution, the best of them is made the current solution, and the process is repeated until the current solution really is superior to all its neighbours.

The name 'simulated annealing' comes from an analogy with metallurgy. When iron is worked, it has to be heated close to melting and then gradually cooled while being beaten continually. That is the way to get a strong implement; if the hot metal is shaped and then cooled down abruptly ('quenched'), it will end up with flaws in its crystal structure, making it brittle. In terms of physics, the desired flawless structure in which all particles are arranged in a completely regular crystalline lattice is a state of 'minimal energy' it is reached from the high-energy, molten state, in which the particles move randomly, by gradually reducing the particles' freedom of movement via cooling. (Hence my choice of symbols T for 'temperature' and f for 'freezing criterion'.) The move-acceptance criterion using the formula $\exp\left(\frac{-d}{T}\right)$, with d representing energy-gain from a small random perturbation of current state, was first introduced by Nicholas Metropolis in 1953 in order to model computationally the evolution of a solid towards thermal equilibrium (Metropolis et al. 1953). But the phrase 'simulated annealing' was coined much more recently, to denote the use of essentially the same algorithm in order to solve problems (such as the travelling salesman problem) having nothing to do with the cooling of physical matter. 'Simulated annealing', in this sense, was apparently invented independently in the early 1980s by Scott Kirkpatrick and colleagues at the IBM Research Centre, Yorktown Heights, New York State (Kirkpatrick et al. 1983), and by V. Černý of the Comenius University, Bratislava (Černý 1985). (An authoritative standard textbook is Aarts & Korst 1989; see also van Laarhoven & Aarts 1987, Davis 1987, Johnson 1989.)

Practical Versus Ideal Algorithms

Rather than one single algorithm, simulated annealing is better thought of as a family of algorithms: on the one hand an 'ideal' algorithm which can be proved to exhibit certain desirable behaviour – but which cannot be executed in real life; and on the other hand various 'quick and dirty' approximations to the ideal, whose 'dirtiness' means that they cannot be the topic of mathematical proofs, but whose quickness means that they can be put to use in real life, and which in some cases share enough of the behaviour of the ideal algorithm to constitute good ways of solving real problems. Domains in which simulated annealing is useful are ones characterized by a high degree of *frustration* (Toulouse 1977), meaning that optimization is difficult because of conflicting constraints: improving one feature of a solution tends to imply worsening another feature or features. Finding a parsetree for a natural language sample is like that: postulating a tagma of category X may be a good way of accounting for the elements that X will contain, but at the same time it may be hard to find a satisfactory way of incorporating an X tagma into the higher-level structure.

In ideal simulated annealing (which I describe here following Hajek (1988), as reported by Aarts & Korst (1989: ch. 3)), there is no freezing criterion (and *a fortiori* no period of exhaustive deterministic neighbourhood search after freezing): the process of randomly generating and accepting-or-rejecting moves simply continues indefinitely, at temperatures which approach zero asymptotically in a manner that depends on an aspect of solution-space geometry known as *depth*. The depth of a local minimum in the solution space, put informally, is the least amount it is necessary to climb in order to get from that point to a lower one – the altitude-difference between the point at the bottom of a cup and the lowest point on the rim. (If a point is not a local minimum, its depth is naturally zero; the depth of the global minimum is infinite.)

For ideal simulated annealing, a constant Γ is selected which must be at least as large as the depth of the deepest local minimum in the solution space, and T is set to the following series of values at successive attempted moves:

$$\frac{\Gamma}{\log 2}, \frac{\Gamma}{\log 3}, \frac{\Gamma}{\log 4}, \ldots$$

– i.e. the temperature for the k'th move is $\frac{\Gamma}{\log(k+1)}$. Various assumptions are made about the geometry of the solution space and about the move-generating function. Each solution must have the same number of immediate neighbours, and the probabilities of generating moves from a solution to each of its neighbours must be equal. For any pair of solutions

a, b, the highest altitude such that all paths from a to b reach at least that altitude – the height of the lowest mountain-pass between the two points, as it were – must be the same as for paths from b to a (in practice this will usually mean that whenever b is a neighbour of a then a is also a neighbour of b, so that paths can be traversed in either direction, though strictly the proof does not require individual moves always to be reversible).

If these conditions are fulfilled and temperature is reduced on the schedule described, then there is a proof that as the number of moves generated tends towards infinity, the probability of the current solution being the optimum solution (or being one of the optima, if there is more than one equally-low lowest point) tends towards 1, i.e. towards certainty.

As a practical computing technique there are two problems with this ideal algorithm (even if the conditions are fulfilled). The non-obvious problem is that the depth of the deepest local minimum, a quantity needed to determine an adequate cooling schedule, is exceedingly difficult to calculate. And the obvious problem is that we cannot wait for ever to finish optimizing an input. Accordingly, practical simulated annealing introduces various approximations and divergences from the ideal, the concept of a 'freezing criterion' which is attained in finite time being one of these. Empirically it emerges that these approximate techniques do yield optimal or near-optimal results with very high probabilities for a wide range of problem-types.

Commonly, cooling is controlled in a way that takes no account of 'depth of deepest local minimum': instead, runs of attempted moves are executed at fixed temperatures, beginning with some more or less arbitrarily chosen initial temperature T_0; after each sequence of L attempted moves, for some constant integer L, the temperature is reduced by multiplying it with some constant cooling factor c between 0 and 1, normally much closer to 1 than to 0. The variables T_0, L, c, and f jointly define an *annealing schedule*: low values of any of them tend to lead to annealing runs which quickly terminate but have a low probability of reaching the global optimum, high values improve the chances of freezing on the optimal solution at the cost of increasing processing time. There is a theoretical reason (which I shall not attempt to explain here) for the system of lowering temperature after runs of move-attempts rather than after each attempted move; but it is treated as an essentially empirical, 'engineering' question what combination of annealing-schedule values for a particular class of problems gives the most satisfactory trade-off between quality of solutions attained and amount of processing entailed (which can be very large indeed).[1] Numerous tricks have been introduced by various researchers in order to preserve the essence of the simulated annealing approach while improving the trade-off between solution-quality and processing (see e.g. Greene & Supowit 1986,

Szu & Hartley 1987, Tovey 1989), and related optimizing techniques have been introduced (e.g. Creutz 1983, cf. Barnard 1987).

One consequence of the fact that 'real' simulated annealing is approximative, with success not guaranteed by mathematical theorem, is that different classes of problem vary in the extent to which they lend themselves to the technique. For a problem to be tractable by simulated annealing, it is important that the shape of its solution space should not be characterized by major cost differentials in the vicinity of the global optimum. Returning to the mountain metaphor: we need the terrain to resemble real hill country, where large near-vertical precipices are rare and lowland contours in particular tend to be gentle; simulated annealing would not work in a terrain like the Witwatersrand, where the gold we seek is found at the bottom of deep, narrow, vertical mineshafts sunk from the top of a high plateau. In such a terrain, the cannonball has no tendency to remain in the vicinity of the global optimum, because points close to it horizontally are mostly very bad. Optimization by simulated annealing depends on not having to examine each solution (if the solution space is small enough for that to be feasible, there will be little point in using a stochastic optimization technique). A system can get away without looking at each separate solution, provided it can pick up clues that it is 'getting warm' by visiting the general area of the optimal solution.

The reason for the unusual shape of the Rand is that men have created mineshafts as artificial modifications to its natural structure. There does seem to be a tendency (though, certainly, a tendency with plenty of exceptions) for natural phenomena to contain few major discontinuities. That is one reason for optimism about the extent of the domain where simulated annealing is potentially applicable (and particularly optimism with respect to our own intended application: human language, I take it, belongs to the realm of natural rather than artificial phenomena). And a larger reason for optimism, perhaps, is that to a large extent solution-space geometry is within our control. The shape of the terrain can be utterly changed by choosing a different method of transforming solutions into other solutions, which defines the neighbourhood relationship between solutions. This choice is not unconstrained: from the point of view of processing economy one would not want to choose a move-set that made the process of generating a neighbour computationally cumbersome; but, even so, there is likely to be plenty of room for manoeuvre when settling on a move-set, and if one move-set induces an unfavourable geometry in the solution space it is quite possible that an alternative move-set will yield a better geometry.

The technique of optimization by simulated annealing was successfully applied to real-world problems very shortly after its invention, notably to the design of chips for electronic systems, where it is desirable to minimize the length of wiring needed to connect circuits but also to satisfy constraints that pull in other directions, for instance to avoid wiring congestion (Kirkpatrick *et al.* 1983: 673ff., Vecchi & Kirkpatrick 1983). Another early application was in the vision domain: optimization by simulated annealing was used for the tasks of cleaning up and interpreting 'noisy' images (Geman & Geman 1984, Sontag & Sussman 1985). For me, what made optimization by simulated annealing particularly attractive was its lack of any concept of 'well-formed' v. 'ill-formed' inputs. The annealing algorithm cannot just fall over if faced with an input for which no good solution exists, as parsers based on the compilation metaphor so easily can: the annealing system goes ahead to seek the best solution available for whatever input it is given, operating in the same way whether the absolute value of the best solution is high or low. Computational natural language processing, I believed, was badly in need of this quality of robustness.

And there was a second attractive aspect of the simulated annealing technique. The amount of processing expended on an input before freezing is roughly determined by the annealing schedule chosen, and it is usual to choose a schedule in such a way that more complex inputs receive more processing. But successful applications of simulated annealing had tended to get good results with schedules that varied quantity of processing linearly with input complexity, or at worst made the former a small power of the latter (Kirkpatrick *et al.* 1983: 679). For natural language processing this is very good news, because compilation-like parsing techniques, while efficient for short inputs, often require processing times that vary exponentially with sentence length. Ultimately, automatic natural language parsers will need to do what human beings do: analyse in real time streams of language which may continue indefinitely, and in which the parser may need to locate sentence boundaries in addition to lower-level construction boundaries for itself, rather than being given a segmentation into high-level units as part of the input data. It is difficult to see how this could ever be achieved with any parsing technique for which processing steps need to increase more than linearly with input length.

For optimization by simulated annealing, 'large' inputs might even be easier to process, because evaluation of a solution would depend on more separate variables, which could tend to make solution-space geometry smoother, less Rand-like.

There were certainly respects in which the parsing problem differed significantly from the problems to which optimization by simulated annealing had originally been applied, and a theoretical linguist would not be slow to notice these. Standard simulated annealing applications, such as electronic chip design, are domains where the important thing is to find *one of the best solutions* – it does not matter whether the solution found is the very best of all. (There are practical reasons why a chip ought not to have circuits whose total length is twice what is necessary, but saving the last fraction of a percentage point of total length has no practical significance.) In natural language parsing, on the other hand, people normally feel that a miss is as good as a mile: a sentence has one correct analysis, and an analysis which is close but not identical is just wrong.

This standard point of view underestimates, I believe, the incidence of grammatical ambiguity in real-life language even when this is edited written prose (Sampson 1987b, 1995: 163–4); very commonly a well-formed sentence will have a number of different interpretations, each of which is defensible. (In speech, what one finds are often not logical message structures at all, but fragments and hints from which a hearer must construct a message as best he may.) What is more, for some practical NLP applications full parsing is not needed; Knowles & Lawrence (1987: 146) argue this in connection with text-to-speech systems, for instance. Nevertheless, even if a parser could legitimately output alternative solutions for an input, there seems to be a sharp boundary between acceptable and unacceptable grammatical analyses of a sentence, not a continuous gradient from better to worse analyses.

That in itself would not matter if an annealing parser could be made to deliver analyses that regularly fell within the acceptable set for the respective input. This would depend on the possibility of finding evaluation metrics which reliably prefer acceptable to unacceptable analyses, and this was another area where parsing was different from typical simulated annealing applications. In the latter, the evaluation metric directly measures the properties that the user is interested in – circuit length, for instance. With parsing, any quantitative measurements are likely to be only a proxy for what the user is really seeking: he wants to know what message a sentence is intended to convey, and although finding an analysis of the sentence which makes its structure statistically typical for the language may be a successful way of locating the intended message logic, the two things are conceptually separate.

But these caveats would have been more serious if the compilation approach to parsing had proved routinely successful when applied to real-life, non-artificial language samples. It had not. The robustness of the simulated annealing algorithm was so attractive a feature, in view of the messiness of real-life usage, that parsing by annealing seemed well worth a try. I decided to carry out a very simple experiment.

A Pilot Experiment

This first attempt had to be designed and programmed single-handed in the gaps of time in a busy teaching and administrative career, so I cut the problem down to the absolute minimum that still retained its essence. I implemented it on what, a decade later, looks like a laughably limited machine – a 'BBC Micro', selected in the early 1980s as the platform for government-sponsored television lessons in computing for the general UK population, which had just 32 kilobytes of RAM. (I had access to 'serious' computing power, but no time to develop software that needed it.) Nevertheless, this toy system exemplified in a small way many of the issues which continue to play a role in the far more complex annealing-parser systems which have succeeded it; the toy system makes a good tutorial case-study, and I shall describe it in some detail.

In such a limited experiment there was clearly no possibility of building a system that would accept input in the form of ordinary unedited text and work out all aspects of its analysis: it was essential that inputs should be heavily 'predigested' and consist of sequences of wordtags (codes for word classes), rather than of the words themselves. Apart from this, the problem was simplified in two further ways.

The vocabulary of parsetree node labels (nonterminal and terminal) was reduced, by merging related labels, to a far smaller number than the vocabulary used in labelling the Treebank from which my data were derived. And the statistical information about the range of structural configurations occurring in the Treebank which was abstracted out to form the system's model of the English language was limited to the simplest category of information that might possibly enable the system to distinguish between plausible and implausible parsetrees.

In the case of the node labels, with a few exceptions I treated any set of nonterminal labels, and any set of wordtags, which shared the same first character in the Treebank annotation scheme as a single label – the structure of that scheme made this a reasonable way of producing an extremely crude classification of words and tagmas. This gave me thirty wordtags (which I represented by lower-case letters, or punctuation marks for the six cases of wordtags representing classes of punctuation mark), and fourteen phrase and clause categories, represented in my experiment by capitals.

By comparison, the Treebank wordtag-set (the 'LOB tagset' of Garside *et al.* (1987: Appendix B)) included 132 distinct wordtags. In the case of tagmatags (nonterminal labels) it is less clear how to calculate the size of the vocabulary used in the Treebank analyses. Treebank tagmatags commonly involved combinations of symbols representing separate grammatical features – the verb group *might not be* in Fig. 2.1 (p. 9) is labelled Vdceb, meaning that it begins with a modal verb in the past tense, is negative, and has *be* as its main verb; and the number of different combinations used was in the hundreds – theoretically the number of possible legal combinations was on the order of 60,000 distinct labels. However, many of the feature symbols were defined in terms of the immediately subordinate nodes (a verb-group node would take the subcategory symbol 'e', 'negative', if and only if one of its immediate constituents was a negative particle, *not* or *-n't*) – since the use of optimization by simulated annealing is to identify features of a solution that cannot be predicted by deterministic rules, arguably these components of the Treebank nonterminal labels were irrelevant for my experiment. But even setting aside the largest possible proportion of nonterminal label elements as deterministically predictable (and many of these elements may in fact have been less completely determined in the annotation scheme than *prima facie* appeared), one would be left with at least 26 nonterminals, almost double the number in my system.

As for the language model, this contained nothing more subtle than statistics about the frequencies of pairwise transitions between daughter labels below a mother label. That is, for any triple of labels MD_1D_2 where M is one of the fourteen nonterminal categories, D_1 is one of the 44 nonterminal and terminal categories or a symbol standing for 'left boundary', and D_2 is a nonterminal or terminal symbol or a 'right boundary' symbol, the language model recorded how frequently in the roughly 40,000 words of the Treebank the symbol-pair D_1D_2 occurred adjacently within the sequence of daughter labels below a mother node labelled M. There are $14 \times (45^2 - 1) = 28{,}336$ possible transitions of this form: the '–1' represents the fact that a transition from left boundary to right boundary is not allowed – every nonterminal in the Treebank analyses had to have at least one daughter. Of these logical possibilities, the data included nonzero frequencies for 1251; for about a third of those cases, the observed frequency was 1. At the other end of the frequency scale, the commonest single transition was 'P [i', representing 'preposition occurring as first daughter of a prepositional phrase', which had a frequency of 4381.

I further simplified things by never inputting a sentence whose correct analysis contained an instance of singular branching, which did sometimes occur within the Treebank annotation scheme: my system restricted itself to exploring solutions in which every nonterminal had at least two daughters. If no constraints are placed on the occurrence of singular branching, then even if an input sentence is very short and the vocabulary of nonterminal labels is very small, the space of possible solutions becomes infinitely large. (A one-word input string could be given a solution in which the word is the daughter of the root node, another solution in which it is granddaughter of the root, another solution in which it is great-granddaughter of the root ... and so on for any finite number of singulary-branching nodes between root and leaf node.) We shall see in due course that, since the fully detailed annotation schemes which have been developed alongside my automatic parsing experiments do permit singular branching in limited circumstances, the more serious parsing systems which have subsequently grown out of the 'toy' system currently under discussion permit solutions to include singular branching, under constraints which guarantee that solution spaces remain finite. My first toy system constrained singular branching in the simplest possible way, by forbidding it altogether.

Reducing the vocabulary of node labels, and limiting the kind of grammatical statistics included in the language model, both help to shrink the dimensions of the annealing-parser development task. If the system knows nothing more about English grammar than how commonly a particular label follows another label within the sequence of daughters below a particular mother label, then there is no possibility of making the analysis-evaluation component of the parser highly subtle in the considerations it uses to prefer one solution to another. Any individual analysis will have to be evaluated through a fairly straightforward calculation, which means that it can be evaluated quickly – very desirable considering that the simulated annealing technique involves long random walks through large solution spaces. And if the vocabulary of node labels is small, the size of the solution space is reduced.

On the other hand, both of these simplifying measures are double-edged swords. Limiting the kind of grammatical knowledge incorporated in the language model makes for simple programming and rapid processing, but at the same time it must tend to reduce the chance for the system to get its answers right, since it has less knowledge to go on. And reducing the label vocabulary means that less information is required in the system outputs, but it also means that less information is available in the system inputs. Since wordtags are given in the inputs, rather than being part of what the system was required to discover, the reduction in the wordtag-set from 132 to 30 members is purely negative from the system's point of view: it reduces the information available about any given input, without offering any compensating advantage. The reduction in the nonterminal label vocabulary does mean that the system has fewer alternatives to choose among when constructing a labelled tree analysis, which in itself makes its task less demanding, but it also means that the analysis will be less securely founded: the appropriateness of a nonterminal label for a node d can be judged only in terms of the labels of the mother and daughters of d, so the less information is available in the mother label and in the labels of those daughters which are nonterminal, the less help they will be able to give in discriminating among alternative labellings for d.

Furthermore, although simplifying the label vocabulary does greatly reduce the size of the solution space, the space remains extremely large. The fundamental motive for applying a stochastic optimization technique to the problem of grammatical parsing was that attempts to state rigid rules about how parsetrees must be configured seem repeatedly to fall foul of the anarchic messiness of real-life language. Accordingly, I saw it as crucial to impose no prior assumptions on the structure and labelling of parsetrees for particular inputs: the solution space should include *any* topologically possible labelled tree, and statistical considerations alone should discriminate between plausible and implausible analyses. An analysis, say, containing numerous nonterminals between root and leaf nodes, every one of which carried the same label G, 'genitive phrase', would linguistically be quite absurd – the label G stands for a phrase like *my wife's*, and English sentences never consist wholly of sequences of genitive phrases containing sequences of smaller genitive phrases nested within themselves. But, for the annealing parser, this absurdity should translate into the fact that such an analysis receives a figure of merit far poorer than the figure assigned to many alternative analyses of the same input, including the correct analysis. The all-G analysis should be included within the solution space, not excluded: it should be treated as one possible analysis, though there should be many better ones.

Specifically, for any given input in the shape of a finite string of wordtag symbols, the solution space which my pilot system explored was the set of all rooted tree structures having one leaf node for each symbol in the input string, and such that each nonterminal node had two or more daughters and bore some label from the 14-member nonterminal vocabulary; except that it was required that the root node should always bear the same initial symbol S, 'sentence'.

Once we know the size of the nonterminal vocabulary, the number of distinct labelled trees in this set depends only on the length of the input. The first input I tried on the system (it will be discussed in more detail below) was 11 words long – quite a short sentence. For an input of this length, there are about 1.9×10^{15} distinct solutions to be explored: that is, 1900 million million (1.9 American quadrillions). This is far fewer than in the case of an average-length sentence as mentioned in ch. 2, but it is not a small number.

Thus the tasks to be solved by the pilot system were not trivial, even though they did omit much of the complexity of English grammar.

The Pilot Algorithms

To specify an annealing system, one must define: a *solution space* (as I have just done); a quantitative *evaluation metric* over the solution space; a method of generating *random walks* through the solution space; and an *annealing schedule* which governs the propensity of the system to make uphill moves at different stages, and provides a criterion for terminating a run.

The evaluation metric is a function from the elements of the solution space into the real number line, which should be such that the desired solution or solutions have better values than any unacceptable solutions. 'Better' does not necessarily mean 'higher'. In fact, for reasons having to do with the thermodynamic analogies which underlie the theory of simulated annealing, it is usual to think of the evaluation metric as measuring the 'cost' of a solution and to arrange for it to assign *low* values to good solutions; annealing systems strive to 'minimize the energy' of a solution. As it happens, my toy system did not do this: a good solution for this system was a solution assigned a high figure of merit. (Either convention can trivially be transformed into the other, but I draw the point to the reader's attention, since both conventions will be encountered in this book.)

I envisaged the task of the evaluation metric as being to give greater preference to a labelled tree, the more it contained daughter-transitions shown by our Treebank to occur with high frequency in English and the less it contained low-frequency transitions. Thus I might simply have used the mean pairwise daughter-transition frequency for all the transitions in the various daughter-sequences below the nonterminal nodes of a tree. Some initial experimentation suggested that this was too simple, and I eventually settled for an evaluation metric that did rather more calculation than this with the individual transition frequencies. Specifically, my function gave a value for an individual nonterminal node by taking, not the simple mean of its various transition frequencies, but the reciprocal root mean square reciprocal of those frequencies, in order to try to ensure that one or two 'bad' transitions made a large negative impact on the overall value of a node most of whose daughter-transitions were 'good'. Because (as we saw above) many transitions have an observed frequency of zero, before carrying out this calculation all transition frequencies were increased by 0.1, in order to avoid dividing by zero when taking the reciprocal of the frequency of an unobserved transition. The function then gave a value for an entire tree by averaging not the simple values of its various nonterminal nodes as thus calculated, but the logarithms of those values: again this was intended to ensure that a few bad nodes would drag down the overall value of a tree, most of whose nodes were good.

At the time, I saw it as a purely empirical issue how best to juggle frequency figures to get an evaluation metric which could be relied on to prefer correct to incorrect analyses of inputs. We shall see in due course that, as this line of research grew from a one-man hobby into a larger-scale team effort, colleagues educated me into understanding that there is theory that can be applied in this domain, and that my initial evaluation metric was not just less than ideal but fundamentally misguided. However, my task at present is to explain what I actually did in the early days, not what I should have done. At this point I had a great deal to learn.

A mechanism for generating random walks through a solution space must have two parts: (i) a way of choosing an initial solution, and, more interestingly, (ii) a way of generating a new solution from any current solution.

For my pilot system (i) was very simple: any input string was automatically assigned the *flat tree*, in which each leaf node is directly dominated by the root node (and the root node is labelled S, which is true throughout the solution space).

In the case of (ii), the move-generation mechanism, there is a potential misunderstanding to be averted. Linguists who hear that an annealing parser is based on a process in which parsetrees are repeatedly transformed into other parsetrees often relate this idea to their existing tradition of grammatical theorizing by supposing that the steps from one tree to the next must be chosen to make some kind of logical sense – that perhaps trees are transformed into trees having related meanings, as in 'transformational grammar'.

Nothing like that is intended here. An annealing parser simply needs some way of making small local changes to the shape and/or labelling of trees, considered as abstract mathematical objects, such that from any tree in a solution space one can get to any other tree in the solution space via a chain of permissible moves. We shall see later that, for successful simulated annealing, some definitions of 'permissible move' work better than others, but the relevant considerations have to do with the abstract logical geometry induced in the solution space by a particular move-set – they are not to do with the linguistic interpretation of solutions when simulated annealing is applied to the specific problem of natural language parsing. The moves generated by the pilot annealing system normally make no sense at all in terms of semantic relationships between the trees they cause to succeed one another in a random walk, and they are not intended to make this sort of sense.

To explain the move-generation mechanism used in the pilot system is slightly complicated (though, like the pilot evaluation metric, it is simpler than the mechanisms which replaced it in later, more 'serious' versions of the annealing parser). Intuitively, a move involved detaching a randomly chosen tree node from its mother, reattaching it at one of the points where it could be attached without 'crossing lines' in the tree, and randomly relabelling its new mother.

To define this class of moves explicitly is most easily done if we postulate that a parsetree is always represented as a data structure in which the input word-string is preceded and followed by boundary markers, which as leaves of a parsetree are always immediately dominated by the root node and form the first and last daughters of the root. These two additional terminal nodes make no difference to the size of the solution space or to the evaluation of solutions (they are ignored in evaluating root nodes), but they enable the class of moves from solution to solution to be defined without needing to describe special cases.

Given any labelled tree over a string, a move to a different tree is generated as follows:

- Choose at random with equal probabilities one of the terminal or nonterminal nodes of the tree, other than the root node or the two boundary markers. Call this node *d*.
- Delete the link[2] between *d* and its mother, *m*. Node *d* will now be the root of a separate subtree below an 'arch' of nodes and links leading from the terminal node immediately preceding the subtree up to a 'keystone' nonterminal node and down to the terminal node immediately following the subtree. (The keystone node is the lowest node dominating both of the terminal nodes just mentioned.)
- Choose at random with equal probabilities one of the nodes or one of the links contained in this 'arch', other than the two terminal nodes at its base, or the link immediately above a terminal node if that node is one of the boundary elements.
- If a node of the arch is selected, call this node *e*, and create a new link joining *e* as mother to *d* as daughter.
- If a link of the arch is selected, create a new node *e* 'in the middle of the link', and create a link between *e* as mother and *d* as daughter. That is, if the chosen link joined node *f* as mother to node *g* as daughter, the new node *e* should have *f* as mother and should have *d* and *g* as daughters (in whichever order those nodes occurred before the tree was modified).
- In either case, assign node *e* a label drawn at random with equal probabilities from the nonterminal vocabulary (replacing the previous label if node *e* is not newly created).
- If the original mother *m* of *d* is left with only one daughter, delete *m* and convert the daughters of *m* into daughters of the mother of *m*.
- If *m* is the root node and is left with only one daughter other than the two boundary markers, delete that daughter and convert the granddaughters of *m* into daughters of *m*.

For instance, in the tree on the left-hand side of Fig. 3.1, node 17 has been chosen and the link between nodes 16 and 17 deleted. The 'arch' surrounding node 17 then passes from terminal node 5 through nodes 15, 14, 12 to the 'keystone' node 11, and down through node 16 to the terminal node 8. Of the two trees shown on the right, one has resulted from reattaching node 17 to node 15, the other from reattaching node 17 to a new node 18 created on the link between 11 and 16.

It is not difficult to show that the move-set I have defined is closed, that is, that any possible tree can be reached by a chain of moves from any other possible tree (Sampson 1989c: 193).[3] It certainly does not meet the

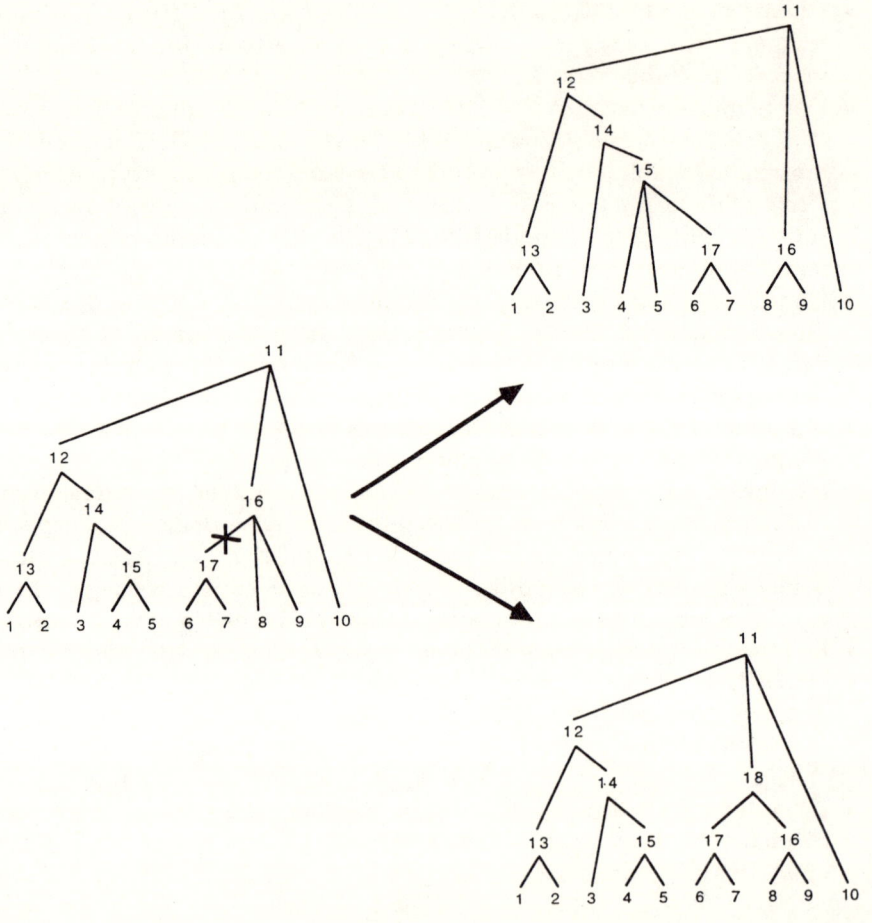

Figure 3.1 Alternative steps in the solution space for the pilot system

conditions discussed above for 'ideal simulated annealing'. For instance, with this move-set, solutions have very different numbers of neighbours (depending on the length of the arch created when the chosen node *d* is detached from its mother). I do not believe this is a peculiarity of the particular move-set I chose to use in the pilot system; I very much doubt whether there is any straightforward way to define a class of moves through the space of labelled trees over a string that would induce a logical geometry in which each solution had an equal number of neighbours. If my doubt is justified, simulated annealing applied to the parsing problem must always be an empirical craft rather than a theoretically pure science – but then that is usually so even for applications where in principle it would be possible to make the solution-space geometry and move-generation mechanism conform to the requirements of the theoretical model.

This means that the detailed figures which define an annealing schedule are a matter of trial and error rather than of principle, and they tend to be of little general interest outside the laboratory in which they are applied. Nevertheless, for the sake of completeness I give the schedule used for my first serious attempt to run the pilot system over a sentence. The initial value for T was 1.0, and T was reduced by 3% after every fiftieth (accepted or rejected) move. A run was terminated at the first temperature drop at which each of the preceding 100 proposed moves had either been rejected or had left the tree-value unchanged.[4]

First Results

The first input I gave this system, on the New Year evening described in ch. 1, was the typist's practice sentence *The quick brown fox must jump over the lazy dog.*[5] In terms of the 30-member wordtag-set this was submitted to the system as the string:

```
d j j n o v i d j n .
```

– the codes translate as:

    d   determiner
    j   adjective
    n   singular noun
    o   modal verb or *do*
    v   main verb
    i   preposition
    .   sentence-final punctuation mark

The initial tree, [Sdjjnovidjn.], had the value −2.26.

50 Evolutionary Language Understanding

A	T	Ch	Value	Current Tree
100	0.970	93	-1.31	[Sdjj[Rn[Lo[G[Fvi][J[N[Gdj]n].]]]]]
200	0.913	93	-1.52	[S[Wd[D[Jjj]no]][Fv[Vidj]][Pn.]]
300	0.859	92	-1.02	[S[Pd[Dj[Jjn]][Nov]i[R[Adj]n]].]
400	0.808	88	-2.30	[Sd[Dj[V[Fjn][P[V[Gov][Ji[Ldj]]n].]]]]
500	0.760	82	0.01	[S[Vdj][Njn[W[Tovidj]n]].]
600	0.715	90	-0.54	[S[N[Jd[T[Pjj][S[N[Tn[Jov]][Tid]]j]]]n].]
700	0.673	66	1.64	[S[Sd[Njj[Nn[No[Vvi]]]d[Njn]]].]
800	0.633	69	-1.51	[S[N[Nd[Sjj]]no][J[A[Tvi][Tdjn]].]]
900	0.596	73	-0.06	[S[N[D[F[Ad[S[Fjj][Nno]]]v][Tid]j]n].]
1000	0.561	75	-0.98	[Sd[D[L[Gj[Njn]][Wov]][F[F[Lid]jn].]]]
1100	0.527	58	1.50	[S[P[Mdj][Njn][Jovi][Ndj]n].]
1200	0.496	66	-0.18	[S[Ndjjn][Novid]j[Mn.]]
1300	0.467	63	0.67	[S[N[Dd[Njj]n]ov[Lidj]n].]
1400	0.439	54	0.33	[S[Nd[Njj]n][P[Jo[Rvi[Sdj]]n].]]
1500	0.413	57	0.76	[S[Nd[V[Njj]n]o][S[T[Tvi][Dd[Njn]]].]]
1600	0.389	18	4.93	[S[Ndjjn[F[Vov][Pid]]][Njn].]
1700	0.366	8	5.21	[S[Ndjjn][F[Vov][Pi[Nd[Njn]]]].]
1800	0.344	11	5.46	[S[N[Ndjjn][F[Vov][Pi[Ndjn]]]].]
1900	0.324	7	5.70	[S[Ndjjn][F[Vov][Pi[Ndjn]]].]
2000	0.305	5	6.63	[S[Ndjjn][Vov][Pi[Ndjn]].]
2100	0.287	5	6.63	[S[Ndjjn][Vov][Pi[Ndjn]].]

```
A:   attempts
T:   temperature
Ch:  changes
```

Figure 3.2 The first annealing parser run

Fig. 3.2 gives a snapshot of the situation after every hundredth attempted move (that is, after a hundred moves had been proposed by the move-generator and either accepted or rejected). In the early stages the system visited areas of the solution space where values are poor; the current tree after the first hundred attempts, for instance, analyses *the lazy* as a genitive phrase and *jump over* as a finite subordinate clause, and treats the full stop as part of an adjective phrase. After 400 attempts the system reached a solution worse than the one it began with; and there are large falls as well as rises in the immediately following series of recorded values. From attempt 1400 onwards, though, solution-value increases steadily (though undoubtedly with smaller up-and-down fluctuations between the points recorded), and after attempt 2000 the system has settled (the five moves recorded as accepted between attempts 2000 and 2100 were null moves of the sort described in footnote 4) on the high-valued analysis which it outputs:

```
[S[Ndjjn][Vov][Pi[Ndjn]].]
```

This is the correct analysis, according to the Treebank annotation scheme from which the system derived its language model. *The quick brown fox*, and *the lazy dog*, are noun phrases, N; *must jump* is a verb group, V; and *over the lazy dog* is a prepositional phrase, P. (In the Treebank scheme, there is no internal structure in a phrase such as *the quick brown fox*.)

This is a simple sentence and, once established, its structure looks trivial. It is a thoroughly well-formed example (for this first attempt I simply input a coded version of the first sentence that came into my head), and a fragile compiler-like parser should have little difficulty in analysing it. But the annealing parser knew none of the rules that a compiler-like parser would use to work out the analysis: it had only statistical knowledge of a kind that could be deployed also on an input that was not perfectly well formed. And although the structure may seem trivial, the system found its way to it as one among almost two quadrillion alternatives. From the system's point of view, this analysis (which we human onlookers know to be uniquely correct) was not flying a flag saying, 'Here I am, you've found me!' The system settled on this solution because, having reached it through a chain of moves from one solution to another slightly better solution, it then failed despite many attempts to find a still better solution in order to continue the chain.

As a first result this was obviously very heartening. It did involve a measure of beginner's luck. My computer had time to execute three annealing runs, using different random-number seeds, on the same input during the hours I was at that New Year party; the second and third runs were less successful. The second run yielded the analysis [Sdjjnov[Pi[Ndjn]].], value 4.43 (at temperature 0.270, after 2200 attempted and 1328 accepted moves): part of the structure has been correctly built, but no structure at all has been found in the first part of the sentence. The third run gave [Sdjjn[Vov]id[S[Njn].]], value 4.18 (at temperature 0.166, after 3000 attempted and 1378 accepted moves). In this case some of the structure created is just wrong: the words *lazy dog.* have been analysed as an embedded main clause consisting of a noun phrase followed by a full stop, an implausible configuration whatever wording lies behind the codes.

But these runs, though clearly failures, were not too worrying, because their output analyses were much lower valued than the correct analysis. If the only problem with an annealing experiment is that it does not consistently locate the solution with the best value, then there is every possibility of curing this through adjustments to the annealing schedule or (via modifications to the move-set) to the geometry of the solution space. The larger issue for an annealing parser is whether an evaluation metric can be found which succeeds in preferring correct to incorrect solutions sufficiently reliably to make 'best valued solution' an acceptable proxy for 'correct analysis'. The metric based on daughter-transition frequencies was so very simple that I did not imagine it would do for realistically complex inputs, but the results just reported gave no evidence of its limitations. Thus far, the concept of parsing by stochastic optimization seemed at least worth more serious consideration.

Notes

1. Although cf. Huang *et al.* 1987, Basu & Frazer 1990.
2. The conventional term for the lines joining nodes in a tree structure is *arc*; however, in other contexts this term has such strong connotations of curvature that it is not particularly natural in this use, and it would be specially confusing in the present context where the term *arch* will be important in a different sense. I therefore call the lines between tree nodes *links* rather than arcs.
3. In the reference cited, I used the term *ergodic* for the property here called 'closed'.
4. A proportion of moves in the class defined above leave the tree unaltered: they reattach the chosen node *d* to the same mother node from which it was detached, and relabel that mother node with the same label that it had previously. In the pilot system described here, the move-generator was allowed to propose 'moves' of this type (it would have complicated the programming to exclude them); and the nature of move-acceptance decisions in simulated annealing means that such 'moves', when proposed, are invariably accepted. Thus it was not possible to define a freezing criterion in terms of long uninterrupted sequences of move-rejections: such sequences never occurred. (In more recent work it has proved desirable for independent reasons to arrange that any move proposed by the move-generator makes a real difference to the current solution.)
5. In fact the standard sentence including each letter of the alphabet has *jumps* rather than *must jump*, but the correct analysis of the *jumps* sentence has a singulary-branching V node dominating *jumps*; I therefore substituted the wording shown above.

4 An Early System

Parsing for Speech Recognition

One could argue for a long time about what, if anything, follows from results with a toy system such as the one described in the previous chapter, but I could not realistically take the annealing-parser concept much further as an individual part-time researcher. In 1986 I looked for sponsorship for a more serious research effort which would employ a software engineer full time. At this period, the compilation paradigm was sufficiently dominant in the computational linguistics community that research funding agencies concerned with this field were disinclined to take seriously the idea that stochastic optimization could have anything to offer. To illustrate the spirit of the times, I recall one visit I made to a leading university linguistics department to give a talk on my plans, where a respected academic stood up at the end, stated indignantly, 'This is not parsing!', and departed. I had supposed that parsing meant taking language samples as input and outputting their grammatical analyses, and that what happens in between is an empirical issue about what works best; but in the 1980s, for some people, rule-based compilation was not just one approach worth exploring – it was required by definition.

Fortunately for me, however, there existed another research community whose attitudes were quite different: speech researchers. To an outsider it might seem odd that 'language' and 'speech' should be regarded as different research areas, but at this time they were entirely separate. Practitioners in either field usually knew little about developments in the other, and were sometimes no more than marginally aware of its existence. For human beings, speech rather than writing is the more natural communication mode, so that the economic benefits potentially available from successful, reliable automatic language-processing systems are likely to be particularly large in the case of systems that accept input and produce output through the spoken mode. But natural language researchers almost invariably worked on analytic systems whose raw material was electronic text, in which the identities of the words were not in doubt and the issue was only what grammatical, semantic, and pragmatic structures or functions underlay the sequences of words. Conversely, speech researchers were concerned with resolving speech signals, as patterns of airwaves, into word sequences (or, in the case of work on speech synthesis, with generating the airwave patterns) – they tended to see their task as complete if they could move from speech signal to string of words, and sometimes showed little awareness that there is more linguistic structure to an utterance than a linear word-string. (For a survey of the speech field, see e.g. Holmes 1988.)

Speech researchers differed sharply from natural language researchers also in terms of their methods. There had once been a time, while the dominance of the compiler metaphor was at its zenith, when phoneticians supposed that even speech analysis ought to be based centrally on subtle logical rules relating to the meanings of utterances; researchers who argued for more empirical, statistically-based techniques were on one famous occasion condemned in the *Journal of the Acoustic Society of America* as 'mad scientists and untrustworthy engineers' (Pierce 1969: 1050). But the aspects of physical reality which speech researchers work with are so very messy and imperfect that the need to use empirical, quantitative techniques which look for 'the best analysis available' rather than 'the unique correct analysis' is hard not to recognize in that domain. By the mid-1970s it was universally accepted by the speech-research community (partly as a consequence of an initiative by the American research-funding agency, DARPA,[1] which set up an objectively judged competition in which the statistical approach convincingly beat the logic-based approach) that empirical techniques were the right way forward.

As I learned more about the mathematical techniques used by speech scientists, I found that they had a battery of methods for locating statistically optimal analyses that worked deterministically and therefore far more efficiently than any stochastic optimization technique could hope to do; J. K. Baker's dynamic programming approach (Baker 1979) was one notable example. But, as mentioned in ch. 2, these techniques depended on the availability of probabilistic language models which obeyed specified formal constraints. Baker's technique, for instance, required the statistical properties of a grammar to be definable by associating probabilities with the rules of a context-free grammar in 'Chomsky normal form' (Aho *et al.* 1974: 74).

Even if the statistical properties of our Treebank could be adequately represented in terms of a probabilistic context-free grammar, the rules of such a grammar would often have more than two symbols to the right of the arrow; I could find no theorem guaranteeing that a probabilistic context-free grammar containing such rules could be converted without loss of information into a probabilistic grammar in Chomsky normal form. But in any case I believed that a parser capable of achieving the kind of grammatical analysis I was interested in would need a language model containing information that could not be expressed naturally (and perhaps could not be expressed at all) in context-free form. Even if the parser is required only to find the correct analysis of word-sequences that do occur, and is not required to reject word-sequences that do not occur in real-life usage, it seemed likely that the parser would need to know, for instance, that when a verb group is split into separate parts by Subject-Auxiliary Inversion (***Has he been seen* . . . ?**) the nature of the part of the verb group remaining to the right of the subject depends on the nature of the verb which has been shifted to its left. Victor Yngve (1960) had identified an asymmetry in English parsetree structure whereby right branching is allowed without limit but left branching is restricted; it seemed likely that the language model could be improved by building in a statistical bias which would assign poorer values to analyses with more left branching, and this related to a global property of trees rather than a context-free property expressed by particular productions.[2]

Theoretical linguists had spent decades developing theories asserting that natural language grammars obeyed various formal constraints, but repeatedly these theories seemed to have been proposed on inadequate evidence and were refuted as soon as they were seriously tested (see e.g. Hagège 1976: 88ff., Sampson 1980a: 40ff., 1980b: 125). What the discipline needed was an optimizing technique which made the fewest possible assumptions about the formal nature of the material it dealt with, so that it could continue to be applied whatever fresh surprises might crop up to challenge linguists' assumptions about natural language grammatical structure. Simulated annealing was attractive as offering a high degree of the needed theoretical impartiality.

In Britain the leading government centre for electronics research is the Royal Signals and Radar Establishment at Malvern (descendant of the Second World War Telecommunications Research Establishment, birthplace of radar), whose Speech Research Unit had in 1986 just been augmented through the merging into it of the speech group from GCHQ Cheltenham.[3] Together with colleagues at Lancaster I had been working with written English samples, which was the only kind of corpus we had; but the Speech Research Unit saw the general technique of parsing by stochastic optimization as a potentially valuable way of improving the performance of speech analysis systems. As discussed in ch. 2, a speech-recognition system which uses exclusively knowledge about how individual words are apt to be realized as patterns of sound waves usually will not be able to resolve a speech signal into a single unambiguous string of words. It will offer alternative interpretations for various stretches of the signal, with some sort of numerical estimate of how well each word-hypothesis fits the respective stretch of sound. We humans recognize the words we hear because we know what makes sense in context, and part of that knowledge involves understanding which grammatical word-patterns are plausible and which word-hypotheses can be discarded because they imply a bizarre grammatical sequence; the word-hypothesis which offers the best fit to a stretch of speech signal, in terms of similarity between predicted and observed wave-patterns, may give a poor fit in terms of contextual appropriateness. Thus a robust parsing technique which worked quantitatively and avoided making strong assumptions about perfect grammatical well-formedness (which do not hold for spoken language) offered a good match to the kind of system the Speech Research Unit was developing.

Beginning in late 1986, the Speech Research Unit arranged for my annealing-parser project to be sponsored by the UK Ministry of Defence. Except for an interruption caused by an unplanned career hiccup in 1990, the work has been sponsored directly or indirectly by the same source ever since. I recruited a software engineer, Robin Haigh, who (subsequently assisted by others) worked on the project until I left the University of Leeds in 1990. The progress made since 1986 has been due chiefly to Robin Haigh, and to Miles Dennis who succeeded him in a similar role after I resumed the research at the University of Sussex in 1992.

When our research project began life in December 1986 as a formal entity with a budget, staff, etc., we baptized it 'APRIL', standing for 'Annealing Parser for Realistic Input Language'.

To my astonishment, the APRIL project impacted on the national media even before we began work. 'Parsing' to the educated layman has an exclusively humanistic connotation, being associated for many people chiefly with dim memories of the Latin lessons of their schooldays. The *Daily Telegraph*'s 'Peter Simple', scourge of every social innovation much newer than the mid-nineteenth century, spotted my recruiting advertisement for a software engineer to work on the parsing of unrestricted English, and led his daily *Way of the World* column with a denunciation of the shocking state of affairs revealed at Leeds University: 'The word "unrestricted" suggests that English expressions will be used which are unsuitable for family reading . . . The word "simulated" with its suggestion of underhand practices – and, I fear, worse – is most distasteful. Our columnar workers would be shocked at the idea of using a machine for parsing . . .' As a Peter Simple fan of long standing, I felt chastened.

APRIL began by reimplementing my toy system in an efficient programming language (the C language) on powerful computing equipment, but almost immediately moved on to replace it with a succession of systems which preserved the general concept of using simulated annealing as an optimization technique to find the most plausible analysis of an input in terms of a statistical language model, but which grew increasingly sophisticated with respect to the nature of the analyses produced and the nature of the machinery used to seek the target analyses. We continued to work mainly with written English, because of the much better research resources available for this than for spoken language (although in the period immediately before the work was interrupted in 1990 we had begun to develop an analysed corpus of spoken English); and, in view of the success of the CLAWS word-tagger at transforming raw text into sequences of grammatical word-class codes, we felt justified in continuing to simplify the total task by omitting this stage of linguistic analysis from the APRIL system and giving it inputs in the shape of strings of wordtags. But, in other respects, the research quickly left the toy pilot system behind.

The Structure of an Early System

It would not be appropriate here to go through all the details of each of the successive systems that were built between 1986 and 1990; in chs 5 to 7 I shall give rather complete details of the system currently being developed at the University of Sussex, which is designed to reflect the lessons we learned from experience with earlier versions. However, the current system has at the time of writing not yet begun to produce assessable results; so let me here describe in outline one of those earlier versions whose performance can be illustrated: the system we called 'APRIL Mark 2', which was operational by the first half of 1988.

As compared to the pilot system, APRIL Mk 2 in the first place worked with a more refined scheme of grammatical annotation. The distinctions recognized between wordtags in the input were not much increased – they rose from 30 to 44 distinct tags; but the range of distinct tagmatags recognized in the language model and included in the output was considerably enlarged, from 14 to 185 distinct tags. Almost every distinction made in the Treebank annotation scheme was reflected in the APRIL Mk 2 language model. By comparison to the SUSANNE scheme exemplified in Fig. 2.1 (p. 9), which later developed from it, the Treebank scheme certainly had its limitations; in particular, it gave a purely formal, surface grammatical analysis, making no attempt to indicate the function of constituents as subject, object, etc., or to show disparities between logical and surface grammar. But one could at any rate claim that the target output analyses for APRIL Mk 2 were defined independently for other purposes – they did not represent a scheme that had been deliberately made simple to ease the task facing an annealing parser. For some NLP applications, surface grammatical parsing, if done reliably, may well be adequate – though unquestionably there are other applications which depend on deeper, logical analysis.

It would take too much space to give full details here of the Mk 2 target annotation scheme; it is described in outline in Garside *et al.* (1987: 88–9), and in the present work it will be enough to mention the meaning of particular symbols as they arise. One particular change, relative to the annotation used for the pilot experiment and the Lancaster-Leeds Treebank annotations, does need to be explained. Those annotations had treated 'S', for 'sentence', as the largest unit of analysis, so that the root node of a parsetree was invariably labelled S and (because punctuation marks as grammatically significant elements were allotted their own nodes in parsetrees) the last daughter of a root S would normally be a sentence-closing punctuation mark such as a full stop or question mark. In the Mk 2 output annotation scheme, a tagma labelled S excluded the sentence-closing punctuation mark, and the letter O was used as the initial symbol of a tree: root nodes were labelled O, and they typically had two daughters, an S tagma and a punctuation mark.

There were two motives for this change. One was simply to achieve consistency in the meanings of labels. Sentence-like sequences sometimes occur embedded within larger sentences, for instance as interpolations, and are commonly not terminated with punctuation marks such as a full stop when they occur in embedded positions. In the Treebank scheme, these embedded sequences were also labelled S, but this created a contrast between S constructions having closing punctuation and those without – it was better to use 'S' consistently for sentence-like word-sequences (we gloss the symbol as 'main clause' to stress that an S is not always a maximally inclusive construction), and to make the punctuation terminating a typographically independent sentence a sister rather than daughter of the S tagma. (Other tagma-bounding punctuation marks were always analysed in the Treebank scheme as sisters rather than first or last daughters of the constructions they bounded.)

But a more significant motive was the intention to move towards a version of the annealing parser which accepts a continuous flow of input, and treats sentence boundaries as one of the analytic features it must discover, rather than finding them already marked in its input data. Human hearers can deal with speech which continues indefinitely; they do not require speakers to break utterances into clearly delimited sentence units, and speakers do not do that. Mitchell Marcus 1980 has shown that English grammatical structures have the property that parsing can proceed left-to-right and will rarely need to 'backtrack' to reconsider an earlier analytic decision in the light of wording that comes in more than a very little later than the point when the decision was made. Accordingly, we believed that ultimately the most desirable configuration for an annealing-parser system would be to have continuous input text moved through an annealing 'window', and to bias the move-generation process with respect to the location of nodes in the window: the process would be less likely to propose a change to a node as the node grew 'older', so that the bulk of processing time and effort would be concentrated on the area where worthwhile tree-changes are most likely to be found.[4] For this style of processing, any tagma whose boundaries the system is required to locate – including sentences – would need to be subordinate to an overall root node dominating the entire input. We shall see in ch. 7 that under the SUSANNE annotation scheme which serves as the output target for newer versions of APRIL, the symbol O, glossed 'paragraph', dominates indefinitely long sequences of sentences interspersed with sentence-closing punctuation marks. The Mk 2 annotation scheme adopted a compromise position, in which in effect inputs were provided in the form of single-sentence paragraphs.

The literature on optimization by simulated annealing suggests (e.g. Aarts & Korst 1989: 82) that the technique works best if each solution in the solution space has a large number of immediate neighbours (solutions which can be reached by a single move). Therefore another innovation in the Mk 2 system allowed a wider range of individual moves than the pilot system. In the pilot system, each move involved detaching a node from its mother and reattaching it to a new mother. In APRIL Mk 2, this was just one type of move, called the 'Reattach' move, and there were three other types called 'Hive', 'Merge', and 'Relabel'. In a Hive move, a nonterminal node having three or more daughters is selected, and some subsequence of two or more of its daughters become granddaughters through the creation of a new intermediate node dominating them. A Merge move is the reverse of a Hive: a nonterminal is eliminated and its daughters turned into daughters of its mother (see Fig. 4.1). A Relabel move simply involves choosing a nonterminal node and replacing its label with some other label.

A Hive move requires a label to be created for the new node, and Reattach and Relabel moves involve choosing new labels for existing or new nodes. The simulated annealing literature suggests (e.g. Tovey 1989: 396ff.) that the technique can be helped by biasing the generation of moves in favour of generating moves that are likely to improve rather than worsen solution-value; therefore, instead of choosing new labels from the nonterminal vocabulary with equal probabilities, APRIL Mk 2 chose from a probability distribution determined by statistics on mother-label/daughter-label relationships – a label was more likely to be chosen for a node if many of the daughter nodes bore labels that often occur below that mother label. This was still a far cry from building rigid rules into the language model specifying that certain label sequences can and others cannot occur as expansions of a particular nonterminal – any label might be chosen with some positive probability; but it gave the system a helping hand out of the mountains and into the favourable areas of the solution space.

60   Evolutionary Language Understanding

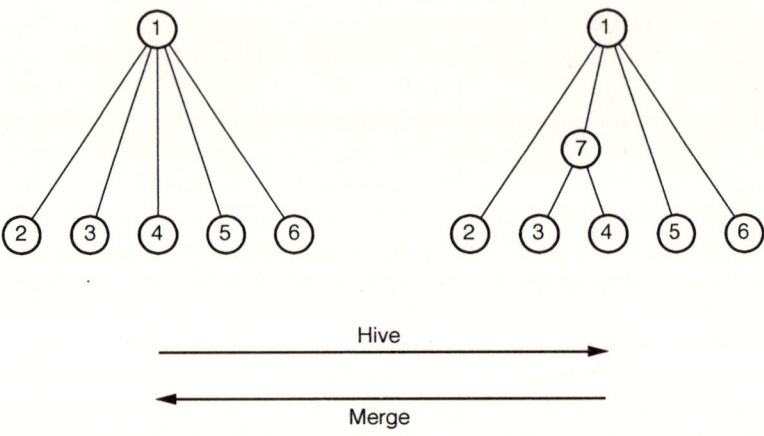

Figure 4.1   Hive and Merge moves in the Mk 2 system

The most important development concerned the nature of the language model by which solutions were assessed. Evaluating constructions purely in terms of pairwise transitions between adjacent daughter labels is an extremely crude technique, even if the label vocabulary is more refined than in the pilot system. Consider, for instance, the well-known fact that many linguistic constructions consist of a unique head element surrounded by variable numbers of modifiers. Transition-based evaluation systematically ignores this fact. Within a clause, a transition from a noun phrase to a verb group (sequence of auxiliary verbs and main verb) frequently occurs, and so does a transition from a verb group to a noun phrase; the noun phrases in the respective transitions will commonly be clause subject and object respectively. A language model which knows only about pairwise transitions will predict that V + N + V (using our symbols for verb group and noun phrase) should be a likely sequence within a clause, since both transitions within this three-symbol sequence are individually likely. But, except in the special case when a single verb group is split into two parts, for instance by Subject-Auxiliary Inversion, a single clause will *never* have multiple verb groups: the verb group is the head of a clause, almost every clause has one of them, and no clause has more than one.

It is true that an automatic parser such as APRIL is required only to find an appropriate analysis for what does occur in the language – not to distinguish between word sequences that do occur and word sequences that do not. But that does not mean that it is harmless for the APRIL system to take V + N + V as a well-formed subsequence of clause daughters. English sentences often contain multiple clauses, and if grammaticality were assessed in terms of transitions alone then the system could treat as plausible an analysis of, say, *I **was watching** Mary **practise** her backswing* which identified the entire sequence as a single clause. Such an analysis will occur in the APRIL solution-space, along with all sorts of other crazy analyses, and it is unlikely that the system will give good results unless its language model is capable of recognizing in such a case that the two verb groups are a clear indicator of two clauses.

Consequently, the APRIL Mk 2 language model was based not on tables of transition probabilities, but on probabilistic finite state networks. For each mother label, a network was designed which provided distinct pathways for the elements which occur with high frequency as daughters of that mother, but which also included paths for 'any other label', so that any label-sequence whatever could be accepted, deterministically (that is, along one and only one route), by any network.

As an example, Fig. 4.2 shows the APRIL Mk 2 network for the nonterminal category Tg, present-participle clause. The initial state is represented by the circle at upper left labelled T20. A particular sequence of daughter-labels for a Tg mother is accepted by moving rightwards along horizontals starting from T20, consuming an element of the input sequence for each horizontal having a label (unlabelled horizontals are 'jump arcs' traversed without consuming any input element), making a choice (guided by the identity of the next input element) whenever one encounters a vertical having alternative horizontals leaving its right-hand side, and arriving at a terminal state (a circle with a diagonal across it) when the entire input sequence is consumed. (Intermediate states, e.g. S35, S76, are shown at more than one place in the diagram to avoid the need for a confusing tangle of arcs.)

The notation uses an asterisk to mean 'any label other than those on arcs departing from the same state as this arc', and it uses the ellipsis mark '. . .' to mean 'subcategory symbols occurring as part of the label already accepted on the preceding arc'. Thus, among the four alternative arcs departing from the initial state T20, the uppermost accepts any of the symbols N (noun phrase), G (genitive phrase), R (adverb phrase), or EX (existential *there*), the second accepts a present-participle verb group (Vg), the third allows the input string to terminate (as might be appropriate if this point in the network had been reached via traversal(s) of either of the arcs looping back to the initial state), and the fourth accepts any label other than N, G, R, EX, or Vg. If state S30 is reached, the next arc traversed depends on whether the Vg just accepted is a Vgb (present-participle verb group ending with a form of *BE*, e.g. *being, having been*), a Vgp (passive present-participle verb group, e.g. *being eaten, having been eaten*), or some other type of Vg (an active present-participle verb group ending in a verb other than *BE*, e.g. *eating, having eaten*).

The gate symbol # means 'any label ending with a plus or minus sign', which in our annotation scheme represents conjuncts.

Once such a network is designed, its arcs are assigned probabilities by driving the productions in the database over it, and counting the number of times each arc is traversed; the various arcs which depart from any one state are assigned probabilities summing to one in proportion to the number of traversals of the respective arcs. (As in the pilot system – cf. p. 45 above – a small positive quantity is added to the figures for observed traversal frequencies for each arc, in order to avoid producing a language model which assigns zero probabilities to some transitions.) A node in a parsetree is then assigned a value representing the product of the probabilities of the arcs traversed when its daughter-label sequence is driven over the network for its mother label.

I shall not discuss the workings of these networks at length here, because we shall see in due course that they were later replaced by networks of a more specialized type that will be described in detail; but notice that the finite-state network formalism makes it easy to avoid problems such as the one about multiple verb groups within a clause. If V, verb group, is the head of a clause, then an arc labelled V will link an area of the network containing pre-V states with an area containing post-V states. Provided one avoids creating an arc allowing a move back from the post-V to the pre-V area, it would be easy to prevent V arcs from being traversed more than once per clause.

In fact our aim in designing such a network is not to prevent sequences containing multiple V symbols from being accepted, but rather to ensure that they are assigned very poor figures of merit. A run of the annealing parser will throw up all sorts of absurd analyses in the early stages, including analyses within which a Tg dominates multiple V nodes; our network must accept such structures, in order to be able to give them poor values. Consequently, the network of Fig. 4.2 explicitly includes V arcs where one might not at first sight expect to find them, in the 'post-V' area of the network. The two alternative Vg arcs entering state S30 represent the present-participle verb group which is expected to occur as the head of a Tg

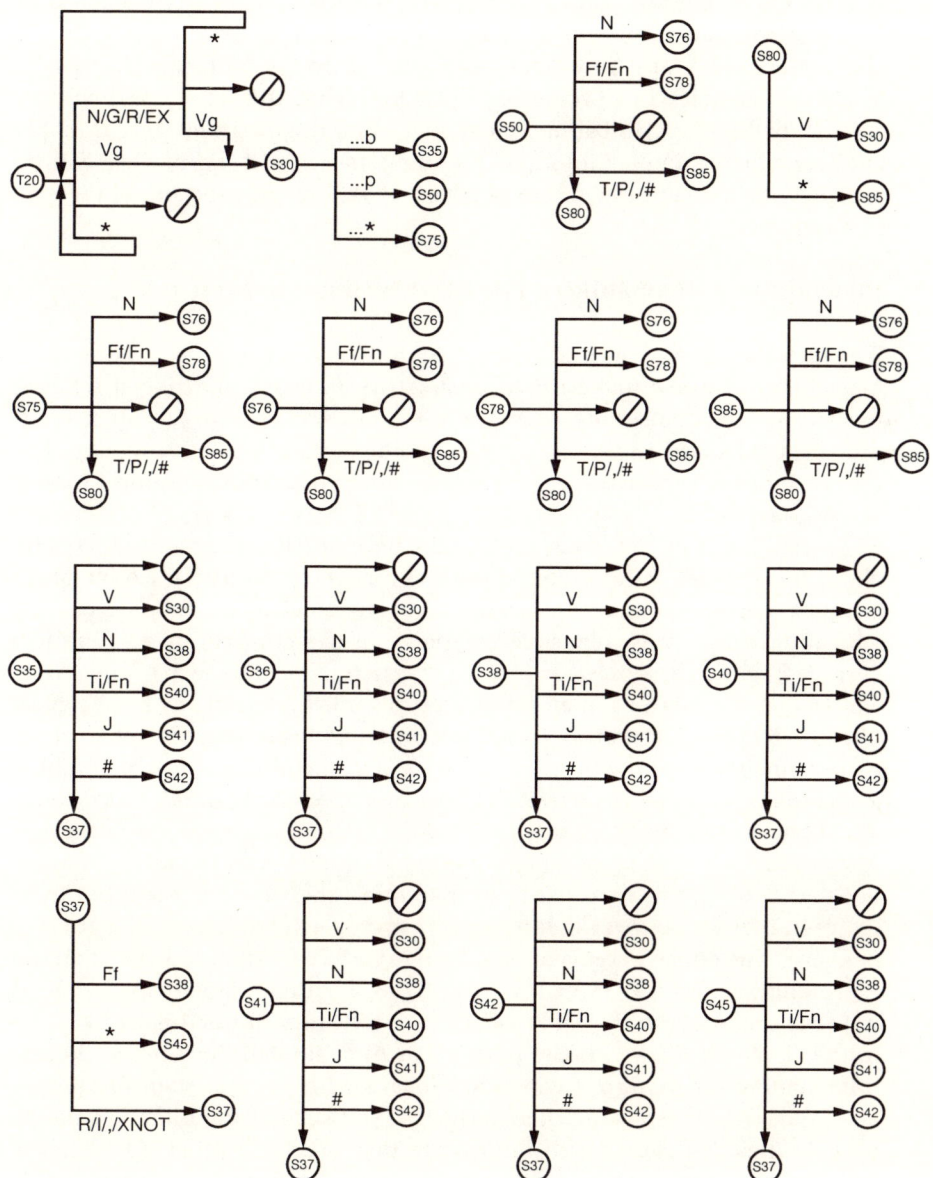

Figure 4.2 Mk 2 transition network for the category 'present-participle clause'

clause (and accordingly these arcs will have fairly high probabilities). But, whichever route is taken after leaving S30, it is then possible to reach a later V arc: thus, states S50 and S75 both give access to S80, which offers a choice between V and 'any label other than V'. In the S80 subnetwork, the V arc will be assigned a probability close to 0 while the arc marked with an asterisk will have a probability close to 1: so a linguistically unreasonable analysis which includes multiple V daughters below a Tg mother will be accepted with a very low figure of merit, as the overall working of the system requires.

Plausibility v. Probability: The Mk 2 Evaluation Metric

The question of how to put together figures representing the grammatical plausibility of individual parts of a parsetree, in order to arrive at a figure measuring the plausibility of the entire tree, was the subject of a long-drawn-out debate. In this debate, my point of view was quite wrong, but (because of my seniority) was for a long time taken more seriously than it should have been.

To me, the raw statistics that could be extracted from the Treebank about frequencies of local configurations within correctly parsed language samples represented measures of the extent to which a tree proposed by the annealing parser was 'plausible', 'typical' of the configurations found in correct English parsetrees, or 'similar' to such trees. The task of the parser was to find the analysis of an input that was most plausible or most typical of correctly parsed structures. I did not find it natural to use the term 'probability' in connection with these statistics; and the obvious way to combine individual statistics into an overall figure for a tree, to my mind, was to average them, not to multiply them. Indeed, in my pilot system, the numbers associated with individual daughter-transitions were not the kinds of number that could be interpreted as probabilities: they were not real numbers between 0 and 1, but raw counts of transition frequencies.

Even if one chose to replace such figures with individual statistics that did represent probabilities – for instance, by associating a label-triple MD_1D_2 not with the total number of . . . D_1D_2 . . . transitions found below M nodes in the database, but with the proportion of symbols found below M and immediately following D_1 which are tokens of D_2 rather than of another label type, or by replacing the Markovian statistics of the pilot scheme by probabilities associated with finite-state network arcs – then (despite the fact that the correct way to estimate the probability of a compound phenomenon, given the probabilities of its separate component phenomena, is to multiply these probabilities together) there was a good reason *not* to use multiplication to arrive at overall parsetree plausibility figures. Different trees over the same string have very different numbers of nodes, so it seemed that evaluating trees by taking the product of individual figures each between 0 and 1 would build in a large bias in favour of trees with few nodes. However 'good' the individual transitions or nodes of an analysis containing many nonterminal nodes might be, the fact of having many fractions to multiply together would ensure that the overall value was lower than for some tree with few nodes.[5]

As we saw above, I found it necessary in my pilot system to carry out some mathematical manipulations a little subtler than simply taking the arithmetic mean of daughter-transition frequencies, to ensure that individual 'bad' transitions weighed more than proportionately against many 'good' transitions. But I always averaged, I did not multiply.

Others disagreed; and they were right. The figure of merit associated with a parsetree, they urged, should be seen as an estimate of the probability that the category 'Sentence' will be expanded into that particular labelled tree structure rather than any other. Probabilistic finite-state networks (or daughter-transition frequency tables) can be used to estimate conditional probabilities for different daughter sequences, given their mother labels. We know the root node must always be labelled with the initial symbol, so we can estimate the probability of the sequence of daughter labels immediately below the root, given the label of the root; we can estimate the probability of the daughter sequence below each root daughter-label that is not terminal, given that label as mother; and so on down to the wordtags. Our individual figures represent the probabilities of each individual label-expansion, and we are seeking a figure for the joint occurrence of all the label-expansions: so the elementary calculus of probabilities implies that the individual figures must be multiplied together.

Faced with this logic, I eventually retreated from my original position, but my retreat was slow and occurred in stages. (It is this aspect of APRIL research that was used for the sociological study by Greg Myers referred to in ch. 1.) At the Mk 2 stage, I accepted that the figures derived from the finite-state networks for individual nodes must be multiplied rather than averaged, but I still insisted that we should roughly offset the bias in favour of few-noded trees, by multiplying the product of the various node probabilities with a figure (derived from the formulae on p. 27) for the number of distinct labelled trees having the same number of leaves and nonterminal nodes as the tree being evaluated. Later, I was persuaded that this 'tree size correction' is inappropriate: if an analysis has few nodes but is a poor analysis, this should mean that those nodes it does contain will have low probabilities, whose product (although derived from few factors) will be too small for the solution to be optimal. When this is not so, the cure lies in improving the estimation of individual node probabilities, rather than in introducing extraneous correction factors.[6]

Tree values in APRIL Mk 2 were expressed as negative logarithms (i.e. −1 times the logarithms) of the figures derived as above, so that analysis optimization involved seeking the tree with the lowest possible value, as is normal in the simulated annealing tradition. Thus tree values would always have been expressed as positive numbers, without the tree size correction; with it, they were commonly negative.

Word-Ancestor Assessment

In order to judge the performance of successive versions of the APRIL system, we needed a quantitative measure of output accuracy: that is, a measure of the degree of similarity between two labelled trees over the same sequence of terminal symbols (the APRIL analysis of a sentence, and the correct analysis as recorded in our database − system tests were run over samples of our parsed Treebank which had been reserved for this purpose and did not contribute to the APRIL language model). Finding no standard measure in the literature, we developed our own measure, *word-ancestor assessment*, which we believe will always give marks that are broadly in line with intuitive estimates of tree-similarity, while leaning towards conservatism in marking the kind of analyses produced by systems of the APRIL type.

The principle of word-ancestor marking is as follows. Consider in turn each word of the input string. For any such word, in each of the two trees to be compared there is a unique path between the word and the respective root node, and this path gives a sequence of node labels. (The label-sequences for a given word may be of different lengths in the two trees.) We compute the similarity between the two label-sequences by looking for the largest set of labels which occur in the same order (possibly interspersed with non-matching labels) in both sequences, and dividing the number of labels in the two sequences which match in this sense by the total number of labels in both sequences. Thus, if the sequences compared were A B F D E C F G and B D A C, we would count them as containing three matched pairs:

```
A   B   F   D   E   C   F   G
    |       |       |
    B       D   A   C
```

− if one matched the As in the two sequences, this would prevent the Bs and Ds being matched, and the total matches would be only two, so we do not choose that matching. Having found three matching pairs of labels, we score the pair of sequences as 50% similar, i.e. six (three matched pairs) divided by twelve (total labels in both sequences). The mark for a pair of trees is computed by taking the mean of the figures for the various words.

This principle is modified in two ways. First, it would be unfairly generous to allow root labels to match, since in our parsing scheme all trees have the same root label so that this does not need to be guessed by the system. Therefore the label-sequences which are compared for each word omit the label of the root node.

Secondly, as described above the marking scheme could yield 100% similarity figures for non-identical trees, which is obviously unacceptable. If, say, words 3 to 7 form a single noun phrase in one tree, and the other tree is similar except that words 3 to 5 form one noun phrase and words 6 to 7 a separate noun phrase (as it happens this was a rather common type of mistake for APRIL Mk 2), then the marking scheme described will fail to penalize this difference – in both trees the symbol N, noun phrase, will occur in the label-sequence for each of words 3 to 7, and nothing will indicate that two short Ns occur in one case and one long N in the other. To meet this problem, the sequence of word-ancestor labels for any given word w in a particular tree includes up to two additional symbols, left- and/or right-boundary markers, placed in the sequence to identify the highest tagma of which w is respectively the first or the last word. (The respective boundary symbol is omitted from a sequence for a word which is not initial/final in any higher tagma, or which is the first/last word of its sentence.) These boundary symbols are treated as separate matchable items in word-ancestor sequences, on a par with node labels for the purpose of computing the similarity of sequence-pairs.

This method of assessment is a relatively conservative one with respect to the APRIL approach to parsing, because it gives greater weight to accuracy of tagmas high in a parsetree (which form part of the ancestry of many words) than to accuracy of low tagmas which dominate few words. While APRIL is not formally a 'bottom-up' parsing system, as a deterministic technique might be, in practice it manifests a strong tendency to begin by discovering structure low in the tree, and only later to build on this in discovering higher-level structure. Thus we believed that we were not being unduly generous to ourselves in adopting word-ancestor marking to evaluate system performance.

A further virtue of word-ancestor marking is that in principle it can be used to assess the analysis of any sequence of words, which need not necessarily begin or end at a sentence boundary. This will become a very valuable feature when APRIL is adapted to accepting continuous input in which sentence boundaries have to be discovered as part of the analytic process, rather than being specified in the input.

When the percentages yielded by word-ancestor marking are quoted as measures of parser performance, it is naturally appropriate also to quote the size of the vocabulary of analytic labels in the parser's output annotation scheme (as I have done for APRIL Mk 2 above). The more categories a parser is required to distinguish in its output, the harder it is for output trees to match their targets exactly.[7]

A Sample of Mk 2 Output

As examples of Mk 2 performance, Figs 4.3 and 4.4 show extracts from test runs over various LOB Corpus sentences: respectively twelve sentences from official and technical documentation, and six sentences from fiction. (The nine-character code before each analysis identifies the location of the example analysed within the Corpus, with the first three characters naming a LOB text: thus the first example in Fig. 4.3 is taken from text H06.) As indicated in the file header in Fig. 4.3, the annealing schedule for these runs used the values $T_0 = 5.0$ and $c = 0.9999$. Rather than being constant for different inputs, L was set to equal the length in terminal nodes of the current input (so that the amount of processing varied roughly linearly with sentence length). The freezing criterion was somewhat complex, requiring both long uninterrupted sequences of rejected moves (the length again depending on input length) and T below 1.0, to guard against premature freezing triggered by freak sequences of consecutive rejected moves. After a run achieved the freezing criterion, the deterministic neighbourhood search technique described on p. 35 was used to check whether any better solution occurred in the immediate vicinity of the solution at freezing.

In the output analyses, the printout replaces the wordtags that constituted the input to the system with the actual words of the original texts, to enable the human analyst to judge performance.[8] The terms 'tries', 'changes', 'gains' refer respectively to the number of tree-changes proposed by the move-generator on an annealing run, the number of those that were accepted, and the number of accepted moves which improved tree-value. The last two lines below each solution compare statistics of the output and the target analyses.

The overall average mark for the eighteen inputs of Figs 4.3 and 4.4 is 83.1%, which is typical of the performance figures being achieved at this stage – mean scores on test runs were normally in the 80s, sometimes in the high 80s.

There is a moderate correlation between length and mark, longer inputs tending to be less well analysed. This correlation is not very strong, but, once APRIL began consistently delivering mean scores in the 80s, a mild correlation of this sort did regularly occur. (The average length of the sentences in Figs 4.3 and 4.4 is representative for the Corpus as a whole; some much longer sentences received analyses which scored much lower than

```
Mon Apr 18 12:47:22 BST 1988

APRIL Version 2.0

Initial temperature: 5.0 invariant
Cooling: x0.9999 after n tries (n = sentence-length)
Freezing after 10 occurrences of 10n rejected moves
        (temp below 1.0)
        (optimised by neighbourhood search)
Available moves: Merge, Hive, Reattach, Relabel
Labels version 1.0 based on TreeBank 40
Tree-size correction added
Probs version 1.0 based on TreeBank 4.0


H06177052
[O[S[N Improved designs [Po of [N both forms N]Po]N][Vp are being Vp][Tn[Vn tried Vn][R
out R]Tn][P at [N present N]P]S] . O]
Tries  196035      Changes         26966        Gains  13380
Finished at temp    1.000
Final value:  -32.905           Nonterminals:  11       Leaves:  12
Correct parse: Value: -17.219   Nonterminals:   8       Mark:    90%

H10056001
[O[S[R More recently R] , [R however R] , [N the [NN Council , NN][P in [Tg[Vg accepting
Vg][N responsibility N][P for [N the [J Low [N Temperature [N Research N]N]J][NN Station
, Cambridge NN]N]P] , [W-[N the Ditton N][N[NN Laboratory , NN][N+ and the Pest N+][N-
Infestation [NN Laboratory , Slough NN]N-] , N]W-]Tg]P]N][V has moved V][P outside [N the
farm N]P][N gate N][S+ and [V has V][Tn[R thus R][Vn extended Vn][N its interest [P in [N
food N]P]N][Ti[Vi to include Vi][N storage N]Ti]Tn]S+][N+ and preservation N+]S] . O]
Tries  1461411     Changes        169055        Gains  84456
Finished at temp    0.311
Final value:  -116.033          Nonterminals:  39       Leaves:  52
Correct parse: Value: -64.458   Nonterminals:  24       Mark:    71%

H22091001
[Oh[N Television N][N aerials N]Oh]
Tries  32619       Changes         5207         Gains  2587
Finished at temp    1.000
Final value:  -1.611            Nonterminals:   3       Leaves:   2
Correct parse: Value:  -0.490   Nonterminals:   2       Mark:    67%


H27177042
[O[S[N This merger N][V has V][Tn[Vn enabled Vn][J large J]Tn]S][S[N savings [Ti[Vip to
be made Vip][P in [N technical staff N][P+ and in [NN costs , and NN][N the operations
N]N]P+]P][Rw now Rw]Ti]N][V appear V][Ti[Vip to be Vip][Tn[Vn adjusted Vn][P to [N the
likely volume [Po of [N orders N]Po]N]P]Tn]Ti]S] . O]
Tries  578747      Changes         73379        Gains  36695
Finished at temp    0.796
Final value:  -86.040           Nonterminals:  27       Leaves:  31
Correct parse: Value: -66.709   Nonterminals:  19       Mark:    70%


J02010042
[O[S[N Plot N] , [P in [N addition [P to [N Biblical [NN quotations and Philosophical
NN][N Transaction [N references N]N] , N]P]N]P][V alludes V][P to [N[D no less [Fc than
[Nl fifty-two Nl]Fc]D] works N]P]S] . O]
Tries  368103      Changes         56919        Gains  28306
Finished at temp    0.814
Final value:  -46.466           Nonterminals:  16       Leaves:  20
Correct parse: Value: -36.969   Nonterminals:  14       Mark:    86%
```

Figure 4.3 Sample Mk 2 output: official and technical prose

J05044001
[O[S[N This process N][Vp has been discussed Vp][R extensively R][Pb by [N A. [N F. [N Joffé N]N]N]Pb][S+ and [Vp has been applied Vp][Pb by [N him N]Pb][P to [N the study [Po of [N[JJ liquid and amorphous JJ] semiconductors N]Po]N]P]S+]S] . O]
Tries 426078   Changes   56521   Gains 28200
Finished at temp   0.936
Final value: -66.314   Nonterminals: 18   Leaves: 25
Correct parse: Value: -51.868   Nonterminals: 15   Mark: 97%

J11098072
[O[S[Ni It Ni][Rw now Rw][V seems V][Nj clear [Fn that [N the fossils [P from [N[N the Warminster N] Greensand N]P]N][Vb are Vb][J Cenomanian J][P in [N age N]P][S+ and [N the majority N][V did not come V][P from [N Warminster N]P]S+]Fn] itself [S+ but [N[P from [N Maiden N]P][NN Bradley and Mere NN]N]S+]Nj]S] . O]
Tries 526901   Changes   75099   Gains 37553
Finished at temp   0.943
Final value: -74.665   Nonterminals: 25   Leaves: 31
Correct parse: Value: -58.345   Nonterminals: 21   Mark: 75%

J16173013
[O[S[N The possibility [Fn that [N life N][Vb had been Vb][Tn[Vn preserved Vn][Pb by [Nd some [N rare chance N]Nd]Pb]Tn]Fn]N][V would indicate V][N the need [P for [N[D at_least some D] attempt [P at [N resuscitation [P in [N all bodies [Tn[R freshly R][Vn recovered Vn][P from [N water N]P]Tn] , N]P]N]P]N]P][Fc as [Vb is Vb][N the current practice N]Fc]N]S] . O]
Tries 733186   Changes   92665   Gains 46344
Finished at temp   0.632
Final value: -97.862   Nonterminals: 28   Leaves: 35
Correct parse: Value: -74.908   Nonterminals: 23   Mark: 84%

J21025023
[O[S[Nd These Nd][Nf three d Nf][V form V][N the complete intersection [Po of [Nf Q [P with [Nf E , Nf]P][N the polar N] ([Nl 4) [Po of [N g N]Po]Nl]Nf]Po]N]S] . O]
Tries 421179   Changes   63447   Gains 31631
Finished at temp   0.625
Final value: -13.276   Nonterminals: 14   Leaves: 20
Correct parse: Value: 3.830   Nonterminals: 10   Mark: 76%

J23071012
[O[S[Q[S[R Later R] , [N they N][Vp can be set Vp][Ti[Vi to measure Vi][N the length [Po of [N other objects N]Po]N][P in [N the environment [P to [N the nearest foot N]P]N]P]Ti]S] , Q][Fa so_that [Fa if [N an object N][Vb is Vb][J[N[M nearly 3 M] feet N] long J]Fa]Fa][Ni it Ni][Vp is recorded Vp][P as [N a [J full [Y 3 Y]J] feet N]P]S] . O]
Tries 963170   Changes   105673 Gains 52717
Finished at temp   0.437
Final value: -99.834   Nonterminals: 29   Leaves: 39
Correct parse: Value: -79.590   Nonterminals: 24   Mark: 75%

J31158001
[O[S[Fa Since [N the analysis [Po of [N birth [N control [N methods N]N][N+ and contraceptive histories N+]N]Po]N][Vb is Vb][Tn[Vn concerned Vn][R essentially R][P with [N the patterns [Po of [N methods N]Po][Tn[Vn reported Vn][Pb by [N the users N]Pb]Tn]N]P]Tn]]S+ and [R particularly R][N the avowed users N]S+]Fa] , [N we N][V have felt V][Ni it Ni][Tn[Vn justified Vn][Ti[Vi to continue Vi][N the analysis [Po of [N birth [N control [N methods N]N]N]Po]N][P for [N all informants , [Tn[JJ male and female JJ][Vn combined Vn]Tn]N]P]Ti]Tn]S] . O]
Tries 1360921   Changes   143755 Gains 71896
Finished at temp   0.339
Final value: -151.334   Nonterminals: 41   Leaves: 50

Figure 4.3 (Cont'd)

```
Correct parse:  Value:  -109.468      Nonterminals:  33       Mark:   83%


J36048112
[O[S[Fa In_so_far_as [N[JJ social and vocational JJ] roles N][Vp are predetermined Vp][Pb
by [NN race , caste , or family NN]Pb]Fa] , [N the assessment [Po of [N the abilities [Po
of [N the individual N]Po]N]Po]N][Vb is Vb][Po of [N less significance N]Po]S] . O]
Tries   457718          Changes          59276          Gains   29592
Finished at temp        1.000
Final value:   -71.043            Nonterminals:  16       Leaves:  28
Correct parse:  Value:  -71.043   Nonterminals:  16       Mark:   100%
```

Figure 4.3 (Cont'd)

any of these.) This correlation is not surprising, considering that the size of the solution space increases far more than linearly with input length (though it is perhaps a little disappointing in view of my comment above about the need for linear annealing schedules in speech analysis).

These results are far from perfect; only one example (the last example of Fig. 4.3) has been assigned an analysis that exactly matches the target analysis. On the other hand, we frankly expected beforehand that performance at what was still an early stage of system development might be considerably worse than this.

In order to give an impression of what sort of things the system was getting right and what it was getting wrong, Fig. 4.5 displays the J23 example from Fig. 4.3, with the target analysis shown graphically to the right of the vertical column of text, and the APRIL output as in Fig. 4.3 shown to the left of the text. With a mark of 75%, this was one of the poorer results in the two Figures.[9]

APRIL has made a fairly spectacular error in the higher levels of its parse-tree: it has taken the opening words of the sentence, up to *foot*, as a direct quotation, Q. We had arranged for the Mk 2 language model to ignore inverted commas, because (unlike many other punctuation marks such as commas or semicolons, which tend to offer good cues to the surrounding grammatical structure) inverted commas when functioning as 'scare quotes' can hinder more than help the identification of sentence structure. But the corollary of the decision that the system should analyse sequences including inverted commas as if the inverted commas were not there is that it will occasionally analyse a sequence lacking inverted commas as containing a construction to which in reality inverted commas are essential, and that has happened here.

And this fundamental error has led to another. If the material up to *foot*, were a quotation, it could not be the main clause that is modified by an adverbial clause (Fa) introduced by *so_that*: therefore *it is recorded* . . . is

L05077072
[O[S There [Vb are Vb][N[M four M] letters [P for [N you N]P]N]S] . O]
Tries   114555   Changes   12974   Gains 6470
Finished at temp   1.000
Final value: -13.016   Nonterminals: 7   Leaves: 7
Correct parse: Value: -5.555   Nonterminals: 5   Mark: 82%

L08129001
[O[S[Ni It Ni][V did not surprise V][N him N][R very much R][Ti[Vi to find Vi][Fn that Fn]Ti][Q[S[N the door N][V opened V][P on [N the latch N]P]S] , Q][Fa for [Ni it Ni][Vb was Vb][J so old J][Tn+ and [Vn worn Vn][Fn that [Ni it Ni][V offered V][N little security N]Fn]Tn+]Fa]S] . O]
Tries   490252   Changes   68739   Gains 34351
Finished at temp   1.000
Final value: -88.403   Nonterminals: 25   Leaves: 30
Correct parse: Value: -73.580   Nonterminals: 22   Mark: 77%

L12027003
[O[S[N I N][V called V][N myself a louse N]S] . O]
Tries   97870   Changes   16047   Gains 8013
Finished at temp   1.000
Final value: -0.668   Nonterminals: 5   Leaves: 6
Correct parse: Value: 2.242   Nonterminals: 6   Mark: 94%

L16084072
[O[S[Ni It Ni][Vb 's Vb][N a complex matter N] , [J not easy J][Ti[Vi to explain Vi][P in [N a_few words N]P]Ti]S] . O]
Tries   233982   Changes   38606   Gains 19234
Finished at temp   0.964
Final value: -28.682   Nonterminals: 10   Leaves: 14
Correct parse: Value: -14.062   Nonterminals: 11   Mark: 91%

L21153062
[O[S[N I N][V do n't want V][R ever R][Ti[Vi to see Vi][Nd either Nd][Po of [N you N]Po]Ti][N again N]S] . O]
Tries   196087   Changes   25097   Gains 12532
Finished at temp   1.000
Final value: -24.417   Nonterminals: 11   Leaves: 12
Correct parse: Value: -21.369   Nonterminals: 10   Mark: 80%

M01005054
[O[S[N He N][V stared V][P at [N her N]P][R blankly R] , [Tg[Vg mouthing Vg][N an incoherent gabble [Po of [N half words N]Po]N]Tg]S] . O]
Tries   228853   Changes   35000   Gains 17466
Finished at temp   1.000
Final value: -41.121   Nonterminals: 12   Leaves: 14
Correct parse: Value: -34.876   Nonterminals: 11   Mark: 98%

Figure 4.4 Sample Mk 2 output: fiction

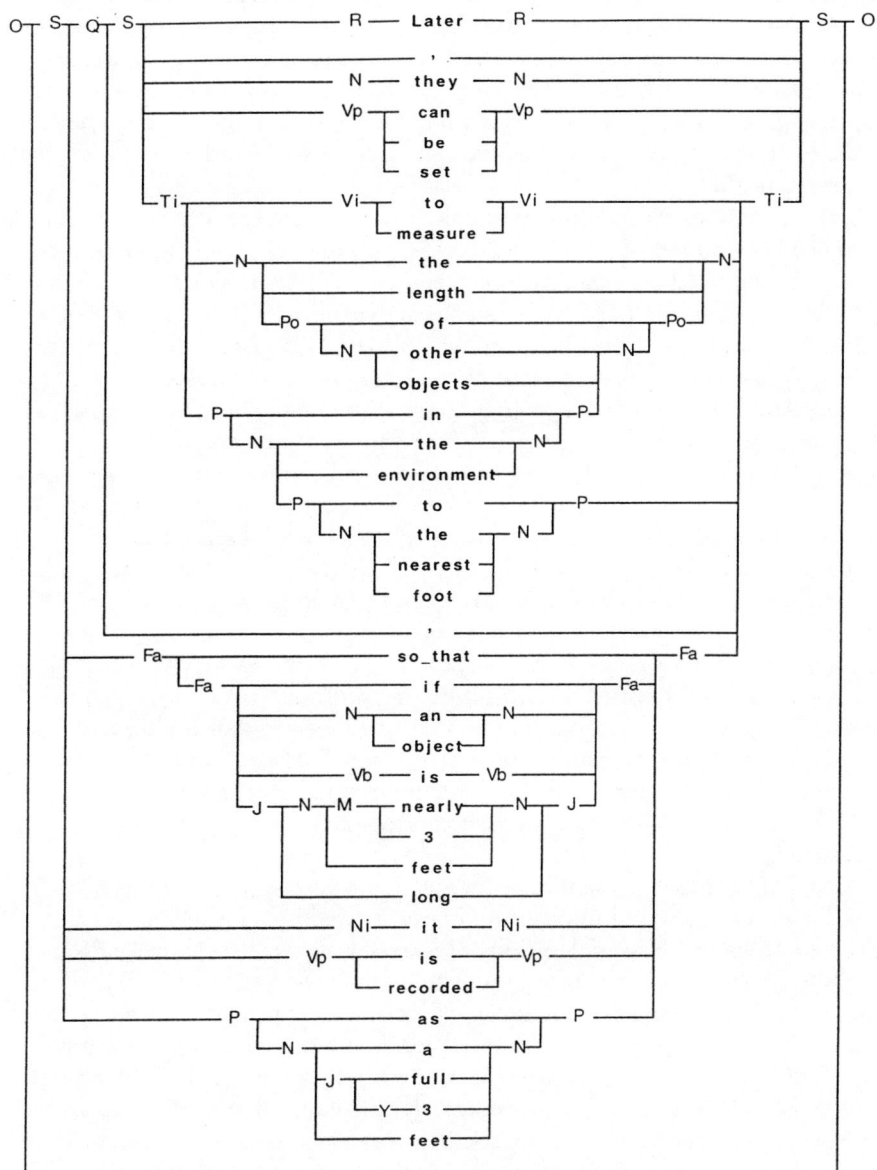

Figure 4.5 A Mk 2 analysis compared with the target analysis

taken as the main clause, which leaves two subordinating conjunctions (*so_that*, and *if*) each of which would normally introduce a clause containing its own verb. There is only one verb available, *is* (*nearly 3 feet long*), hence *so_that* is analysed as having no clause of its own. One might have hoped that this odd outcome would have led the system to reconsider its decision to treat the first part of the sentence as a quotation; but, on this occasion, it did not.

Setting aside these two linked errors, however, the rest of the analysis is far more acceptable. Most of the short phrases are accurately analysed: *can be set* is recognized as a passive verb group (Vp), *the nearest foot* as a noun phrase (N), *nearly 3 feet long* as an adjective phrase (J) consisting of an adjective premodified by a noun phrase *nearly 3 feet*. And where there are mistakes, these sometimes relate to issues that can be resolved only by recourse to information which is lacking in the Mk 2 language model, so that there is no way that the system could be expected to get the decision right. A human knows that *to the nearest foot* modifies the verb *measure*, because that interpretation makes sense; but on the basis of grammar alone, it is equally reasonable to take *to the nearest foot* as a postmodifier of *environment*, as APRIL has done – if the wording were changed from . . . *the environment to the nearest foot* to, say, . . . *the road to the nearest town*, this would be the correct analysis. APRIL has seen only the wordtags, which are the same for either of these alternatives.

In the case of another postmodifier attachment problem, even with human language understanding it is not entirely clear that the discrepancy between output and target represents an error: I take it that *in the environment* was intended by the writer as postmodifying *objects*, but it is not wholly senseless to think of *in the environment* as the place where objects are measured.

APRIL Mk 2 had no semantic knowledge whatever: its language model contained exclusively information about surface grammatical statistics. Therefore, where parsing decisions require semantic knowledge, APRIL is unlikely to get them right more often than chance would imply. This does not mean that parsing by stochastic optimization is intrinsically a 'surfacy' technique. Where parsing decisions depend on word meaning or on underlying logic, there seems to be no reason in principle why an annealing parser should not make such decisions correctly, provided that corpora analysed with respect to the relevant linguistic features are available and can be used to extract statistical language models relating to these 'deeper' levels. If, for instance, humans use co-occurrence restrictions between verbs and their arguments to resolve analytic problems, so that the subject of *drink*, say, is required to be animate except in occasional figurative expressions such as Yorick Wilks's example *my car drinks petrol* (Wilks 1978), then one would hope that a language model derived from a corpus which classified verbs and nouns in such terms could enable an annealing parser to resolve these cases correctly.

The trouble is that, at present, no such corpora exist. Producing usefully large samples of analysed usage is an activity requiring highly intensive and very skilled work, and availability of such resources is always the chief bottleneck for the type of research discussed in the present book. When APRIL Mk 2 was developed, the analysed corpora available were barely adequate with respect to surface grammatical phenomena, and they ignored deeper or more semantic aspects totally. Six years later there has been some progress in this respect (as we shall see in the next chapter), but the progress remains quite limited. Consequently, one must bear in mind when considering the performance of systems of the APRIL type that they can hope to get right only those features of grammar for which data are available.[10]

In some cases errors were caused by shortcomings in the Mk 2 language model that could be cured with the data available to us. The only mistake in the L12 example of Fig. 4.4, for instance, is that *myself a louse* has been treated as one constituent rather than two. A noun phrase beginning with a reflexive pronoun and containing further words is highly implausible, but the wordtags used for Mk 2 input were so crude that they did not code the reflexive feature of the pronoun *myself*. If our language model had recognized every possible grammatical distinction, when spread across so many categories the numbers that emerged from our limited data source would often have been too tiny to be meaningful, but even our Treebank was large enough to make it worth distinguishing reflexive from non-reflexive pronouns; we had begun by guessing which categories were significant enough to incorporate in the language model, and in this particular case we had guessed wrong.

Another error type that was much more pervasive could be cured more easily. We have seen that singulary branching is a significant issue for the APRIL system; the Mk 2 version allowed nonterminals with single daughters to be created freely when the daughters were terminal (a configuration that was common in the Treebank parsing scheme) but disallowed singulary branching higher in a parsetree (where the Treebank scheme did allow it, but rarely). However, although singulary branching at the bottom of a Treebank parsetree is frequent, the scheme lays down rigid rules about where it does and does not occur (cf. Sampson 1995: 172ff.). A node with a single daughter can be labelled with a phrase category, such as noun phrase (N) or adjective phrase (J), only if its mother is labelled with a clause category, such as main clause (S) or present-participle clause (Tg). The analyses of Figs 4.3 and 4.4 contain numerous violations of this rule, which could easily be eliminated by including a simple deterministic postediting procedure after the conclusion of an annealing run to prune out illegitimate single mothers. Consider for instance the first example in Fig. 4.4: this contains two violations of the rule just stated. The word *four* is treated as a one-word numeral phrase, M, within the noun phrase headed by *letters*; and *you* is treated as a one-word noun phrase within the prepositional phrase *for you*. If a postediting procedure had cut out the redundant singulary-branching nodes above *four* and *you*, the resulting analysis would have had a much higher score.

In this example, the analysis would still not have received full marks (though the equivalent correction to the *her* of the M01 example would bring the mark for that analysis up to 100%), because the target analysis for the L05 example specifies that *four letters* and *for you* are sister constituents of the clause, rather than the latter phrase modifying the former as APRIL had it. In reality this target analysis is debatable; it would be difficult to argue that *four letters for you* cannot be regarded as a single constituent, subject of *are*. One factor limiting the performance figures is that APRIL outputs are judged against a very precise standard, which lays down many requirements that go beyond the general linguistic consensus about grammatical structure.

Take, for instance, the phrase *nearly 3 feet* in the J23 example displayed in Fig. 4.5. APRIL has analysed this as containing a subordinate numeral phrase *nearly 3*. The parsing scheme which defines the target analyses lays down explicitly that phrases like *nearly 3 feet* are analysed without internal structure (Sampson 1995: 226), and the APRIL output lost marks accordingly. But the issue is discussed explicitly in the parsing scheme just because linguistic consensus does not make the answer obvious: some linguists might see *nearly 3 feet* as containing internal structure, others not. Repeatedly, features in Mk 2 output which are marked as errors relate to analytic alternatives which were considered at length when the target parsing scheme was formulated, because the arguments for drawing the trees one way or the other were finely balanced. We had to make decisions, and sometimes did so by little more than coin-tossing; in such cases it is hard to view APRIL's choice of the other alternatives as 'errors' in the full sense.

Certainly, there are also many things in these outputs which are bad errors by any standards. But then, it would have been fairly miraculous if there had not been.

Improving the Language Model

The most significant single feature of these outputs is that (in every case except the one perfectly correct analysis at the end of Fig. 4.3) the value assigned to the output tree is better (is a lower number) than the value assigned to the target tree. Instances of the reverse did happen, but on balance it was clear that the chief problem at this point lay not with the annealing algorithm but with the language model: the evaluation function was failing in its task of preferring correct analyses to all rival candidates. Very likely the annealing algorithm was also not consistently locating the best-valued solution – since there was no way of knowing what the optimal solution value for a given input was, this was less apparent (though if different runs on the same input yielded outputs with different values, they could not both be optimal). But we were relatively confident that by adjusting annealing schedules, and changing solution-space geometry by modifying the move-set, this latter problem could be solved. It would not matter, though, how good the annealing algorithm became at finding the best-valued tree, unless – at least in the great majority of cases – the tree assigned the best value by the evaluation function was a tree that human analysts accepted as a correct analysis. So we turned our thoughts to improving the language model.

Here there was a difficulty. The finite-state networks which the Mk 2 language model used to evaluate the plausibility of various expansions of a nonterminal label were complex affairs. Designing them had been a very challenging task, and their intricacy made it scarcely possible for a human analyst to foresee the precise implications of making a particular modification. Any characteristic error in APRIL outputs could very likely be cured by changing some aspect of one of the networks, but it seemed quite possible that such a change would have unanticipated consequences for the analysis of other inputs, so that the net effect of the change might be to reduce rather than increase analysis accuracy. The situation was rather akin to the problem of debugging unstructured 'spaghetti code' in computer programs.

Two developments seemed to be required if the APRIL language model was to become the kind of thing that could be progressively tested and improved with a reasonable expectation that changes would actually have a positive impact on overall performance. First, it was a mistake to represent all the diverse ways of realizing a given nonterminal label within a single unified network. The Treebank nonterminals were broad categories, whose expansions often divided into a number of distinct families or 'clusters', with strong family resemblances between the alternative expansions in one cluster, but little similarity between separate clusters. Expansions of the symbol N, noun phrase, for instance, might be based on a determiner + common noun structure, or on a proper name, or on a pronoun, and so forth – though many individual members of a cluster would contain additional extraneous elements, perhaps a punctuation mark, or an adverbial element (in English grammar adverbials have unusual freedom of location with respect to other sentence components). One way of imposing structure on the finite-state networks would be to separate the networks for separate clusters.

Secondly, it was true that the Treebank data showed a degree of messy anarchy in the alternative symbol sequences that appeared to belong to a single cluster: an element that occurred in most members of a cluster might be omitted in one or a few members, and extraneous elements might intrude in particular cluster members as just discussed. But trying to design networks *ad hoc* to represent the pattern of this messiness separately for each individual cluster again leads to network structures that are hard to understand or improve. We needed to represent the core label-sequences that defined the prototypical profile of a cluster, and the possibility of 'messiness' that allowed actual examples to deviate from the prototypes, by some standard structuring, the same for all clusters and all mother labels, so that if any particular shortcoming was noticed in evaluation-function performance it would be transparently clear which aspect of which network was responsible.

The solutions chosen were the concept of *prototype production*, and the *skip-and-loop* network structure. A prototype production is a canonical sequence of daughter labels for a mother label, such that the various members of a 'cluster' can be seen as derived from the same prototype sequence through insertion of extraneous 'intruder' elements and/or deletion of one or more prototype elements. 'Skip-and-loop' refers to a finite-state network architecture which allows any symbol sequence to be accepted by inserting intruder elements into and/or deleting elements from a prototype sequence, and such that the structure of the network allowing these insertions and deletions is fully predictable once the prototype symbol sequence is chosen.

Fig. 4.6 shows the skip-and-loop network for a hypothetical prototype sequence A B C D. The symbols of this sequence, which may be individual terminal or nonterminal symbols, or may stand for sets of such symbols, appear on horizontal 'spinal' arcs. Loop arcs attached to the start state and every second following state accept intruder symbols: 'V' stands for the entire terminal and nonterminal vocabulary, so each loop accepts any symbol other than symbols belonging to later parts of the prototype sequence. Arcs in grey are jump arcs, transited without consuming input. Thus any symbol-string whatsoever can be accepted by such a network (a string having no symbols in common with the prototype will be accepted through repeated traversals of the loop on the start state, followed by traversal of the successive skip arcs above the spinal line to the end state); and each particular string is accepted deterministically – there is never a choice of valid routes, and no need for a backtracking algorithm provided jump arcs are taken only when a 'black' arc cannot be taken. The structure of the network is modular, so the generalization of its shape to prototype sequences having more or fewer than four elements is obvious.

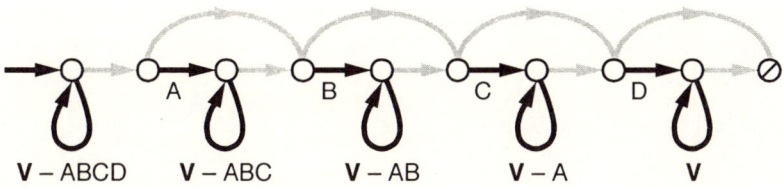

Figure 4.6 Skip-and-loop network for a prototype sequence

Each arc in such a network is associated with a probability – though, since each state has exactly two departing arcs, the language model needs to store probabilities only for black arcs: the grey jump arcs will always have the complementary probabilities. For those black arcs that stand for a range of symbols (the loops, and those of the spinal arcs which represent groups of symbols rather than single symbols), separate probabilities can be stored for the alternative symbols that may cause the arc to be transited. However, in the case of loop arcs the data are likely in practice to be too scanty to give meaningful probabilities for individual intruder symbols on individual loops. For these arcs, and perhaps also for multi-symbol spinal arcs, it will be better to predict the probability of accepting a particular symbol on the arc by multiplying the general probability for the arc with the prior probability of the symbol (the probability of that symbol relative to its alternatives in the language as a whole).

Each nonterminal symbol will be associated with a set of skip-and-loop networks, one for each prototype daughter sequence, which we can think of as subnetworks of a larger network for the mother symbol, arranged as in Fig. 4.7. The arcs radiating like fingers of a hand from the start state are jump arcs leading from the start to the skip-and-loop subnetworks for the respective prototypes, and are associated with probabilities summing to one representing the relative frequencies of the different clusters. The jumps from the start state make the network as a whole nondeterministic; but the nondeterminism is tamed, so that an optimal path can be found without incurring the cost of fully general algorithms for searching nondeterministic networks. Probabilities are assigned to the skip-and-loop arcs automatically, by driving the productions of an analysed database over the networks for their respective mother symbols and keeping count of arc-transitions on the individual skip-and-loop subnetwork which best matches any individual production.

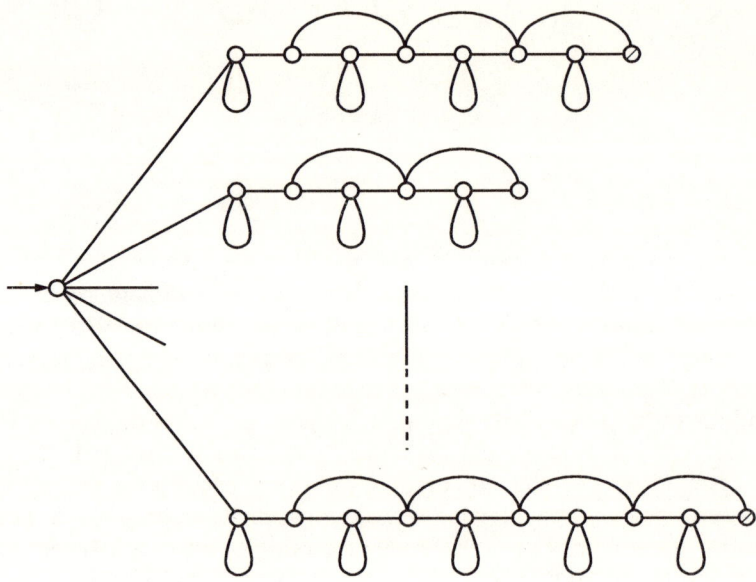

Figure 4.7 System of skip-and-loop networks for a nonterminal symbol

A language model based on skip-and-loop networks structures its total information about the language into units that are manageable and comprehensible to a human analyst. A prototype daughter-label sequence for a nonterminal is readily understandable, being comparable to a production rule in the compiler-like approach to NLP. (The distinction between core prototype expansions and expansions whose acceptance involves intruder loops and/or skips might perhaps be distantly compared to Chomsky's distinction between ideal linguistic 'competence' and imperfect real-life 'performance', though this analogy cannot be taken far – we shall see in ch. 7 that the prototypes actually used in newer versions of the APRIL system are very different indeed from anything that a theorist of linguistic competence would propose as a grammatical rule.) If such a language model performs poorly on some particular type of input, one can edit some of the prototype sequences with a reasonable expectation that this will achieve the overt intention without throwing up unexpected side-effects; and, because the structure of the language model is fully determined by the prototype sequences, after a prototype is edited no human effort is needed to recompile the model. Likewise, one can adjust probabilities for individual arcs, and for alternative symbols accepted on an arc, with some confidence that one knows what one is doing.

Thus we moved on from the Mk 2 version of APRIL with a fairly clear vision of how its performance – which for such a novel technique was already good enough to be interesting, although certainly not yet good enough to be usable in practical applications – might be progressively improved.

Unfortunately, external circumstances turned temporarily adverse. The research marked time for a while as a consequence of staffing rearrangements associated with the completion of one three-year contract and the inception of another; once those complications were surmounted, although I did not know it yet, I was in my last months of employment at Leeds University. Before I left Leeds in 1990 much promising work was done on implementing the new style of language model, and some initial results were obtained from it, but these were too fragmentary to discuss here. Full implementation had to wait until I found another academic post which enabled me to win new research funding in 1992.

In the mean time, the intellectual climate had evolved in a way that was gratifying to those of us involved with the APRIL work. When we began in the mid-1980s, the separation between computational linguists, orientated towards compiler-like rule systems, and statistically minded speech researchers, was still almost total. We did our bit to bring the two camps together – a conference we organized at Leeds in 1987 was, I believe, the first public occasion in Britain explicitly dedicated to encouraging language and speech researchers to exchange ideas and techniques; but for a while it continued to feel like an uphill struggle. Quite suddenly, attitudes changed. In Britain the change seemed to happen virtually overnight, probably as a consequence of somewhat earlier developments in America.[11] At a January 1990 conference at Wadham College, Oxford, computational linguists who for years had been almost aggressively sceptical about the use of statistics one after another testified to their new-found belief in the value of probabilistic techniques.

And yet we still seemed to be the only group internationally to be applying stochastic optimization to the parsing problem.[12] It was good to think that from now on, if I could keep the APRIL research programme alive, it would be judged on its specific merits, not in terms of prior methodological assumptions.

Notes

1. 'DARPA' stands for 'Defense Advanced Research Projects Agency'. At different times in recent American history the word 'Defense' has been added to and deleted from the name of this agency, and its acronym has accordingly varied between DARPA and ARPA; in this book I shall use the name current during most of the period discussed, which included 'Defense'.
2. Recent research using the SUSANNE Corpus to study the incidence of left branching in English (Sampson 1996) suggests that the generalization underlying Yngve's insight may be less 'global' in nature than I supposed at this time.
3. In 1992 RSRE became a branch of the new Defence Research Agency, and is now called 'DRA Malvern'.
4. Alternatively, Bridle & Moore (1984: 321) suggest imposing a temperature gradient across the window, so that adverse changes are less likely to be accepted as nodes grow older until material passing out of the left side of the window is frozen. However, this would not appear to offer a saving of processing effort, as biasing the location of proposed changes should do.
5. One might suppose that, if the elementary statistics relate to daughter-transitions, more nodes in a tree would be offset by the nodes containing fewer transitions apiece. But the compensation is not exact. Each additional node in a tree over a given number of leaves adds two to the total number of daughter-transitions in the tree.
6. The eventual decision to drop the tree size correction factor turned out to introduce a problem of its own. The evaluation measure was better at discriminating between correct and incorrect analyses without this factor; but the geometry of the solution space became less favourable, so that it was harder for the annealer to locate optimal solutions.
7. A further refinement of the assessment technique which becomes increasingly appropriate as the node labels recognized by a parsing system grow more complex and informative would give partial credit for matches between labels that are similar but not identical. Since word-ancestor assessment was developed, alternative measures of parsing accuracy have been proposed, notably by the (American) Grammar Evaluation Interest Group. Ted Briscoe and John Carroll (1996: 144–5) have compared various measures; they find word-ancestor assessment to perform better than the alternatives in delivering numerical scores sensitive to all relevant factors and consistent with intuitive judgments of relative accuracy.
8. Italics and inverted commas were ignored by the Mk 2 system, and are accordingly not shown in these outputs.
9. In the Treebank analytic scheme, *so that* was treated as a 'grammatical idiom' (Sampson 1995: 99ff.) equivalent to a single word, hence it appears on one line of Fig. 4.5.

10. This problem may be slightly less severe in practice than it appears. Fujisaki (1984) gives evidence that, even when alternative tree-structures over a string are nominally 'legal', for instance in the case of postmodifying elements which could be attached to a tree at different levels, writers tend to use the language in such a way that statistics on preferred structural configurations yield good predictions about the interpretation that a human would select on semantic grounds.
11. See, for instance, the successive Proceedings of conferences sponsored by DARPA (*Speech and natural language* (1989) and subsequent volumes in the same series).
12. After beginning my own programme of research I discovered that Bart Selman and Graeme Hirst at Toronto had also used simulated annealing (in a very different way) in connection with natural language parsing (Selman & Hirst 1985, 1987); but their work related to parsing of a subset of English defined by a rigorous and rather simple generative grammar, of the kind that could be handled efficiently by a compiler-like parser. It is not clear to me what advantage stochastic optimization had for them.

5 The Current System: Goals and Standards

Outline of APRIL3

The experiments described in previous chapters established, I believe, that optimization by simulated annealing merits serious exploration as a way of developing robust natural language parsers capable of returning useful analyses even for messy inputs. In the next three chapters I describe the development effort currently under way to convert parsing by simulated annealing from a local experimental programme into an established technique available for assessment and further development at multiple sites internationally.

This effort takes the shape of a research project, initiated at the University of Sussex in 1992 and sponsored jointly by the Science and Engineering Research Council (UK) and the UK Ministry of Defence,[1] whose goal is to produce a self-contained, adequately documented, and fully portable suite of annealing-parser software which will be suitable for distribution to other sites and will make it realistically possible for researchers having no previous involvement with the work to run experiments using their own input texts and choosing their own settings of annealing parameters and similar options. In cases where performance proves disappointing, the software should be sufficiently 'transparent' to enable researchers to formulate ideas about what has gone wrong, and thus the system will promote progress towards better techniques that in due course will doubtless incorporate concepts different from any that our team have thought of. Parsing by annealing is not a 'solved problem', but it has moved beyond the stage where it can usefully remain an essentially private academic hobby by one small group of researchers at a single site.

We use the name 'APRIL3' to refer to the software suite now being developed, to distinguish it from the more limited annealing-parser systems described in previous chapters.[2] The APRIL3 system has the following characteristics, each of which sets it apart from the earlier experimental APRIL versions:

- APRIL3 accepts raw English-language input – that is, it does the whole

task of moving from ordinary English text to a grammatical analysis, looking up words in an electronic dictionary to discover their grammatical properties, whereas earlier versions of APRIL assumed that the dictionary-lookup phase, together with disambiguation of grammatically ambiguous words, had already been carried out by independent systems (the input to those versions consisted of sequences of wordtags).
- Although (for reasons to do with availability of suitable research resources) APRIL3 continues to be geared to written-English inputs, its text-segmentation and parsing routines are based on the concept of *word-hypothesis lattice* which is central to automatic speech recognition: the data-structures which the APRIL3 front end creates and delivers to its parsing machinery are the same general kind of structures which speech-recognition systems commonly output as their partially complete attempts to resolve physical speech signals into linear sequences of words. We have already seen that much of the impetus for the APRIL research programme has lain in the hope that its robust probabilistic approach will be specially useful for grammatical analysis of spoken language; this structural feature of APRIL3 is intended to make it relatively easy to incorporate APRIL into speech-understanding systems, once adequate grammatical data on spoken language become available and allow suitable language models to be developed.
- The analyses output by APRIL3 are expressed in terms of a precisely defined, detailed published standard. (By contrast, the less-detailed Treebank analytic norms used in the earlier APRIL work were never publicly documented – when an APRIL output was correct, readers essentially had to take our word for it that we had a specification of 'correct output' independent of 'observed APRIL output'.) Thus, although at the time of writing it remains to be seen how successful APRIL3 will be at hitting its targets, we can at least say that the issue cannot be fudged: the properties of target outputs for given inputs are fully and clearly specified, whether the inputs are the particular samples used by our team for testing purposes, or any other examples of English which users elsewhere may choose to experiment with. Furthermore, the target analytic standard is one which specifies all aspects of English grammar, including 'logical' or 'deep grammar' considerations that were totally ignored by earlier APRIL versions (though they are often very important for practical applications of NLP technology); the APRIL3 system will not attempt to identify all aspects of the logical grammar of input texts (that would be too ambitious a goal at this stage), but it will make a significant advance in this direction by comparison with the purely surface analysis of earlier APRIL versions.
- The statistical model of English used by APRIL3 in order to assess

proposed analyses is generated automatically from an analysed corpus of text. APRIL Mk 2 used a hand-crafted language model, and the work of producing this proved to be a major development bottleneck; the task was massively more demanding than anticipated in advance. As well as using simulated annealing to optimize an analysis for a given text input with respect to a language model, APRIL3 uses simulated annealing in a second way to optimize a language model (in the form of sets of daughter-sequence prototypes) for a given database of analysed language. If parsing by annealing is destined to be a widely used technology, users will often need to develop new language models as fuller data on grammatical statistics become available; language models will need to be adapted to different schemes of grammatical notation, different genres of English, and perhaps even to other languages. In view of earlier experience we believe that for this to be realistically feasible requires the process of creating a language model to be at least partly automated.

- The work of developing the APRIL3 system is being executed in conformity with the principles of modern software engineering practice. Computer programming began as a craft carried out by individuals with few explicit guidelines governing their working methods, and at the research level within universities and elsewhere it commonly remains such even today. But in more practically oriented industrial settings it has come to be understood that this style of working is not well suited to producing, within time and budget constraints, software that succeeds in achieving its intended goals and which is capable of being used, maintained, and extended by people other than those who wrote it. We believe this is just as true for software developed for research purposes; research environments typically have different working relationships from those which obtain in settings geared to developing software for profit, and these relationships may explain why software engineering disciplines have been slower to take root in the research community, but the need for them is just as great there.[3]

In the remainder of this chapter and in the following chapters I shall expand on these points; but, in order to produce a coherent account of the working of the APRIL system, they are best taken in a different order. Below, I take up the issues of software engineering, and input and output standards. Word-hypothesis lattices are discussed in ch. 6, on the analysis algorithms; the language model is discussed in ch. 7.

Software Engineering

For a survey of software engineering techniques, see for instance Sommerville 1992. There exist a number of highly specific named 'recipes' for executing the software development process; however, these tend to make assumptions about the properties of the task which real-life tasks do not always fully meet, and probably most practical software development exercises are somewhat eclectic in their use of named techniques, as the APRIL project is. Nevertheless, various principles are common to virtually all software engineering styles.

In part, these agreed principles are intended to ensure that unclarities or hidden inconsistencies in initial plans are brought to light and resolved as early as possible in the process by which abstract concepts are converted into specific algorithms, and certainly that substantive decisions should no longer remain to be taken at the stage when algorithms are realized as concrete program coding. Software engineering disciplines seek to control what might be caricatured as the hacker's instinct: take an interesting idea and move more or less straight to the keyboard to get some version of it running quickly; treat the inevitable finding that the first version behaves in ways different from what is really wanted as a series of problems to be solved by *ad hoc* reprogramming as they arise; leave documentation as a disagreeable necessity to be fitted in to whatever time remains at the very end of a project.

This is a style of working which is natural and attractive to many people who enjoy working with computers, but it routinely fails to deliver the goods. In building a house it is probably obvious to anybody that one needs to plan everything in detail before the first brick is laid, and that putting up a few walls and then pondering what to do next, or changing one's mind about the layout partway through the building process, would be a very bad idea. Because of the 'soft', intellectual rather than material character of computer programs, it is less immediately obvious in their case that there are heavy costs involved in not getting them right first time; but experience in the software industry has abundantly shown that this is so. Boehm (1981: 39–41) quotes the expense of error elimination as increasing by as much as a hundred to one depending how late in the development lifecycle the errors are detected. More importantly, if unclarities in the specifications emerge only at the coding stage, the probability becomes quite high that the project will never succeed in producing a working system at all.

Since natural language parsing by annealing is a research task, neither our team nor anyone else can guarantee to produce a system which delivers sufficiently accurate outputs for a sufficiently high proportion of inputs to be a useful component of practical NLP applications – mankind simply does not yet know whether optimization by simulated annealing using daughter-sequence prototypes is capable even in principle of delivering analyses with the required degree of accuracy. But what should be possible, and what we need software engineering disciplines in order to achieve, is a suite of software which reliably tests the concept of parsing by annealing, so that if the performance of APRIL3 should ultimately prove disappointing this will be because of limitations in the abstract technique rather than because of flaws in the implementation of the technique on the computer.

One implication is that, in effect, documentation should be done first rather than left to the end. Early stages of the project consist of developing specifications on paper to increasing degrees of refinement: ideally, by the time that coding is undertaken, the paper specifications to be realized as lines of program code are themselves so complete that the possibility of logical errors in the programming scarcely arises – bugs should be limited to little more than typing mistakes. Time is invested in the specification process in order to maximize the chance of achieving coding that succeeds in doing the intended task, but a by-product is that, when the software is complete, little additional time needs to be invested in documenting it for the ultimate users; to a large extent it is already documented through the specifications.

The APRIL3 project involves the following categories of documentation:

- A *Requirements Definition*, which describes the desired system and its functionality in plain English, in terms that can be followed by potential users who have no interest in entering into details of how that functionality is achieved. The Requirements Definition also covers non-functional requirements such as error trapping, and portability (which is achieved for instance by requiring all source code to conform to ANSI standard C, and by disallowing use of graphical user interfaces).
- A *Requirements Specification* – a more substantial document rendering each aspect of functionality identified in the Requirements Definition fully precise (often by means of tables or other symbolic material) even in areas where a typical potential user wanting to know what the system does would be satisfied with a general indication or example of functionality. For instance, the Requirements Definition takes just a couple of lines to state that the annealing system develops a parse by choosing and modifying its choice of a path through a word-hypothesis lattice and a labelled tree structure over that path; the Requirements Specification uses several pages to formalize the precise method by which a solution is initialized and what steps are allowed in exploring the solution space. The Requirements Specification can be thought of as a contract between

system developers and procurer. In many software development environments, it would be the basis of a legal contract; in a university research setting the legal relationships are different – both the 'principal investigator' who wins the research grant by means of a successful proposal to a funding body, and the 'research fellows' or 'research assistants' whom he takes on to execute the proposal, are all employees of the same institution, so that no legal contract exists between them – but on the APRIL3 team we have nevertheless found it a useful mental discipline to agree to act as if the principal investigator were commissioning a system from the research fellows on the basis of the Requirements Specification.

- A *Software Specification,* which states how the requirements are broken down into a set of interacting programs, including for each program details of its decomposition into components and a specification for each component. On a larger software development project, the Software Specification would ordinarily be considerably longer than the Requirements Specification. On the APRIL3 project, where almost all sections of coding are the responsibility of single individuals, this is not necessary, and much of the detail that would ordinarily be included in a Software Specification is replaced by full and systematic commenting within the software itself.
- A *Quality Plan,* laying down organizational arrangements for the management and execution of the project, governing matters such as meetings and reviews, production of progress reports, standards and style requirements for documentation, and the management of paper and electronic filing systems.
- *Coding Guidelines,* governing layout, naming conventions, use of comments, and so forth within APRIL software, with the intention of ensuring that all APRIL3 source code shares a common 'look and feel', making it clear and maintainable.[4] The Coding Guidelines could logically form part of the Quality Plan, but because on our project there is much more to say about coding standards than any other single area within the Quality Plan it was convenient to make the Coding Guidelines a separate document.

In due course there will also be a *Test Plan* laying down a regime of tests for checking that the software performs to specification, and a *User's Guide*; at the time of writing these have not yet been produced, but the latter will largely be derived from the documents listed above, which were brought close to completion before any APRIL3 code was written.

Ideally, these documents would have been fully complete and stable before coding began. Reality commonly falls short of this ideal, and did so in our case: the experience of coding forced reconsideration of some specification details, and changes were made in various of the formal documents (under the rules of the Quality Plan a careful log is kept of successive document versions). But the fact that 'documentation before coding' was adopted as an ideal meant that modifications of this sort have been much fewer than one would otherwise have expected on a project of comparable logical complexity, and it has been possible to ensure that where modifications are unavoidable they do not trigger uncontrolled chains of consequential changes to other components of the system. The debugging process as software components are coded up has to date been relatively painless.

Many academic researchers might tend to see this level of prior documentation (versions of the documents current at the time of writing the present book total about 170 pages, and are by no means yet complete) as rather 'over the top' for a project staffed by two researchers who share an office and see the principal investigator on a virtual daily basis. It is very likely true that the documentation does include some items which could adequately have been left to be understood informally among such a small team, even if they would need to be written down explicitly on larger software development projects involving separate groups of workers who rarely interact. But even within small groups, matters that are understood informally often are not really understood, or are understood differently by different members (or by the same individual at different times). We would argue that it is better to err on the side of writing too much down rather than too little.

The time taken for this level of prior documentation should be recouped through the speed with which successful code can be generated once the coding process starts. In the context of academic research there is, however, another cost in doing things this way which is not so easy to recoup, and which may help to explain the slowness of some research environments to accept software engineering disciplines. Successful long-term programmes of academic research depend on a research leader's ability to win a series of grants and contracts, each of which will last for a limited period (typically about three years) but which ideally should follow immediately on from one another or overlap, without gaps when funding dries up, impetus is lost, and research teams break up and move to other jobs. An academic looking for new funding wants to be able to point to results at least of a preliminary kind flowing from his current project at an early stage, because it takes many months to get from an initial proposal to the inauguration of a new project even when the proposal is successful. There is therefore a real tension between the precepts of good software engineering practice (which delays the point at which research begins to yield concrete results) and the social organization of science, which tends to reward premature coding.

The APRIL3 team have resisted the latter pressure: we have decided that we would rather try to get things right than get something out quickly. But the pressure is real, and one cannot always resist it with impunity. The point deserves to be pondered by those who have influence in the commissioning of information-technology research. In Britain during recent years we have heard much about the need to encourage academics to choose research topics with a potential economic payoff, but arguably a more significant issue is the lack of encouragement for researchers to produce software that is solid and reliable, whether the application is practical or abstractly academic.

Input Text

APRIL3 is designed to accept input text in the form of paragraphs of ordinary written English. (Since inputs may be quite long, they are taken from files rather than entered at the keyboard.) The paragraph is the largest grammatical unit recognized in the SUSANNE scheme, and will normally be a fairly clearly discrete section of a written text. Ultimately, the location of sentence boundaries within a paragraph is intended to be one of the analytic problems which the system is required to solve. Initially, however, we are simplifying the task confronting the system by requiring inputs to contain markers for the beginnings of sentences; this is the only way in which APRIL3 inputs differ from ordinary text.

'Ordinary written English' is a vague concept. The APRIL3 project renders it more precise by defining the style of text which the system is required to cope with as 'English as it would conventionally appear if typed on a traditional British typewriter' – not including 'special symbols' whether these are available on modern computer keyboards (e.g. '<') or not (e.g. 'é', 'µ', '½'), and indicating both opening and closing inverted commas and apostrophe by undifferentiated single or double marks. Before the advent of computer equipment into offices in the 1980s, the conventions for encoding written English into the set of characters provided on a standard typewriter were rather well established. The larger character-sets provided by modern word-processing equipment, and the fact that word-processing equipment is now commonly used by people who have not undergone a secretarial training with formal instruction in clerical skills, have introduced a measure of orthographic anarchy into current writing habits which has not yet settled down into a new set of conventions: one can sometimes nowadays see writers using quite diverse systems for spacing adjacent to punctuation, for instance, and even varying inconsistently within a single document. Some writers continue to use undifferentiated opening and closing inverted commas, others write ` . . . '. If we required APRIL3 to cope with that sort of thing, the difficulty of its task would be greatly increased, and yet the problem is of limited interest in the context of our overall research goals. We believe that the specified style of input will in fact commonly coincide with the style that would be used spontaneously by, say, a visitor at a system demonstration who is invited to type a piece of English text with no special instructions about format.

The requirement on input texts is enforced by routines which reject inputs containing disallowed characters. If a text is orthographically deviant but uses only permitted characters, the system has no way of rejecting it, but we would not regard poor analytic performance on such an input as reflecting badly on the system. This may seem inconsistent with the idea that APRIL is designed to deal robustly with messy language, but the messiness we are interested in dealing with relates to the grammatical construction of sentences, where deviance occurs in both writing and speech and is indeed much more salient in the latter. Indiscipline with respect to surface orthographic details, such as spellings or the placement of spacing and punctuation marks, is a phenomenon that relates exclusively to the written medium; dealing with these matters (as commercial grammar-checking software tries to do, with limited success at present) is a large separate problem that our project cannot afford to take on board.

The SUSANNE Analytic Scheme

The early annealing-parser research reported in preceding chapters produced analyses annotated with the symbols developed for use in the Lancaster parsing project discussed in ch. 2, which were private to our group: many of our symbols have other meanings for other computational linguistics researchers, and although we supplied brief definitions of the elements of our annotation scheme in Garside *et al.* (1987: 88–90), these were by no means complete enough to allow an outsider to be sure how the symbols would be applied in numerous debatable cases.

This might seem an odd way to proceed. If developing an automatic parser for English is the worthwhile goal that I have argued, surely doing it properly ought to mean producing analyses couched in the standard descriptive notation. However, no standard notation existed. In this respect, computational linguistics has been in a state comparable to that of biology before Linnaeus. When researchers belonging to different local traditions wanted to communicate with one another about the elements of their language samples – the word-classes, the grammatical constructions, and so forth – they had only traditional, ill-defined, and sometimes quite ambiguous terminology in which to do so; in so far as grammatical terminology was sharpened up at individual research sites, this was done largely through interpersonal discussion and rarely publicly documented. There was not even a standard comprehensive listing of the grammatical elements of English, let alone a standard set of symbols for representing those elements. (And what was true for English was undoubtedly true also for other languages; English has received far more attention by computational linguists than any one other natural language.)

Within computational linguistics, it has been the norm for each individual research group to make its own independent decisions about the intended output of its parser, in such a way that one group's analyses are not just notationally distinct from but usually substantially non-equivalent to those of other groups. Furthermore, description/definition of target analysis schemes has tended not to be a high priority, so it is quite difficult for an outsider to know just what structural properties of English a particular group's parser aims to specify; researchers have usually been far more concerned to publicize their parsing *system* (the nature of the software they have created in order to move from raw input to analysed output) than to publicize their parsing *scheme* (the nature of the structural analyses comprised in the output of a parsing system) – indeed, it is not always seen as important to codify the latter explicitly even for a research group's internal purposes. And it is clear that the (explicit or implicit) parsing schemes of virtually all groups are highly incomplete: any such scheme will offer no specific analyses for very many phenomena that frequently occur in English.

There are (at least) two reasons for this state of affairs, both stemming from aspects of the recent history of linguistics. First, computational linguists have tended to treat their subject as a branch of theoretical linguistics, and theoretical linguistics has for decades been concerned with rival notational systems for capturing highly abstract generalizations about a limited range of 'core' grammatical constructions, such as relative clauses, or verb complements. To a theoretical linguist it is simply not part of his goals to use an analytic system which comprehensively covers everything that occurs in the language in practice, which represents analytic distinctions in a maximally straightforward, self-explanatory fashion, or which coincides with the notations used by rival theorists. There are valid intellectual reasons why these should not be goals for theoretical linguistics; but the result has been (since it is largely the same people who practise both disciplines) that they have not become goals of computational linguistics either, where their lack is unfortunate.

Secondly, we have seen that theoretical linguists have until very recently been uninterested in working with corpora; yet it is only through corpus work that the analyst is forced to confront the great diversity of linguistic phenomena that occur in practice and to seek an analytic scheme comprehensive enough to cope with them. If the linguist relies on data invented by himself in his role as a native-speaker of the language, as has been more usual (not because linguists are lazy, but as a consequence of methodological axioms about 'competence' and 'performance' which may be respectable within theoretical linguistics though, again, they are less relevant to practical NLP research), then it is near-inevitable that the linguist will focus on a limited range of phenomena which the research community has picked out as posing interesting problems, while overlooking many other phenomena that happen never to have struck anyone as noteworthy.

Because the agenda of theoretical linguistics gave that discipline little reason to spend time on developing comprehensive, explicit taxonomies of the elements of real-life language structure, some theoretical linguists have in the past been not just uninterested in but positively hostile towards such activity: consider for instance the tone of remarks by J. J. Katz (1971: 31ff.) on 'taxonomy' and linguistic 'botanizing'. But, for practical, economically useful NLP purposes, 'botanizing' seems quite a good description of what is currently needed.

The target for APRIL3 outputs is based on an annotation scheme (exemplified in Fig. 2.1 above, and defined in Sampson 1995) which was developed under a separate project, SUSANNE,[5] that aimed to do for the English language something rather akin to what Linnaeus did for botany. (For further discussion of the analogy between linguistic and biological taxonomy, cf. Sampson 1992.) It is worth taking a page or two to explain the nature of the gaps which this SUSANNE scheme is intended to fill.

Limitations of the Analytic Tradition

One consequence of the theoretical orientation of computational linguistics research has been to overlook various aspects of natural language that ought not to be ignored. Many researchers, for instance, have excluded written-language punctuation from grammatical analysis. NLP applications often concern written rather than spoken language, and the sentences discussed by theoretical and computational linguists commonly involve the formal, elaborate style characteristic of the written mode; but theoretical linguists have scarcely ever discussed punctuation,[6] and there is no consensus among computational linguists about how (or whether) to include punctuation marks in parsetrees (despite the fact that for automatic analysis of written language, punctuation marks are highly significant, comparable in importance to grammatical words such as *of* or *the*). Some computational linguists have explicitly urged that punctuation should *not* be included (see e.g. Taylor *et al.* 1989; cf. Sampson 1992: 443–4). Again, real-life (written and spoken) language contains many high-frequency phenomena such as dates (*August 7th 1992*), weights and measures (*five foot ten*), Harvard-style bibliographical references in academic literature (*Greenberg (1963: 90) wrote . . .*), addresses (*10, Bridge Rd, Ambridge, Borsetshire BC21 7EW*), etc. etc., which have their own characteristic structures in different languages (compare the varying national formats for postal addresses, or compare Portuguese *2$50* with American *$2.50*, for instance); but theoretical linguists – and indeed those who produce language descriptions of a more traditional type, such as (for English) the series of grammars by Randolph Quirk and his collaborators culminating in Quirk *et al.* 1985 – perceive them as peripheral, and for these phenomena too there is no consensus about how they should be analysed. Yet for practical NLP applications they will often be as important as many of the constructions that theoretical linguists see as part of the 'core' of language.

The neglected areas just listed relate chiefly to written language; but there are as many or perhaps more phenomena characteristic of spoken English which tend to fall outside the purview of computational linguistics, with its focus on relatively formal, impersonal language (cf. Allwood *et al.* 1990). It is clear, for instance, that word-classification schemes developed for tagging written English words are likely to be inadequate for tagging the words of spoken utterances, which are full of items serving discourse rather than logical functions (good work has been done in this area by Swedish researchers, e.g. Stenström 1990, Altenberg 1990).

Roger Moore, of DRA Malvern, has urged (Moore 1992) that speech science and technology have now developed to the point where they face 'an overwhelming need for agreed standards' in transcribing the structure of everyday, extempore speech; he notes that no such conventions are currently known to exist, and suggests that speech scientists themselves are not best qualified to devise conventions relating to structural features. One problem is that speech – particularly 'private' speech such as face-to-face or telephone conversations, as opposed to lectures, broadcasts, etc. – contains a high incidence of phenomena such as speech repairs and hesitations which tend to be invisible in standard grammatical description, since this is usually based on a 'competence' version of linguistic behaviour that excludes them. The limited work we have done in this area to date (see p. 183 below) suggests that existing attempts to specify notations for these phenomena (notably Levelt 1983, and cf. Howell & Young 1991) are unsatisfactory: they depend on spoken language conforming to patterns which, in practice, are frequently violated.[7]

Both in the case of writing and in that of speech, NLP applications require the ability to penetrate beyond the surface grammar of a text or utterance to disentangle its logic. Great attention has been paid to this issue by linguistic theorists in recent decades with respect to the 'competent' language characteristic of writing, where it largely involves the reconstruction of deleted items whose identity is implied by the surface grammar, and recovery of the logical position of 'transformationally moved' items. In addition to these matters, though, spoken language involves a large extra layer of surface/logical contrasts having to do with the unannounced changes of tack, breaking off of utterances before their logical completion, production of logically confused utterances, etc., which are frequent in speech but are normally edited out of writing. It will be a long time before automatic language processing systems are capable of dealing adequately with naturalistic speech in which such phenomena are salient; but a prerequisite for advances in that direction is availability of databases showing what patterns the phenomena fall into in practice, and this in turn presupposes adequate annotation schemes.

Furthermore, even in the areas of language which are shared between writing and speech and which linguists would see as part of what a language description ought (at least ideally) to cover, there is a vast amount to be done in terms of listing and classifying the phenomena that occur. Many constructions are omitted from theoretical descriptions not for reasons of principle but because they are not very frequent and/or do not seem to interact in theoretically interesting ways with central aspects of grammar, and although they are mentioned in traditional grammars they are not systematically assigned places in explicit inventories of the resources of the language. One example among very many might be the English *the more . . . the more . . .* construction discussed by Fillmore *et al.* 1988, an article which makes some of the same points I am trying to make about the tendency for much of a language's structure to be overlooked by the linguist. Discussion between research groups about the grammatical resources of a language is hampered by the fact that traditional terminology is used in inconsistent and sometimes vague ways. For instance, various English-speaking linguists use the terms 'complement' and 'predicate' in quite incompatible ways. Other terms, such as 'noun phrase', are used much more consistently, in the sense that different groups agree on core examples of the term; but traditional grammars devote little attention to defining clearcut *boundaries* between such terms that would allow unclear cases to be assigned predictably to one category or another. The work of producing the tagged version of the LOB Corpus of written British English forced Stig Johansson to produce a short book-length specification of boundaries between the 136 tags used to classify English words;[8] this work (Johansson 1986) was so far as I know unique in English linguistics. Johansson's manual is by no means the last word to be said on word classification, and there is as much or, in my view, even more to be done in the area of classifying grammatical constituents.

Unlike the writers of traditional language descriptions, theoretical linguists are in one sense heavily concerned with the definition of boundaries between grammatical constructions. A theoretician might well be interested in the question whether or not (to borrow an example from Garside *et al.* 1987: ch. 7) the wording following *is* in the sentence *A dog is as much God's handiwork as a man* should be classified as a noun phrase. But the sense in which a theoretician would address himself to this question is different from the sense in which it requires an answer for the purposes of the linguistic stocktaking advocated here. For the theoretician, the question would be whether *as much God's handiwork as a man* 'really is' derived from the same node as core examples of noun phrases, such as pronouns or proper names, in the most psychologically correct or explanatorily adequate formal definition of English. A question of this sort is very deep, and can be answered only provisionally and for a limited number of grammatical phenomena. For NLP purposes, the most pressing need is for an explicit, comprehensive classification scheme to be *imposed* on a language, without too many worries about whether its details are psychologically or otherwise correct, so that we can all talk about the elements of the language using a common notation and knowing that we mean the same thing by our notational categories and that the set of categories is reasonably exhaustive.

Logical Structure

While theoretical and computational linguists have not striven for comprehensiveness of coverage, they have put considerable effort into identifying divergences between the 'surface structure' of natural language utterances and their 'underlying structure' or 'logical form'. (To illustrate this distinction via the classic example: *John is eager to please* and *John is easy to please* share the same surface structure, but logically their grammar is quite different: in one case *John* is the logical subject and in the other case the logical object of *please*. Likewise it might be said that active/passive pairs such as *John ate the toast* v. *The toast was eaten by John* are distinct in surface grammar but logically equivalent.) For many NLP applications, identifying the underlying logic of an input is a necessary stage of analysis; only for a few special cases such as text-to-speech systems is surface parsing alone arguably sufficient. However, there is much more divergence between various theorists' conceptions of logical form than of surface structure. It is probably safe to say that everyone agrees on representing the surface grammar of sentences by means of labelled tree structures (or some notation clearly equivalent to labelled trees), though the alphabet of node labels would differ considerably from research group to research group, and to a lesser extent the shapes of the trees drawn for particular sentences would also differ. In the area of logical form, however, although some researchers would again use labelled trees to represent the facts others would use quite different methods of representation (for a survey, see Winograd 1983).

Sometimes it is not clear whether these differences are notational or substantive. Thus, Winograd (1983) represents the logical forms output by the Augmented Transition Network parsers which he deals with at length by means of diagrams that look superficially quite unlike labelled trees, and which are never brought into relationship with the trees that Winograd displays in connection with other systems of analysis he discusses; yet these diagrams can be mechanically converted into labelled tree structures that are unorthodox in only one or two minor respects.

By contrast, in other areas differences between notations for logical form are entirely real and hard to resolve. An example would be the question of how to distinguish the various arguments of the predicate element (usually the verb) of a clause. The arguments include the items that appear as subject, direct object, etc. in surface grammar, but some researchers regard these categories as unhelpful for specifying the logic of a clause (note that the grammatical subject of a verb is by no means always the 'doer' of the action). Numerous alternative proposals are available in the literature; many are couched in terms of Fillmorean 'case theory' (Fillmore 1968), but they diverge widely with respect to the sets of cases recognized, and other schemes again use concepts other than case.

The importance of logical analysis for NLP applications, already alluded to, might suggest that any project orientated towards such an application would be forced to develop a well-defined analytic approach in this area. Surprisingly, this is not always true of even the largest projects. The European Communities' EUROTRA project for machine translation between all the official languages of the member states was probably the largest and most expensive NLP project anywhere in the world (after a pilot phase lasting several years it was fully established in 1982 and subsequently employed on the order of 100 full-time researchers at any time, spread over all EC member states). According to Bente Maegaard (1989: 44), even at that late date the EUROTRA representations of source- and target-language logical structures resolved the issue discussed above about identifying the various arguments of a verb simply by labelling them 'arg1', 'arg2', etc. – i.e. they said nothing substantive at all about this important aspect of logical structure and merely tried to rely on the accident that Western European languages usually order corresponding arguments of corresponding verbs in the same sequence. This is a striking illustration of the way in which *the level of sophistication of natural language analysis targets has been lagging behind the sophistication of the software being created to execute natural language analysis.*

The Emergence of Standards

Whatever the past situation, it is clear in the 1990s that taxonomic work and standards definition for natural language is an idea whose time has come. In some areas great strides have been made in the last few years. Thus, the Unicode Consortium is developing a standard (Unicode Consortium 1991–2) that enables us to move beyond the severely limited ASCII encoding of written characters (in which, for instance, marks as distinct in function as apostrophe, prime sign, and acute accent are lumped together under a single code, and a system must know what language a document is written in in order to decide whether to display a given code on the screen as, say, a Roman letter D or a Greek delta) by defining a systematic 16-bit encoding scheme providing a distinct code for every distinct written character of all the world's languages, together with the symbols of language-like systems such as the alphabet of the International Phonetic Association; the Unicode scheme is now in effect adopted as an international standard, ISO/IEC 10646-1, published in 1993. The SGML standard (ISO 8879:1986, cf. Goldfarb 1990, van Herwijnen 1990) has for almost a decade given us a well-defined way of representing the logical structure of the formatting of natural language text; and more recently the Text Encoding Initiative (Sperberg-McQueen & Burnard 1994) has attempted to extend SGML techniques from high-level matters such as paragraphing and heading relationships to more directly linguistic features of text content.

The centrality of parsing for NLP means that something akin to these efforts is needed for the grammar of natural languages, and my SUSANNE scheme offers a first attempt in this direction. The SUSANNE scheme is used as the target to which APRIL3 output analyses are expected to conform (though, just as earlier versions of APRIL omitted some of the detail of the Treebank annotation scheme, so APRIL3 currently omits some of the much richer detail in the SUSANNE scheme; SUSANNE is intended to provide a method of representing all aspects of English grammar, irrespective of whether it is practical for a specific language-processing system to deal with particular aspects).

The initial goal of the SUSANNE project was to create a parsed sample of English more adequate for statistical NLP purposes than the Lancaster-Leeds Treebank. This aim was achieved; but, as the work proceeded, it became increasingly clear that the chief value of the project lay in the rigorous taxonomic scheme that was developed to ensure that an analysis was available for any phenomenon occurring in the language and that analyses of different texts were always consistent with one another. By the time the

SUSANNE project was complete, there were a number of parsed English corpora in existence, the largest of which (Mitchell Marcus's Pennsylvania Treebank, see Marcus *et al.* 1993) dwarfs the 130,000-word SUSANNE Corpus; but the explicit SUSANNE taxonomic scheme is so far as I am aware the only extant large-scale attempt at a rigorous, comprehensive grammatical taxonomy for any natural language which is *reproducible*, in the sense that two analysts both armed with the scheme and faced with the same sample of real-life text but working independently must annotate the grammar of the text identically. Only because the corpus is limited in size was it feasible to examine its contents with the degree of intensity needed in order to produce and document an annotation scheme which approaches the ideal of being sensitive to the full range of grammatical subtleties found in the language it represents.

The SUSANNE Corpus does evidently still have value as a statistical database (apart from its use as the source of grammatical statistics for the APRIL3 language model). The Corpus was first released by the Oxford Text Archive via anonymous ftp (file transfer protocol) in October 1992, and by early 1994 it was being accessed by about sixty different academic, commercial, and governmental research sites a month, spread over at least four continents; although it is smaller than some comparable resources, it includes categories of information which they omit.[9] But, as I now see it, the main *raison d'être* of the corpus is as a guarantee of the fact that the parsing scheme is developed from and applicable to realistic data, rather than being a mere aprioristic invention. (I stress that this scheme cannot claim to be more than a first attempt; even if it achieves a degree of recognition in the research community, it unquestionably leaves a great deal of room for extension and improvement in time to come.) A rigorous and explicit set of parsing standards offers many benefits for NLP technology (Sampson 1995: 7–10) apart from the possibility of extracting consistent statistical information from a corpus to which they have been applied.

Since the chief point of the SUSANNE annotation scheme is the rigour with which it is defined (Sampson 1995 is a book of almost 500 pages), it would be inappropriate to try to summarize the scheme in a few paragraphs here. Its wordtags and formal tagma categories are more refined than those of the Treebank scheme (for instance, about three times as many distinct wordtags are recognized); and, as we saw in ch. 2, the SUSANNE scheme contains resources for indicating the logical grammar of sentences as well as their surface structure. The current APRIL3 language model includes some of the SUSANNE logical annotation, but not all. The language model recognizes distinctions between clause complements (subject, direct object, indirect object, predicate complement, etc.), though it ignores the SUSANNE distinctions between adjunct functions (adverbial of Place, of

Time, of Manner, etc.); and APRIL3 does not at present attempt to reconstruct 'ghost' elements, such as the invisible logical subject following *seemed* in Fig. 2.1 above (p. 9).

Likewise, for the APRIL3 language model the wordtags and the formal parts of tagmatags are simplified relative to the full SUSANNE annotation – but the APRIL3 language model retains more distinctions than occurred in the Mk 2 model.

In all, the current APRIL3 language model distinguishes 105 wordtags, and 317 tagmatags. The workings of the language model are detailed in ch. 7.

Notes

1. SERC reference number GR/J06108, 'A full natural-language annealing parser'. In 1994 the role of SERC was inherited by the new Engineering and Physical Sciences Research Council.
2. There have been more than three versions of the APRIL parsing system; the name APRIL3 is chosen to reflect the fact that the current research contract is the third in sequence.
3. These remarks are not intended to imply a crude contrast of the kind 'industrial practice good, academic practice bad'. The industrial sector may on balance have gone further than the academic sector towards converting software development into a professional engineering activity, but *all* sectors still have far to go in this direction (see e.g. Gibbs 1994).
4. We acknowledge with gratitude the help of Martyn Lovell of Brameur Ltd in developing the APRIL3 Coding Guidelines.
5. The SUSANNE project was sponsored by the Economic and Social Research Council (UK), reference R00023 1142.
6. Nunberg (1990) is a recent exception.
7. Johansson *et al.* (1991) have compiled a survey of existing conventions for speech transcription, Stig Johansson being convener of a three-man group (with Doug Biber and myself) charged with formulating recommendations in this domain for the US/EC-sponsored Text Encoding Initiative.
8. The difference between the figure of 136 quoted here and 132 quoted above in connection with the CLAWS system relates to a slight difference between the tagset of the Tagged LOB Corpus, as published in Norway, and that used by the Lancaster project which created CLAWS.
9. The SUSANNE Corpus is available from ota.ox.ac.uk, directory /pub/ota/public/susanne. Please note that the address quoted in Sampson (1995: 461) is out of date.

6 The Current System: Front End and Parsing Algorithms

We use the term *front end* for the component of APRIL3 which takes in an English text and uses an electronic dictionary and other information in order to output a lattice in which each pathway represents a possible segmentation of the text into identifiable words with specific grammatical properties, annotated with figures representing the certainty of the identification.

Word-Hypothesis Lattices

The concept of word-hypothesis lattices has been familiar to speech researchers for many years. Speakers encode linear sequences of words into airwave patterns, and the task of an automatic speech recognition system is normally taken as being to derive, from a speech signal (a stretch of airwave patterns), the sequence of words which gave rise to that signal. However, the relationship between words and physical speech signals is so indirect and complex that this goal is usually not fully achievable. Instead, a speech recognition system will tentatively identify various stretches of the signal with particular words, assigning probabilities to the identifications depending on how well they fit, how common the words are, and what other competing words are available as interpretations of a stretch. Alternative word-hypotheses may imply different locations for word-boundaries within the continuous signal, hence the result is a branching data structure standardly called a word-hypothesis lattice.[1] For instance, an utterance of the sentence *Do as your father says* might give rise to a lattice such as Fig. 6.1.

Any path through Fig. 6.1 between the boundary symbols represented by '#' corresponds to one way of segmenting the signal into stretches identified with particular English words: the speaker's actual words lie along one path, but other paths analyse the signal as e.g. *doers your far versus*, or *do azure far the said*. This is an artificial example invented to illustrate the word-hypothesis lattice concept; outputs of real speech recognition systems tend to be more highly ramified, with very many alternative paths for even a fairly short utterance.

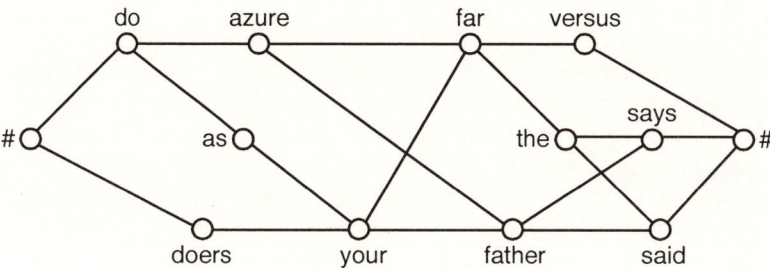

Figure 6.1 A word-hypothesis lattice

(In a lattice such as Fig. 6.1, nodes represent word-hypotheses, and the links between nodes represent boundaries between words. Word-hypothesis lattices are often represented in the converse fashion, with nodes representing time-points at which word-boundaries may occur, and links labelled with hypotheses about the identity of the word which accounts for the material between two time-points. This second representation method yields lattices with fewer nodes and links, and taken in isolation is arguably more natural. For APRIL, however, the first kind of lattice is more convenient, because nodes of a lattice such as that of Fig. 6.1 will become terminal nodes of the parsetree to be constructed by the system.)

In Fig. 6.1, there are no numbers associated with the nodes; but in practice there would be a probability for each node, representing some estimate of the 'goodness of fit' between the word and the respective stretch of the speech signal. The probability of a path through the lattice will then be estimated as the product of the probabilities for the various nodes on the path. In principle, the probability figures for the various nodes in such a lattice ought to be normalized so that the summed probabilities of all distinct lattice-paths is 1; this is a complicated operation, and in practice if one's interest lies in the *relative* probabilities of alternative lattice-paths there may be no reason to normalize.

Prima facie, the concept of word-hypotheses may seem inapplicable to written language: provided that text is typed rather than handwritten then all the characters are unambiguous, and they are divided into words by spacing. However, this view is over-simple. Consider the character-sequence:
in.

Out of context, this might be either the preposition *in* followed by a sentence-closing full stop, or an abbreviation for the unit *inch*. A hyphenated word may be a single dictionary entry such as *co-opt*, or a one-off linkage of independent words not forming a standard phrase, such as the hyphenation in *the aunt-nephew relationship*. And even if the boundaries of a written word are clear, the letter sequence may represent any of several grammatically contrasting homographs, as in the case of *round* discussed on p. 6.

APRIL3 uses the word-hypothesis lattice concept in order to represent analytic uncertainties such as these, before resolving them. The parse annealer seeks not just the best tree over a given linear sequence of leaf nodes but, rather, the best tree available over some path through the lattice: in evaluating a solution, the annealer weighs not only the probability of a particular parsetree over a sequence of wordtags but also the probability of the particular lattice-path which provides that wordtag sequence.

It is probably fair to say that APRIL3 word-hypothesis lattices tend to be considerably less ramified than those generated by large-vocabulary speech recognizers in the current state of technology. If we were considering only the task for which APRIL3 is directly designed, the word-hypothesis lattice machinery might seem an unduly cumbersome solution for the problems it deals with. But we have incorporated this solution precisely because of the central role of the lattice structure in speech recognition. By giving APRIL an organization based on optimizing lattice-paths, we make it relatively straightforward to adapt the system in due course to speech parsing, where the lattice concept will be crucial.

In any case, APRIL3 word-hypothesis lattices, while less ramified than speech recognition lattices, are by no means trivially simple. Consider for instance the character-sequence *lady's-maid*, which occurs as an entry in the APRIL3 electronic dictionary. An input text containing this sequence will trigger the creation of the microlattice of Fig. 6.2. (We use the term *microlattice* for a lattice covering a stretch of text which normally corresponds to a 'typographic word', that is a stretch of text bounded by whitespace[2] – the full word-hypothesis lattice for an input text is derived by linking together the microlattices for its various typographic words. We use the term *logical word* to refer to a stretch of text associated with a terminal node of a parsetree, having its own wordtag, in contrast to *typographic word* as a stretch of nonblank characters surrounded by spaces. A typographic word may comprise more than one logical word, and we shall see later that a logical word may comprise more than one typographic word.)

At this stage, character-sequences whose wordtags need to be established by consulting the dictionary have not yet been tagged; but the system has discovered that the *'s* sequence is three ways grammatically ambiguous as between the reduced form of *is* (VBZ), the reduced form of *has* (VHZ), and

The Current System: Front End and Parsing Algorithm

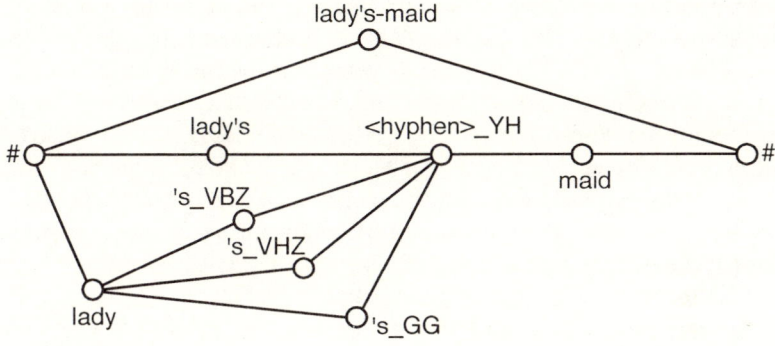

Figure 6.2 Microlattice for a single typographical word

the genitive suffix (GG). The hyphen may be part of a single dictionary word (the uppermost node in the Figure), or it may require to be treated as a terminal parsetree node in its own right, wordtagged YH. When the dictionary is subsequently consulted, one node will be eliminated: the node *lady's* represents the hypothesis that this character-sequence is a single grammatical atom which happens to include an apostrophe character (compare *o' clock*), but the dictionary will list no such word (whereas it will of course list a word *lady*). Even with the elimination of one node, however, the microlattice for this single typographic word will contain four distinct paths.

Furthermore, the lattice for an entire text will not consist exclusively of a series of microlattices linked in sequence: under the SUSANNE scheme, some parsetree terminal nodes will correspond to stretches of text that include internal spaces – most notably, the scheme recognizes many 'grammatical idioms' (Sampson 1995: 99ff.), sequences of typographic words which behave as single words with a special grammatical function, such as *in all* which functions like an adverb (*there were twelve statues in all*) – so the word-hypothesis lattice for a text containing such a sequence will include a path bearing a single node representing the idiomatic interpretation, parallel[3] to one or more paths bearing multiple nodes corresponding to interpretations in which the same words function with their separate non-idiomatic values (*there were mottoes in all the crackers*).

After input text has been validated by checking for disallowed characters, the front end passes it though three successive subcomponents:[4]

- The *Segmenter* divides the input into character sequences which might correspond to logical words. Using information about the possible roles with respect to word-boundaries of various characters (e.g. a hyphen may link separate words, or may occur internally within a single word) and special character sequences (e.g. '*s* can be a suffix if preceded by alphabetic material and followed by space), the Segmenter constructs a microlattice for each typographic word. (The microlattice will often be trivial – if the sentence includes the word *cat* between spaces, because this character-sequence contains no internal complications such as punctuation marks which may or may not represent separate logical words the microlattice will consist merely of a left boundary node, a node for the string *cat*, and a right boundary node in linear sequence.) In certain cases such as '*s* the Segmenter identifies wordtags for input segments.
- The *Word Tagger* takes a microlattice as input, and looks up in the dictionary the character-strings associated with its various nodes (in cases where these have not already been tagged by the Segmenter, as in the case of '*s* discussed above). When the Word Tagger discovers from the dictionary that a string is grammatically ambiguous, it creates additional nodes in the microlattice so as to provide a set of parallel paths, one for each alternative tagging of the word. When the Word Tagger discovers that the string associated with a node does not exist as a dictionary word, as in the case of *lady's* considered as an atomic unit rather than a sequence *lady* + '*s*, in certain cases to be discussed below it eliminates the node and the path which passes through it from the microlattice. (This does not mean that the system assumes that an input text will contain only words known to the dictionary; in many cases, microlattice nodes not corresponding to dictionary words are retained and tagged by default word-tagging rules, as we shall see.) The Word Tagger uses various fields in the dictionary entries in order to add further categories of information apart from wordtags, for instance probability figures, to the microlattice nodes.
- The *Word-Hypothesis Lattice Builder* takes the microlattices output by the Word Tagger for successive typographic words of the input text, and integrates them into the word-hypothesis lattice which is built up for the text as a whole. Minimally, this involves joining the new microlattice to the word-hypothesis lattice as constructed so far by eliminating the right boundary node of the latter, the left boundary node of the former, and adding arcs from each sister node of the deleted word-hypothesis lattice

boundary to each sister node of the deleted microlattice boundary. But in addition the Word-Hypothesis Lattice Builder checks whether a microlattice can be interpreted as completing a grammatical idiom, or a 'word-level co-ordination' such as *black and white*, which under the SUSANNE scheme (Sampson 1995: 318ff.) are treated as units labelled with tags of word rather than phrase rank – in such cases a single node is created for the sequence of typographic words, parallel to the paths carrying separate nodes for the individual words.

Of these three subcomponents, the Word Tagger needs to be described in more detail.

The Word Tagger

The Word Tagger depends on a lexical resource developed for the APRIL research programme mainly on the basis of Roger Mitton's CUVOALD machine-readable version of the Third Edition of the *Oxford Advanced Learner's Dictionary of Current English* (Mitton 1986).[5] CUVOALD has a separate entry for each inflected form of a word; and it includes many entries, such as frequent proper names, not included in the published Oxford dictionary. In the 1992 version of CUVOALD, common abbreviations are included in alphabetical sequence along with unabbreviated words. We have adapted CUVOALD to our own purposes, producing a resource we refer to simply as the *probabilistic dictionary*.

The probabilistic dictionary has three special features by comparison to CUVOALD from which it derives:

- grammatical information is expressed in terms of the wordtags of the SUSANNE analytic standard; CUVOALD used a grammatical coding system invented by Mitton which expresses just those grammatical distinctions indicated in the published Oxford dictionary, which in the case of closed-class 'grammatical words' (e.g. determiners, conjunctions, as opposed to nouns or verbs) are very crude by comparison to SUSANNE wordtags;
- the probabilistic dictionary includes information, derived from the Tagged Brown and LOB Corpora, on the frequencies of various word/wordtag pairings, enabling one to check frequencies both of individual wordforms and, in the case of grammatically ambiguous words such as *round*, frequencies of the alternative uses of the form;
- headwords in the probabilistic dictionary are recorded and sequenced in a 'stripped-down' form, omitting non-alphabetic characters such as hyphen and Continental accents, and reducing capitals to lower case: the

'secondary orthographic details' stripped off the headword are placed in a subsidiary field within the entry. The purpose for this is to facilitate lookup of forms occurring in real-life texts, whose orthography will not always perfectly match the form of a dictionary entry. A word borrowed from a foreign language in which it has an accent, such as *détente*, will in English sometimes be written with and sometimes without its accent; usage in a real-life text will not reliably coincide with the usage chosen by the Oxford dictionary compilers. Likewise, the use of hyphens is subject to great individual variation: a word may easily be listed in the Oxford dictionary as *wineglass* but appear in a text as *wine-glass*, or be listed in the dictionary as *wing-span* but appear in a text as *wingspan*. And capitalization is not only a lexical but also a grammatical phenomenon: any word listed in the published dictionary with a lower-case initial will be capitalized when it occurs in a text at the beginning of a sentence. Accordingly, the most efficient way to locate dictionary entries as possible matches for a wordform found in a text is to reduce the text form to a stripped-down version without secondary orthographic details, and look up the result in a dictionary whose entries are similarly stripped down; any entry located is a candidate, and subordinate routines can be used to downgrade the probability of a match, or eliminate a candidate altogether, if the respective secondary orthographic details differ in ways that cannot be accounted for in terms of orthographic variation or grammatical capitalization.

Apart from these overall structural differences from CUVOALD, the probabilistic dictionary also contains various extra individual entries added by our team. It currently comprises almost 86,000 entries.

The easiest way to give the reader a clearer impression of the contents of the probabilistic dictionary is to show a selection of entries: see Fig. 6.3.[6] (The entries shown in Fig. 6.3 are of course not contiguous in the dictionary itself, which for instance contains 71 intermediate entries between the last *in* entry and the *inc* entry.) Each entry has ten fields; ' | ' or ' – – ' appears as a placeholder for a field containing no information in a particular entry. The fields can be briefly identified from left to right as follows:

1   headword
2   entry batch indicator
3   American/British flag
4   secondary orthographic details
5   pronunciation
6   wordtag
7   inflexion pattern
8   Hornby valency codes

9   tagged-word distribution
10 tagged-word frequency

The probabilistic dictionary is intended as a general NLP resource, and a number of these fields (fields 2, 3, 5, 7, 8) play no part in the APRIL3 project, though they have been or are likely to be important for other work.[7] Those fields which are relevant for the present work are discussed in more detail here.

The *headword*, which determines the alphabetic sequence of entries, is the stripped-down form of a word as already explained; and the secondary orthographic details of the word as it appears in the published Oxford dictionary are coded in field 4. For instance, the first four lines of Fig. 6.3 represent words that are listed in the form *in* in the Oxford dictionary, but the fifth line represents the chemical symbol *In* for indium, and the sixth line represents the abbreviation *in.* for *inch*, which is written with a full stop in those publication styles that mark abbreviations with stops. The code −6 indicates that the dictionary lists *income-tax* with a hyphen after its sixth stripped-down character; #2#9 mark the word-spaces in the idiom *in defence of*; ! 1 ? 2 ! 3 encodes the alternative forms *I.O.W.*, *IOW*, *I.o.W.*, *IoW* as abbreviations for *Isle of Wight*; and so forth.

Field 6 normally shows a SUSANNE wordtag, and whenever a headword is grammatically ambiguous there is a separate entry for each wordtag. For instance, the word *in* is ambiguous as between preposition (II) and adverbial particle of place (RP); the tag NNU represents a unit noun; JJj represents an abbreviated adjective used as final element of a corporation name, such as *Inc*, *Ltd*, or *Pty*; NP1p is a singular 'province' name (American state, English county, etc.). An entry in the wordtag field beginning with the > character shows that the wordform occurs as the first word of a listed 'grammatical idiom'. An entry beginning with ~ shows that the headword is an American spelling of the word whose British spelling follows. An entry beginning with a full stop indicates that the entry, although a single typographic word, represents a sequence of more than one logical word: *isn't* for purposes of grammatical parsing must be treated as two words *is not* tagged VBZ XX respectively.

The last two fields contain probabilistic information about the word/wordtag pairing represented by a given entry. The *tagged-word frequency* is the number of instances of the headword with the given wordtag among the rather over two million word-tokens of the Tagged Brown and Tagged LOB Corpora. Each of these corpora comprises 500 text-extracts of roughly equal length; the *tagged-word distribution* shows how many of the altogether 1000 text-extracts contain at least one instance of the word/wordtag pair.

in	0	N	—	In	II	--	--	1000 39460
in	0	N	—	In	RP	--	--	459 926
in	5	A	—	--	>indefenseof	--	--	0 0
in	5	B	—	--	>indefenseof	--	--	0 0
in	5	N	*1	--	FOc	--	--	0 0
in	5	N	.2	--	NNU	--	--	28 110
inc	5	N	*1.3	INk	JJj	--	--	15 22
incometax	0	N	-6	'INk@m-t&ks	NN1n	7	--	2 2
indefenceof	2	B	#2#9	--	II	--	--	10 10
indefenseof	5	A	#2#9	--	~indefenceof	--	--	0 0
iow	9	N	!1?2!3	--	NP1p	--	--	0 0
iq	5	N	!1:2	,aI'kju	NN1c	--	--	1 1
is	0	N	%1;1	aIz	ZZ2	--	--	0 0
is	0	N	—	Iz	VBZ	--	an	987 23035
is	5	N	*1.2	--	NNL	--	--	0 0
isnt	5	N	;3	--	.VBZ_is.XX_not	--	--	.987.995 .23035.14018
jackolantern	0	N	-4'5-5	dZ&k-@-'l&nt@n	NN1c	6	--	0 0
nonetheless	2	N	+4+7,#4#7	--	RR	--	--	31 37

Fig. 6.3

Figure 6.3 Some entries from the probabilistic dictionary

The Current System: Front End and Parsing Algorithm 111

The purpose of recording distribution separately from frequency may be illustrated by a hypothetical example. The word *or* is obviously extremely common in English as a co-ordinating conjunction; but it has another use as an adjective meaning 'gold' in the specialized terminology of heraldry: within that domain, wording such as *Sable a pale or* is a well-formed statement (it means '[The coat is] black with a vertical gold stripe'). Within the total stream of English prose, heraldic usage is not common; but if one of the 500 LOB extracts had happened to be drawn from a work on heraldry, then the adjectival use of *or* might occur repeatedly in that one extract, so that the simple frequency counts could suggest that the adjectival use is common enough to be considered as a plausible alternative to the conjunction usage as an interpretation of *or* in input texts. In reality the adjectival use of *or* is so rare in English as a whole that for a general-purpose NLP system it is almost certainly best ignored; and the distribution data give us a check on this. If an entry has a respectable tagged-word frequency but an extremely low tagged-word distribution, this suggests that the frequency is an artefact of the particular choice of texts in the Brown and LOB Corpora, rather than a true reflection of frequency in English in general. I noted that the example was hypothetical: in fact the Oxford dictionary, and hence our probabilistic dictionary, does not include an entry for *or* in the heraldic sense, and no LOB or Brown extract represents the language of heraldry. But the example illustrates in an extreme (and therefore clear) form an issue which arises, though with less extreme differences between true usage frequencies, for many word uses that the dictionary does list.

The APRIL3 front end does not consult the probabilistic dictionary directly. One reason is that it would be inefficient for dictionary lookup to use a resource, many of whose fields are irrelevant for this system. A more important reason, though, lies in the fact that any particular version of the APRIL3 system uses a reduced set of wordtags. The full range of wordtags defined in the SUSANNE scheme comprises about 350 members, allowing not only the obvious distinctions between word uses but also many quite subtle distinctions to be marked. However, APRIL can use a particular distinction only if it has meaningful statistical information about the occurrence of the alternative usages. Availability of large quantities of accurate statistical data on grammatical usage is always a major problem for probabilistic NLP approaches, and the data available to APRIL3 (the parsetrees of the SUSANNE Corpus, less 2% of paragraphs reserved for testing), while believed to be qualitatively rather accurate, are very limited in quantity. Consequently APRIL3 needs to make its figures meaningful by collapsing together minor grammatical distinctions, both at the level of wordtags and at the higher, tagmatag level; and which distinctions to retain or to merge is one of the open research questions confronting the APRIL3 project.

For these reasons, the system uses a piece of software that converts the full probabilistic dictionary into a smaller resource, retaining information only from those fields which APRIL exploits, and replacing SUSANNE wordtags by their equivalents in whatever reduced tagset is currently used. The output of this conversion software is called the *APRIL Dictionary*; I do not discuss its format here, but details are given in the system documentation.

After looking up in the dictionary the strings identified by the Segmenter, the Word Tagger must decide what to do about any strings not listed in the dictionary (and not already tagged by the Segmenter, as in the case of *'s*). It is clear that realistic input texts will contain many words unlikely to be found in any electronic dictionary – numerals and proper names, for example. Our dictionary does contain a number of significant proper names, such as the names of the English counties; but it would be impractical to expand it to include every British surname or the name of every village and stream. Numerals in principle cannot be finitely listed, and it would be inefficient to list even the lower ones – one can tell that they are numerals rather than dictionary words from the fact that they are composed of digits rather than letters. (Roman numerals, on the other hand, *are* included in the dictionary.) There is also the possibility of ordinary non-proper words in a text which happen not to be included in our dictionary. Research on a sample (Sampson 1989a) has suggested that the *Oxford Advanced Learner's Dictionary* is surprisingly complete in its coverage of the non-proper alphabetic words occurring in practice in modern English writing; but of course there are gaps, both systematic (this dictionary lists few negative words in *un-*) and sporadic (*downstream, inevitably, lithium* are a few fairly common words that are not included, and of course a writer may always chance to borrow some obscure word from another language when referring to a foreign cultural phenomenon).

On the other hand, sometimes we want the Word Tagger to decide that a microlattice path should be pruned. Consider the case of *lady's* (see p. 104, above): it is true that some dictionary words (such as *o'clock*) incorporate an internal apostrophe, but it would be foolish for the system to maintain the possibility that there is an atomic word *lady's* which happens to have escaped the compilers of our dictionary, when an alternative analysis of the string into the dictionary word *lady* and the (grammatically ambiguous) suffix *'s* is available. The rule therefore is that a node in a microlattice which remains without a wordtag after dictionary lookup will be pruned out, unless the microlattice contains no parallel path (so that a traversal of the microlattice from left to right boundary must pass through that node). Thus *lady's* in Fig. 6.2 will be pruned, but an Arabic numeral (whether occurring as an isolated typographic word or written continuously with material forming a separate logical word, e.g. *£1700* in which the SUSANNE scheme prescribes that pound sign and numeral are two logical words) normally will not be pruned. When a node is pruned, any left or right sister nodes that can be reached only along paths which also pass through the pruned node are likewise eliminated, leaving no 'dead ends' in the lattice.

The untagged nodes that remain are assigned wordtags (or in many cases are assigned sets of alternative wordtags, in which case the node in question is replaced by a set of nodes on parallel paths, one for each candidate tagging) by reference to a list of *default word-tagging rules* worked out by studying the character-patterns in the non-dictionary words found in a sample of tagged text.

The default rules are an ordered sequence of 80-odd character-patterns, some rather general and others very specific, each of which is associated with one or more pairings of wordtag and probability. The Word Tagger tags a non-dictionary word by running through the default rules in sequence until it finds the first one which fits the wordform. For instance, the first pattern is 'string starting with a capital and ending with a sequence of consonant, lower-case *s*, and full stop', which is associated with the single wordtag NNSS (plural of a noun of style or title, such as *Sens.*, *Cols.* abbreviating *Senators, Colonels*) with probability 1. On the other hand, the sixth pattern is 'string starting with a lower-case letter and (ending with full stop and/or not containing a vowel)'; this is associated with the following alternative wordtag/probability pairs:

NN1c .40 (singular countable noun, e.g. *i.d.*)
NNU .40 (abbreviated unit noun, e.g. *ml*)
NNL .20 (abbreviated noun used as head of proper name of place, e.g. *av.*)

Near the end of the list are a set of several dozen patterns applying to strings of multiple lower-case letters, possibly linked by hyphens; for instance, if such a string begins with *un* . . . and fits no earlier pattern then it is tagged as an adjective with probability .67, as a singular common noun with probability .33. (The limited range of English verbs in *un-* have all been added to the probabilistic dictionary.) An alphabetic string of this kind that contains no special indicator such as *un* . . . is tagged as a singular common noun .88, adjective .08, base form of verb .04. And the final default rule provides that a string not fitting any of the defined patterns (and therefore, for instance, not composed wholly of lower-case letters) is tagged FO, 'formula'.

After the Word Tagger has completed its task, each microlattice node bears the following information:

- The dictionary form of the word, enabling the system to print out its eventual analysis showing the text words in a normalized orthography.
- A wordtag (from the mapping of full SUSANNE wordtags into the reduced wordtag-set in current use).
- Information specifying how well the wordform in the text matches the dictionary form (in the case of words tagged from the dictionary). In the case of speech analysis, this would be a very important category of information, identifying how closely the wave-pattern observed in the speech signal resembles the template or other available information about the expected wave-pattern given for the word in the system lexicon. In analysing written language, the analogous information is less significant: because the elements of writing are discrete, in the majority of cases text form and dictionary form match perfectly. But there can be mismatches with respect to 'secondary orthographic details', and in particular a word listed in the dictionary with a capital initial will be a relatively poor match for a text word which is identical in its stripped-down version but which is uncapitalized in the text. APRIL uses a simple algorithm which attributes different scores to various types of orthographic mismatch, and calculates a rough estimate of the degree of similarity between dictionary and text spellings in terms of the relationship between mismatch total and length of word. Thus *In*, the chemical symbol for indium, would be counted a very poor match for a text form *in*, whereas with a longer word such as *Danish* the same type of mismatch would give a better similarity score for a text form such as *danish* (which might occur in *danish pastry*, say). If the mismatch exceeds a threshold and the lattice contains a less-mismatched parallel node, the mismatching node is pruned out of the lattice, as a way of keeping the size of the solution space within bounds. (If the text contains the form *in*, which is a perfect match to two high-frequency dictionary entries tagged II, preposition, and RP, adverbial particle of place, we do not want the parser to waste time considering the hypothesis that *in* is an orthographically deviant version of the symbol for indium.) If the mismatch figure falls below the threshold, it is used to reduce the plausibility value for the node (see below).
- A flag identifying wordforms that have an initial capital other than by virtue of their dictionary entry, and wordforms that begin with a lower-case letter. These are not 'discrepancies' relative to the dictionary – a word which appears with a lower-case initial in the dictionary will standardly be capitalized at the beginning of a sentence, or as part of a name, and the lower-case flag takes no account of dictionary form; but the parsetree evaluation function will use these flags in order to downgrade analyses in which the case of an initial letter conflicts with a word's position in a parsetree relative to sentence and proper-name tagmas.

The Current System: Front End and Parsing Algorithm

- A figure giving a plausibility value for the node, to be multiplied with the figures for other nodes on the lattice path, and with the values of nonterminal nodes in the parsetree, to give an overall value for an analysis. So far I have not been explicit about how terminal parsetree nodes are evaluated quantitatively, and this has proved to be one of the more complex issues confronting the project. The following section discusses this.

Terminal Node Evaluation

For APRIL3, the evaluation function which estimates the plausibility of a labelled tree analysis of an input string must take into account not only the wordtags and tagmatags of the tree structure but also the fit between the wordtags in the analysis and the character-strings of the input. (We have seen that earlier versions of APRIL accepted input in the form of wordtags, not raw text.) Integrating values for terminal nodes into the overall evaluation function turned out to involve large conceptual problems.

In determining a structure of hypotheses to account for a set of concrete observations, the natural way to exploit probabilistic information seems to be via conditional probabilities $p(a|b)$, meaning 'probability of a given b', where b is either a directly observable phenomenon or one relatively closely tied to observation, and a is a more theoretical phenomenon: one uses conditional probabilities to work outwards from observations, which are certain, to theoretical hypotheses, which are ascribed more or less reliable probability estimates.

A parsetree for a text is an unusual entity in this context, because it has 'certainty at both ends'. We know that the label of the root must be O, 'paragraph' (and although this symbol relates specifically to the SUSANNE scheme, it is normal within any tradition of grammatical analysis to use some fixed initial symbol, commonly S, 'sentence'). On the other hand, at the bottom of the tree we have the strings of characters comprising the input, which are given rather than needing to be discovered.

In the middle of the tree, we have been assuming that elements of tree structure will be assessed in terms of conditional probabilities working downwards from the known root label to the unknown structuring and labels of lower nodes. One might quarrel with the particular way in which we estimate the probability of a daughter-sequence, given a mother label, but if one grants that we have some way of doing this (and leaving aside the possibility that non-context-free considerations may need to be involved) then it surely follows that the natural way of evaluating a tree structure is to say: 'We know what the root node must be; given that label as mother, its sequence of daughters has the following probability relative to alternatives; given each of those labels in turn as mother, its sequence of daughters has the following probabilities . . .' – and to multiply together the probabilities thus calculated to get an overall measure of tree probability. However, at the bottom of the tree, the character-strings are not theoretical postulates but observed inputs, and the type of conditional probability which we can easily calculate are probabilities of particular wordtags, given particular character-strings. On the face of it there is a puzzle about how to integrate 'downward-looking' conditional probabilities in the bulk of the tree with 'upward-looking' conditional probabilities at the bottom.

My initial assumption was that this should be addressed by means of Bayes's Theorem: that for any a, b, $p(a|b) = p(b|a).p(a) \div p(b)$. Let us write s for the occurrence of a particular character-string, and t for the occurrence of a particular wordtag immediately above it in the parsetree. Then the resources described earlier give us a straightforward way to estimate $p(t|s)$. If we can derive $p(s|t)$, which is a 'downward-looking' conditional probability, from this quantity, then we can multiply the $p(s|t)$ figures for the various words of the input together with the downward-looking conditional probabilities for the higher structure of the tree, and obtain a single logically coherent probability figure in which all the terms that are multiplied together are of the same general type.

From Bayes's Theorem we have $p(s|t) = p(t|s).p(s) \div p(t)$; and we can calculate $p(t|s)$. But then arguably we can ignore $p(s)$. This term represents the probability of encountering a particular string of characters, and the characters are common to all paths through a lattice. For that matter, not only should the relative values of alternative lattice-paths be unaffected by the absolute probabilities of the character-strings, but those probabilities should perhaps actually be regarded as 1, since we know that we have encountered the successive substrings – we are not interested in estimating the probabilities of alternative English texts, but of alternative analyses for a given text. So it would appear that the figures to be associated with the terminal nodes of an analysis should be $p(t|s) \div p(t)$, both terms of which are fairly easy to estimate. It is difficult, on the other hand, to estimate accurately the probability of occurrence of a specific character-sequence.

The only complication would be that, because word-boundaries are sometimes uncertain and parallel lattice-paths can have different numbers of terminal nodes, the probabilities $p(t|s)$ might need to be normalized by raising them to the power of the number of input characters in the string s, ensuring that overall probabilities for alternative lattice-paths are the product of equal numbers of individual probability figures and are thus commensurable (cf. McInnes *et al.* 1989: 463).

Unfortunately, experimental calculations using small 'toy' languages defined to have known statistical properties have demonstrated that (as my researchers at Sussex suspected from the beginning) the above reasoning is fallacious. With or without normalization, the technique outlined does not deliver accurate figures for probabilities of alternative analyses for structurally ambiguous strings; in some cases it predicts that an analysis is less likely than an alternative when it is in reality more likely, and *vice versa*. It is not easy to identify the logical flaw in the reasoning which suggested the $p(t|s) \div p(t)$ formula, and I have been rather surprised to find via e-mail enquiries among the speech research community that this does not seem to be a recognized problem with a standard answer. However, it is evidently a mistake to suppose that because character-strings are given in the input their probabilities can therefore be treated as unity. We cannot escape from the need to estimate specific probabilities for particular strings in English, no matter how irrelevant to our task these probabilities appear intuitively to be. We must envisage our task as being not to estimate the conditional probability of a labelled tree, given the characters associated with its leaf nodes, but to estimate the absolute probability of a tree, including the probabilities of the character-strings below its leaves. The only way in which being given a particular input string simplifies the task is by limiting the class of trees whose probabilities need to be estimated.

In that case, Bayes's Theorem gives us no help. For each terminal node we need to calculate $p(s|t)$, and converting this to $p(t|s).p(s) \div p(t)$ gets us no further forward because estimating $p(s)$ involves the same sort of difficulty as estimating $p(s|t)$. Rather, we use the two million words of the Tagged Brown and LOB Corpora to make the best estimates we can of the probabilities of particular strings with particular tags. By an elementary rule of the probability calculus, $p(s|t) = p(s\&t) \div p(t)$, where $p(s\&t)$ and $p(t)$ can be estimated by looking at the number of occurrences of the string, bearing the relevant tag, and the number of occurrences of the tag with any string, in relation to the total number of word-tokens in the Corpora.

Clearly, with only two million words of tagged data, there will often be gaps in our information. Many words that are listed in our dictionary and might appear in a text never occur in Brown or LOB; in such cases we have to postulate a small positive probability. (This is not done in an arbitrary fashion, but I defer discussion of the statistical principles involved to ch. 7.) In other cases, the character-string is not a dictionary word at all and has to be tagged by the default rules. Here there is no basis whatever for estimating string probability, but fortunately (because of the lattice-path pruning discussed on p. 00) a node tagged by default rules will never be parallel in the lattice to a node tagged from the probabilistic dictionary, for which some estimate of $p(s|t)$ is available. Since default-tagged nodes will be parallel only to alternative default taggings of the same non-dictionary strings, in these cases $p(s)$ is arbitrarily set to the same figure as is used for the probability of a dictionary word that does not occur in the Corpora, and we do use

Bayes's Theorem to estimate $p(s|t)$ as $p(t|s).p(s) \div p(t)$, with $p(t|s)$ estimated via the default rules.

Although we believe that our probability estimates are as accurate as they can be given the data resources available to us, it has to be admitted that the need to use $p(s|t)$ figures means that APRIL3 probability estimates are by no means as reliable as we should like them to be. Two million words of tagged text are just not enough to give good figures on the frequencies of individual words. (We could get more reliable estimates of simple word-form frequencies from the various much larger corpora which now exist, but to measure $p(s|t)$ one needs *tagged* text; and furthermore, since our dictionary and other research resources all use a particular tradition of word-tagging, in practice it is difficult for us to exploit a resource such as the Penn Treebank which tags large numbers of words but using an independently evolved tagset.)

But it is better to use poor estimates of the correct quantities than accurate estimates of inappropriate quantities. Through calculations with 'toy' languages of known statistical properties we have established that the assumption $p(s) = 1$ leads to a systematically misleading analysis-evaluation function, while assigning terminal nodes the probability $p(s|t)$ yields a well-behaved function. At the time of writing it remains to be discovered whether the limited accuracy of our $p(s|t)$ estimates will have disabling consequences for system performance. I discuss on pp. 135–9 below the technique we use to squeeze the best probability estimates we can out of our limited data.

The Parse Annealer

Like APRIL Mk 2, the APRIL3 parser seeks an optimal analysis for an input by executing a random walk through a solution space of alternative parsetrees, assessing each solution encountered by reference to a language model comprising a set of skip-and-loop networks based on *prototype daughter-sequences* for each nonterminal label, and biasing the random walk via the simulated annealing algorithm.

In APRIL3 the prototype daughter-sequences, and hence the language model based on them, are derived automatically from a corpus of analysed language samples, rather than being hand-crafted. This is a major innovation in APRIL3, to which I devote a separate chapter, ch. 7. In the following pages we examine the mechanisms by which the annealing parser explores the solution space and settles on an output, once it has been provided with a language model.

The Solution Space

Any (correct or incorrect) solution for an APRIL input comprises:

- a particular path through the word-hypothesis lattice for that input, defining a segmentation of the input text into logical words and a mapping of those words into wordtags;
- a labelled tree structure over the wordtag sequence thus defined.

Under the SUSANNE analytic scheme, the root node of the tree over any paragraph must be labelled 'O'; other nonterminal nodes will bear labels drawn from the set of tagmatags defined in the SUSANNE scheme, except that (as already mentioned) any particular version of APRIL3 will be operating with a mapping of the full range of distinct SUSANNE tagmatags into a much smaller set of simplified tags, because our data on grammatical statistics are far too limited for it to make sense to deal with every distinction recognized in the SUSANNE system. (Both at tagmatag and at wordtag level, we regard choice of mapping as an open research question at present.)

If APRIL3 were to attempt to produce analyses including 'ghost' nodes such as the 's152' node following *seemed* in Fig. 2.1 (p. 9, above), such nodes would need somehow to be inserted into the node-sequences defined by word-hypothesis lattice-paths: the annealer would need to experiment not merely with alternative constituency structures over the fixed set of terminal nodes on a lattice-path, but with the possibility of creating extra 'ghost' terminal nodes. At this stage, that seems too ambitious. The space of solutions available to APRIL for an input does incorporate limited aspects of logical analysis, but there are no ghost elements, and no 'indices' linking constituents that are marked grammatically as co-referential. This means that there will always be only finitely many distinct wordtagged input segmentations in an APRIL3 solution space: each such segmentation corresponds to a distinct lattice-path, and the number of distinct paths must be finite because a word-hypothesis lattice has no loops and each of its nodes has only a (small) finite number of sister nodes on either side.

There are also finitely many distinct candidate parsetrees over any given lattice-path. The ways in which singular branching occurs in the scheme allow us to constrain APRIL solution spaces so that they remain finitely large. Many words will be immediately dominated by singular-branching phrase nodes: for instance a main verb unaccompanied by auxiliary verbs will be analysed as a one-word verb group, V. APRIL parsetrees are accordingly allowed to contain singular-branching nodes which immediately dominate terminal nodes: this in itself does not make the solution space infinitely large. The scheme also involves singulary branching at higher levels in a tree, but in these cases the labels of mother and sole daughter fall into a few recurring patterns; for instance, an infinitival clause (Ti in the SUSANNE scheme) will often consist of an infinitival verb group (Vi) and nothing else: [Ti [Vi *To err*]] *is human*. One consequence is that a sole daughter will virtually never itself be the mother of a sole daughter (unless the latter is a leaf node).[8] Imposing this restriction on the class of trees considered by the parser guarantees that the class is finite.

Initialization

After the word-hypothesis lattice for an input is completed, an annealing run over that input is initialized by choosing a random path through the lattice and building an initial tree over that path. The data structure representing the lattice contains a pointer for each lattice node other than the right boundary, identifying one of the node's right-sister nodes as the *currently-following node*. Therefore, by setting *each* lattice node's pointer initially to a randomly chosen one of that node's right sisters, one defines a lattice-path (from the left boundary node to the left boundary's currently-following node, from that node to its currently-following node, and so on); and whenever the setting of any one node's pointer is altered, a complete new path will immediately be defined (the new currently-following node will itself be pointing to some successor node, although this pointer may never previously have contributed to the definition of the current lattice-path).

After the lattice-path is initialized, there are two choices for how the system should build an initial tree over the terminal-node sequence on that path. It could either create a constituency structure at random, or impose some standard initial structure, such as a flat tree in which each terminal node is immediately dominated by the root node. Random tree-initialization is unattractive for two reasons. First, when (as in our case) trees are not limited to binary branching, it is surprisingly difficult to design an efficient algorithm for constructing a tree over a given number of terminal nodes which genuinely gives each possible distinct tree-shape an equal chance of emerging; most techniques that look as though they should work turn out to involve subtle biases in favour of one kind of structure rather than another, and we certainly do not want a system such as APRIL to incorporate analytic biases that we have not chosen and do not control. Perhaps more important, even if we could find an algorithm that generated trees with equal likelihood for each distinct structure, it might often happen that the initial tree was one with a reasonably good score – we might find ourselves releasing the cannonball over a valley rather than a peak. In an experimental situation where we have yet to establish what annealing

The Current System: Front End and Parsing Algorithm   121

schedule is suitable, good initial solutions are dangerous, because they may lead us to choose too low a figure for the initial temperature. The only function of an initial solution in an annealing run is to be abandoned, so it seems wisest deliberately to choose initial solutions which are poor and *must* be abandoned.

A problem about initializing with the flat tree is that, among the full range of possible tree structures, the flat tree (while rarely the optimal solution) tends to be nearer the good than the bad end of the scale. APRIL3 tries to guarantee a poor initial solution, by initializing on the *maximally left-branching tree*: that is, for any string of terminal nodes indicated by asterisks, the APRIL3 initial solution will have the structure:

[... [[[[* *] *] *] *] ... *]

As already mentioned, it has been well known since Yngve (1960) that English grammar has a strong propensity to avoid left-branching structures.

A left-branching tree has nonterminal nodes below the root which must be assigned initial labels. Again we ensure a poor initial solution by assigning each of these nodes the label Iq, 'tag question' – in reality tag questions do not occur embedded within one another, nor are they ever the leftmost daughter of the tagma within which they occur.

Move-Set

Once the initial solution is created, the system executes an annealing run under the control of a schedule which is input together with the text to be analysed. For APRIL3, the range of moves from which one is selected at each step of the random walk is more complex than in earlier APRIL versions, since now we have the possibility of changing the lattice-path as well as changing the tree structure over the current lattice-path.

Considering first tree-changes: APRIL3 uses the full set of move-types discussed in ch. 4, Merge, Hive, Reattach, and Relabel. The Hive and Relabel moves, and those Reattach moves which create an additional node, require the system to choose a new node label; as discussed on p. 59, in order to achieve schedules which succeed in optimizing inputs within reasonable lengths of time it is probably desirable not to make such choices equiprobable, but to incorporate a general bias in favour of good choices. Earlier APRIL versions used tables showing the probabilities of finding different mother labels, given a particular daughter label; when a node needed a label, this was selected from an overall probability distribution derived by merging the individual probability distributions of the labels of the various daughters of the node. This is a good way of ensuring that plausible labels are picked more commonly than implausible labels, but it involves intensive calculation and is therefore slow.

APRIL3 does it the other way round. A node is labelled by reference to the label of its mother. The system uses tables showing the relative probabilities of different nonterminal labels for a daughter node, given a mother label; since any node has only one mother, no merging of probability distributions is needed. Thus, simplifying things for clarity: suppose the analytic scheme had only three nonterminal labels, A, B, and C; and suppose that, among all daughters of A nodes in our treebank, 10% were themselves labelled A, 20% were labelled B, 30% were labelled C, and the remaining 40% were terminal nodes. Then, when an annealing run called for a label to be selected for a node and the mother of the node was labelled A, one of the set {A, B, C} would be chosen randomly with $p(A) = .17$, $p(B) = .33$, and $p(C) = .50$: the probabilities sum to 1 and are proportional to the observed frequencies of *nonterminal* A daughters (we know that the node to be labelled is not terminal).

As it stands, this method of label-choosing assumes that every nonterminal label occurs in our data with some positive frequency below any given mother label. That is not so; in fact for the great majority of tagmatag pairs (M, D) the data include no instance of a node labelled D below a node labelled M. We do not want to rule out any label absolutely when a new label is chosen (if we did, there would be a risk that the move-set might not be closed). Consequently, when APRIL3 chooses a node label it first decides whether or not to use a mother/daughter pairing instantiated in the data, with a low positive probability for the 'no' decision; if the decision is no, one of the daughter-labels not instantiated below the mother is chosen with equal probabilities, otherwise it chooses one of the instantiated daughter-labels as in the preceding paragraph.

The other kind of move is a *Pathswitch*, that is a change of lattice-path. In itself, changing the path merely involves choosing one of the nodes on the current path that has more than one right neighbour (not the right boundary node, which has no right neighbour, and not a node such as *as* in Fig. 6.1 which has only the *your* node as right neighbour), and resetting its pointer to a different right neighbour, choosing at random with equal probabilities in the case of a node which has three or more right neighbours.

However, the more interesting issue is what becomes of the current tree structure when a Pathswitch is executed. The old tree will now have some terminal nodes on and some off the current path, but all terminal nodes of an acceptable solution must be on the current path (and all nodes on the current path must be terminal nodes of the current solution tree).

In principle, it seems important to consider that, after an annealing run has progressed for a time, all parts of the current solution will embody useful work which if possible should not be thrown away. Any particular area of the current solution may be wrong, but at least work has been done which has increased its probability of being right, relative to the situation at the start of the run.

When a lattice-path is changed, there will be parts of the current tree which dominate exclusively terminal nodes that remain 'live' (that is, that continue to lie on the current path), other parts of the current tree which dominate exclusively terminal nodes which are now 'dead' (they have been switched out of the current path), and there will also be nodes in the higher reaches of the current tree which dominate some terminals that remain live and others that have died. Obviously subtrees of the first kind, which continue to dominate live terminals, should be retained in the new solution tree. But it seems desirable also to retain subtrees of the second kind within the data structure manipulated by the annealing system: these subtrees will not form part of the current solution tree in the immediate future, but there will be many further Pathswitch moves in the course of an annealing run and the terminal-node sequence dominated by such a subtree may well become part of the current path again – in that case it would be better for annealing to continue from the structure it had previously reached, than to begin from scratch.

Furthermore, it could hardly be sensible to discard structure worked out for the upper parts of the solution tree merely because some of the terminal nodes were no longer live. At one (not infrequent) logical extreme, a Pathswitch might involve substituting a single node in the middle of a long path of terminal nodes for another single node parallel to it in the lattice; the plausibility of a node near the root of the solution tree might be affected hardly at all by the switch, so to eliminate the high-level node automatically and reanneal the upper structure of the tree would be to squander hard-won information.

The solution adopted is to say that, in a Pathswitch, all existing elements of tree structure should be preserved except for links which connect a node dominating at least one live terminal with a node dominating only dead terminals. Consider for instance, in Fig. 6.4, a switch from the lattice-path running through nodes *a p q r b* to the path running through *a x y b*. The links from *H* to *F* and *G* to *r* will be deleted: *r* is a dead node and *F* dominates only dead nodes, but *H* and *G* both also dominate *b*, which remains live. However, the nodes *J*, *H*, and *G*, and the undeleted links below them, are retained (as are all nodes and links above and to the left and right of *J*); and the structure below *F* is also preserved, although it plays no part in the new solution tree. In order to complete the new solution tree, the newly live terminals *x* and *y* must be linked in somehow; we specify that such nodes are automatically linked to the nonterminal dominating both ends of the switched path, node *J* in this example.

Before

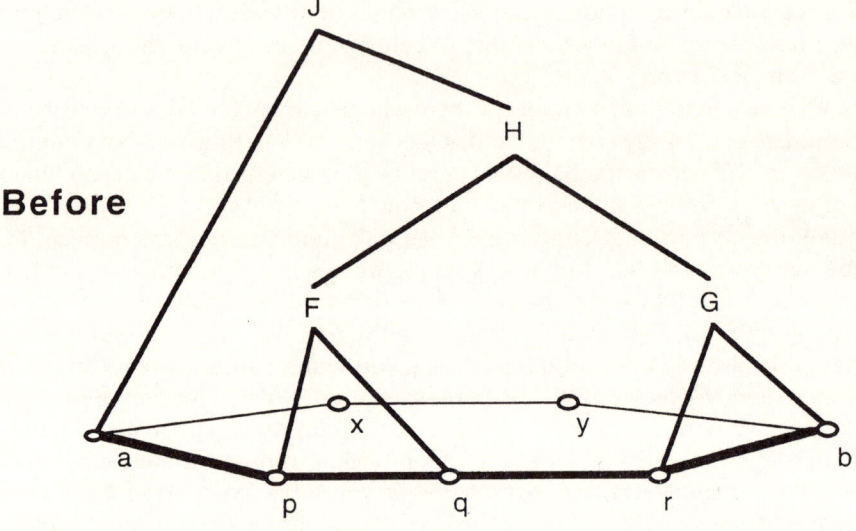

After

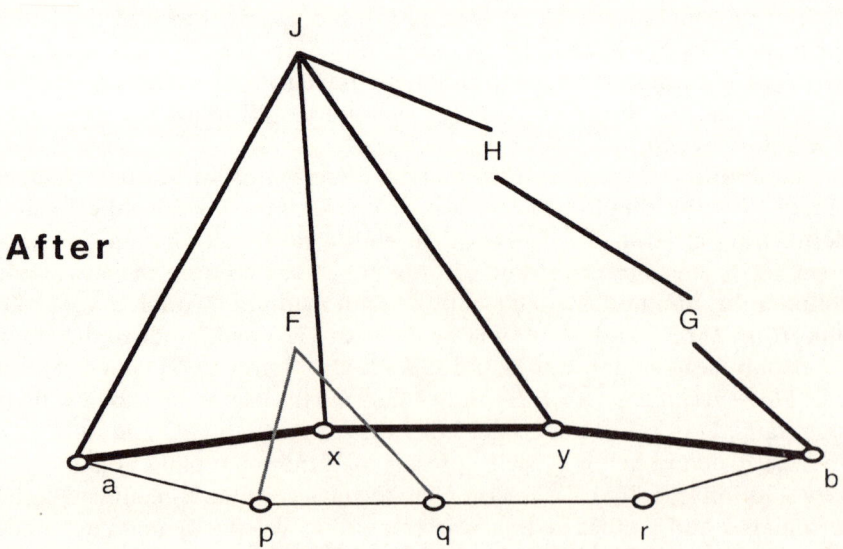

Figure 6.4 Switching paths through a word-hypothesis lattice

After numerous Pathswitch moves have been executed in this fashion on an annealing run, many subpaths in the lattice will have 'dead' structure above them, such as the F node above the p–q subpath in the 'after' side of Fig. 6.4. Then we say that when a further Pathswitch brings a subpath into the current path which did not previously form part of it, the elements on that subpath which are to be made daughters of the node dominating the ends of the subpath are not necessarily the terminal nodes on the subpath, but the highest nodes dominating the newly live terminals. In the move of Fig. 6.4, x and y were linked directly to J because, before the Pathswitch, there was no structural material above x or y; but if, in the 'after' situation of Fig. 6.4, a later Pathswitch returns the current path to $a\ p\ q\ r\ b$ again, then the nodes that will become new daughters of J will be not p, q, and r, but F and r. In this way, alternative lattice-paths can be explored with minimal waste of information.

(The algorithm for 'repairing' the current tree after a Pathswitch has to be a little more complicated than this, since otherwise the annealing run would depart from the space of permissible solutions. If a Pathswitch creates a forbidden singular-branching configuration, this is eliminated by cutting out the node which both is and has a sole daughter.)

Move Generation

Having defined the class of legal moves, it remains to explain how APRIL3 selects a particular move at each step of the random walk. An ideal approach might be for the system on each occasion to work out the full set of available legal moves and choose one of them at random with equal probabilities. This would be computationally very expensive, for a procedure that needs to be executed repeatedly and must therefore be fast. Furthermore, the Pathswitch move-type is computationally much more 'costly' than the moves which modify a tree above an unchanged lattice-path; in an algorithm for which speed is of the essence, we cannot afford to allow complex and therefore slow moves to be executed as frequently as others.

Accordingly, the move generator first decides whether to propose a Pathswitch move or some other type of move, with a low probability for the Pathswitch choice. If Pathswitch is chosen, then a node is chosen at random with equal probabilities from the set of nodes on the current lattice-path at which pathswitches are possible, and a new path at that node is chosen at random with equal probabilities. If the move-type Pathswitch is not chosen, then the move generator chooses at random with equal probabilities some node d in the current tree, other than the root node, and chooses one member of the three-element set {Hive-or-Merge, Relabel, Reattach} from a probability distribution (again, Reattach is a more 'expensive' type of move than the other types, and our assumption is that one Reattach move might be proposed for three of each of the other choices). If Relabel or Reattach is chosen, the proposed move applies the respective move-type to d. If 'Hive-or-Merge' is chosen, then a node e is chosen at random from the set of daughters of the mother m of d. If d and e are first and last daughters of m, the choices are interpreted as the proposal to Merge m out of existence; otherwise, they are interpreted as a Hive proposal involving creation of a new node f below m and dominating the subsequence of m's daughters bounded by d and e. (If $d = e$, f will be a singulary-branching node.) This procedure ensures that the system chooses Hive moves more frequently with many-daughtered nodes to which Hive can be applied in many different ways.

If the node selected is in a configuration to which the chosen move-type is not applicable, the selection process is repeated until node and move-type are compatible. (For instance, a leaf node cannot be Relabelled; a Hive cannot be executed when $d = e$ if the result would be a forbidden singulary-branching configuration.) One of the individual moves of the chosen type is then selected at random (for instance, in the case of the Reattach move, one particular location for reattachment is chosen equiprobably from the possible sites in the arch surrounding d). Where the move would require a new label to be created, the label is selected from a probability distribution determined by mother label, as discussed above. After all details of the proposed move are fixed, it is evaluated and accepted or rejected via the standard simulated-annealing decision process.

Unlike in some earlier versions of the annealing parser, for APRIL3 the move generator is constrained so that any proposed move does make a real difference to the current solution — it cannot, for instance, propose Reattaching a daughter node to the same node which was previously its mother, or propose making any change to a 'dead' terminal or nonterminal node such as the nodes labelled p, q, F, on the 'after' side of Fig. 6.4. If moves of these kinds could be proposed, they would invariably be accepted (since their effect on current solution value would be zero, and the annealing algorithm always accepts moves which do not worsen the current solution). Yet the result of such moves might be highly adverse, if a Pathswitch further left in the lattice were subsequently to 'resurrect' the dead structure. In order to ensure that information once gained is not thrown away, it is important to require that any proposed modification to the data structure representing the current solution is 'visible' to the evaluation metric.

Having achieved its freezing criterion, the system executes a phase of deterministic neighbourhood search. The search is deterministic only in the sense that it systematically assesses each distinct tree-*shape* that can be reached by a single move from the current solution, however. Where a move involves choosing a new node label, instead of working exhaustively through each member of the nonterminal vocabulary the system merely operates its random label-choosing routine a set number of times; because label choosing is biased in favour of likely labels, where an adjacent solution superior to the current solution is in fact available this method gives a high probability of locating it, at the cost of considerably less effort than truly exhaustive neighbourhood search.

Finally, once deterministic neighbourhood search has failed to locate a solution better than the current solution, this is subjected to a fully deterministic postediting process which prunes out any singular-branching nodes that are illegal in terms of the SUSANNE scheme, such as the phrase nodes above *four*, *you*, and *her* in the examples discussed on p. 75-6 above.

The APRIL3 system has an interface which allows the user either to specify values for numerous parameters – the values defining the annealing schedule, the file from which an input text is taken, the interval at which diagnostic reports are produced during a run, and so forth – on a command line, or to let individual parameters default to 'sensible' values. Optionally during an annealing run, and always at the end of a run, the solution achieved is reported, and the user can opt to receive various diagnostics; in modes where the system has been supplied not only with a text to be analysed but also with its correct target analysis, it will generate a mark using the word-ancestor assessment system discussed on pp. 66–7. Details on these matters are contained in the system documentation to be distributed with the software. For present purposes, the significant aspect of system operation which remains to be explained is the nature of the APRIL3 evaluation metric, and the process by which that metric was created. These are the topics of the following chapter.

Notes

1. The term 'lattice' is perhaps unfortunate: this word has a well-defined use in graph theory for a rather different structure (a word-hypothesis lattice will *not* normally be a lattice in the algebraic sense). I discuss this conflict of terminology in Sampson 1993. But the usage is so entrenched in modern speech research that it would be impractical to use a different term.
2. There are a few exceptional cases where the text covered by a microlattice is not a typographic word, for instance cases where a line-break immediately follows a hyphen.
3. In connection with word-hypothesis lattices, we say that one path through part of the lattice is *parallel* to another path if the two paths have the same first and last nodes.
4. Dividing the APRIL3 front end into discrete subcomponents, and indeed

describing the front end as sharply disjoint from the parse annealer, somewhat exaggerates the extent to which high-level functions map onto separate software modules; the exaggeration is justified for the sake of clarity of exposition.

5. The dependence of the APRIL dictionary on Mitton's CUVOALD means that the software system described in the present chapter incorporates intellectual property of Oxford University Press, and distribution of the system when complete will be subject to the permission of the Press.

6. Fig. 6.3 in fact gives a slightly misleading impression of the way the information is stored; rather than a single ten-field file we maintain the dictionary as two files each with fewer than ten fields, corresponding lines in which are related via index numbers. This is necessary because of a few dozen entries which differ with respect to fields not taken into account in collecting frequencies: thus our frequency-counting algorithm did not distinguish between the plural nouns *axes* pronounced [' &ksIz] as plural of *axe*, and *axes* pronounced [' &ksiz] as plural of *axis*.

7. The *entry batch indicator* is a resource management field, enabling researchers to establish how a particular entry got into the dictionary in case a query arises about its validity. The *American/British flag* shows whether an entry applies to only one national variety or to both (N = neutral). The *pronunciation* field indicates the word's pronunciation via a coding of IPA symbols into ASCII characters (the coding is Mitton's own, rather than the SAMPA system which has more recently been promulgated as a standard). The *inflexion pattern* is given for base forms of inflectable words, showing how to make their inflected forms (e.g. whether a noun makes its plural by adding *-s*, adding *-es*, changing *-y* to *-ies*, etc.). *Hornby valency codes* are included for verbs and show the patterns of complementation found in clauses headed by the respective verbs, according to the classification of Hornby (1975).

8. The word 'virtually' is included because the statement is not 100% true for analyses conforming to the SUSANNE scheme; but the rare exceptions are such special cases, difficult to detect automatically, that it has seemed reasonable to design the current version of APRIL as if the exceptions did not exist.

7 The Current System: Language Model

In this chapter I discuss the structure of the APRIL3 *language model* – the body of information about English grammar which the system uses to evaluate analyses proposed by the parse annealer; and I explain the technique whereby a language model is derived semi-automatically from data on English *productions* – that is, the pairings of mother labels with sequences of daughter labels found in a database of analysed language samples.

The Structure of the Model

The heart of the language model is a set of skip-and-loop networks of the kind displayed in Fig. 4.6 above, which for convenience is repeated here as Fig. 7.1, with states labelled by numbers for ease of reference.

For each nonterminal label in the vocabulary of simplified labels, the language model contains a skip-and-loop network for each of its prototype sequences. The various prototypes for a mother label are associated with probabilities summing to 1, representing the frequency with which the respective prototype is the best match for a production observed in the database. For each loop arc, the model specifies probabilities summing to 1 for the alternative *intruder* labels that may be accepted on that loop – that

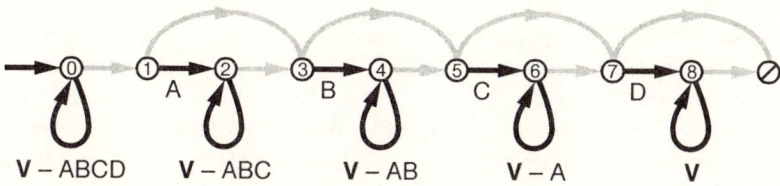

Figure 7.1 Skip-and-loop network for a prototype sequence

is, labels other than elements of the untraversed part of the respective prototype sequence (if the latter are encountered, they will be consumed via spinal rather than loop arcs).

Accordingly, for any production which pairs some nonterminal label with some sequence of nonterminal and/or terminal labels (irrespective of whether the production actually occurs in the structure of real-life samples of English, or is an unnatural configuration thrown up by the random moves of the parse annealer), the language model will efficiently generate a score. With respect to any one of the prototypes for the mother label, the score for a daughter-sequence will be the product of:

- the probability associated with that prototype;
- the various probabilities associated with the arcs traversed in transiting the skip-and-loop network for the prototype; and –
- for each traversal of a loop node, the probability associated with acceptance of the relevant intruder label on that loop.

The overall score for a production will be the highest of the scores given by the various prototypes for the mother label of the production.[1]

The figure of merit assigned to an entire tree over a word-hypothesis lattice will be the product of the scores worked out as above for the productions associated with the various nonterminal nodes of the tree, the scores worked out as discussed in ch. 6 for the various terminal nodes of the tree, and a downgrading factor (a number between 0 and 1 and closer to 0) for each word which is flagged as beginning with a capital letter not explained by its dictionary entry and which according to the parsetree is not sentence-initial or part of a proper name, and for each word flagged as beginning with a lower-case letter which according to the parsetree is sentence-initial or is a major word within a proper name.[2]

It is worth noting that downgrading factors of the kind just mentioned are another way in which the APRIL evaluation function is non-context-free, making it questionable whether an efficient deterministic optimizing technique such as dynamic programming could replace stochastic optimization.

Root nodes (in terms of the SUSANNE annotation scheme, 'O' nodes, representing paragraphs) are a special case. Sentences, and the smaller tagmas which occur within sentences, typically consist of a head element with a small number of modifying elements preceding and/or following the head. Some unpredictable intruder elements may occur, but there will be a limited total number of daughters. A paragraph, on the other hand, will typically consist of a sequence of sentences which may be very lengthy indeed, separated by sentence-closing punctuation marks (full stop, question mark, exclamation mark), which in the SUSANNE scheme are treated as sisters

The Current System: Language Model   131

rather than daughters of sentence nodes. Such a structure cannot be modelled by a skip-and-loop network of a fixed length. A more appropriate model would be based on a cyclical structure, something like Fig. 7.2.

Here, 'S' is the SUSANNE symbol for a declarative main clause, 'S?' the symbol for an interrogative main clause, and YF and YQ are wordtags for full stop and question mark respectively. This is over-simple: the tagmas which occur as immediate constituents of paragraphs are not invariably full clauses, for instance a noun phrase or a prepositional phrase may occur with an initial capital and closing full stop in place of a 'complete sentence', and the SUSANNE scheme will tag such elements according to their form, e.g. as N or P rather than as S. Furthermore, the correlation between declarative v. interrogative grammar and full stop v. question mark is by no means perfect; and as with subordinate tagmas so at the paragraph level occasional 'intruder' elements occur (inverted commas opened in the middle of a sentence may in some styles be closed after the full stop, for instance). But Fig. 7.2 suggests the way in which paragraph grammar is a matter of related pairs of constituents continuing indefinitely, without strong dependencies between one pair and the next.

We have seen (p. 91 above) that the current version of APRIL3 simplifies the analytic task at the root-node level, by requiring inputs to contain

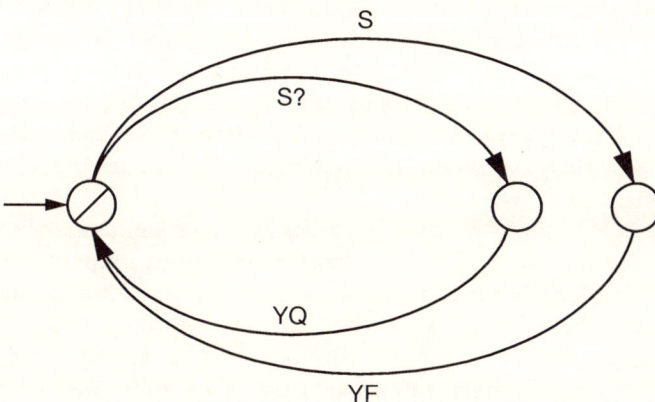

Figure 7.2 Transition network for the category 'paragraph'

explicit markers at the beginnings of sentences (that is, of nonterminal immediate constituents of paragraphs, whether in SUSANNE terms they are main clauses, noun phrases, or tagmas of other categories). Consequently APRIL3 does not need a transition network to evaluate analyses at the paragraph level. At that level, its language model comprises merely a table showing, for each pair (x, y) where x is a nonterminal category and y is a member of the set {full stop, question mark, exclamation mark, no sentence-closing punctuation mark}, the probability of finding x as a root IC given that the immediately following IC is a y. The probability associated with a root node is estimated as the product of these conditional probabilities for each of the non-punctuation constituents immediately dominated by the root.

Another special aspect of the language model relates to co-ordination. Within the SUSANNE analytic scheme, a co-ordination is treated as a main tagma having a second (and, if applicable, a third, fourth . . .) conjunct subordinate to it; thus the noun-phrase co-ordination *the heat and the dust* is analysed as [N *the heat* [Ns+ *and the dust*]], with no separate node for the first conjunct *the heat*. (The tag for a subordinate conjunct ends in a plus sign if the conjunct is introduced by a co-ordinating conjunction such as *and*, in a minus sign if not; and an appositional element is analysed similarly, with the sign '@' in place of a plus or minus sign in its label.) It is a very general property of English grammar that a tagma of almost any category is liable to end with a conjunct, commonly of the same category. Consequently, prototype sequences do not include closing conjuncts as prototype elements: for any mother category, the prototype sequences model the daughters that are apt to occur *before* any closing conjunct. When a daughter-sequence includes closing conjunct(s), this part of the daughter-sequence (together with any associated punctuation) is evaluated by a separate network, having the same structure for all mother categories, shown in Fig. 7.3.

In Fig. 7.3, 'C' stands for the class of all tagmatags ending in +, –, or @; 'Y' stands for the class of all wordtags representing punctuation marks (which in the SUSANNE scheme begin with Y. . .). Separate figures are kept for the probabilities of alternative members of these classes. Closing conjunct sequences are driven over this network backwards (suggested in Fig. 7.3 by placing the start state at the right of the Figure), thus the rightmost arc labelled Y accepts any punctuation mark occurring at the *end* of the daughter-sequence. The overall estimated probability for a production involving closing conjunct(s) will then be the probability of the preceding part of the daughter-sequence, derived from the skip-and-loop system for the mother label in the ordinary way, with the probability of the closing sequence derived from the Fig. 7.3-type network for the mother label (and,

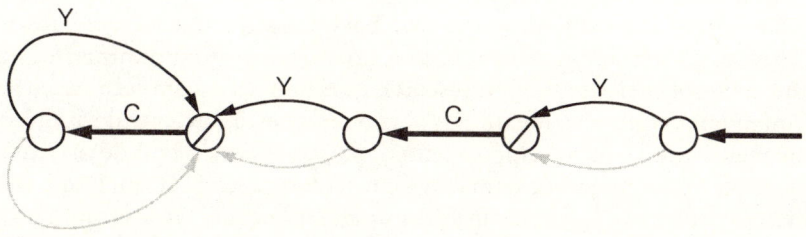

Figure 7.3 Generalized transition network for closing conjuncts below any nonterminal

in the case of a production not containing a closing conjunct, the probability from the skip-and-loop network will be multiplied by the probability associated with acceptance of the null string on the relevant closing-conjunct network).

Because we have only a limited quantity of statistical evidence from which to estimate the many probabilities included in an APRIL language model, it is important to make the most of what we have. For instance, it is not necessary to treat the question of how best to model daughter-sequences via prototypes as an entirely independent issue for each separate mother label. Thus, the SUSANNE scheme recognizes many categories of finite and nonfinite clause; but, with the notable exception of relative clauses (which may omit a relativized element from any part of the clause), most of these clause-types are much more similar to one another at their right-hand ends than at their left-hand ends. An adverbial clause (symbolized 'Fa' in the SUSANNE scheme), such as *although he has informed us of the problem*, has a finite verb group and begins with a subordinating conjunction, but in terms of what follows the verb group (namely, in this case, *us of the problem*) it cannot be distinguished from a present-participle clause ('Tg' in SUSANNE terms) such as *Informing us of the problem (is not enough)*. Since our analysed database provides only so much evidence from which to establish what label-sequences commonly do or do not occur as realizations of any one clause category, we might improve our language model by modelling most clause categories as pairs of half-tagmas, creating one set of prototype daughter-sequences (and hence one set of skip-and-loop networks) for the left-hand end of each separate clause category, up to and including the verb group, but a single set of prototypes (and hence networks) for the right-hand ends of all the clause categories taken together – giving us more reliable statistics on the frequencies of various possibilities to the right of the verb group than we have for any single clause category.

How to combine our data categories to squeeze maximum useful information out of them is an open research question. We want frequencies that are high enough to give meaningful probability estimates, while at the same time we do not want to lump together categories which embody significant differences that might help our system to locate correct analyses. At the time of writing, we have not in fact implemented the suggestion of modelling clauses as pairs of half-clauses. On the other hand, we have implemented another data-merging principle, relating to the intruder loops.

With many distinct nonterminal categories (even in the simplified vocabulary of category labels), and several prototype sequences for each nonterminal category, the set of probabilistic skip-and-loop networks that constitutes the language model will clearly have a very large number of loop arcs. Any loop arc accepts almost any category (the only exceptions being categories occurring in the part of the prototype sequence to the right of a particular loop). To evaluate a daughter-sequence generated by the parse annealer we need estimates for the individual probabilities of each of the different categories accepted on any loop, but, if we estimated these probabilities on the basis of frequencies observed for particular categories and particular loops separately, our data would be so sparse that the estimates would be close to meaningless.

Consequently, our system allows us to specify a grouping of loop arcs into classes, so that probabilities for different intruder labels are estimated jointly for all the loops of a large class, based on the observed frequencies for different intruders on any loop in the class. For instance, one might guess that the kinds of grammatical constituent which typically occur as intruders within clauses will differ, statistically at least, from those which occur as intruders within phrases; in which case one could group all loops in clause networks into one class and all loops in phrase networks into another class. Again, it may well be that different categories commonly occur as intruders at the *beginning* of a prototype daughter-sequence (on the loop attached to state 0 in Fig. 7.1) as compared to the categories which typically occur at any later point, so one might decide on a two-way classification of loops into state-0 loops v. later loops. This classification is orthogonal to the clause-loop v. phrase-loop classification, so if both were adopted we would have four loop classes, hence four sets of estimated probabilities for the incidence of various word and tagma types as intruders. With more loop classes we can build more refined information into the language model about the propensity of different sorts of grammatical item to occur in different environments, but the data allowing us to estimate those propensities will be less reliable.

Estimating Probabilities from Sparse Data

The foregoing paragraphs discuss the importance of not spreading our limited data too thin, by grouping similar categories together so that observed frequencies tend to be large enough to yield meaningful probability estimates. Taken too far, category merging would make the distinctions in APRIL output analyses so coarse that the system, even if it performed accurately, might seem valueless; and anyway, if the categories recognized by the language model are excessively coarse then output analyses probably will not be accurate. But there should be a happy medium which produces usable arrays of statistics by eliminating peripheral distinctions which do little to help the system get its answers right, and have little value if recorded in the output, while preserving the important distinctions.

Nevertheless, with this research as with many other kinds of statistical research on natural language, however we group data categories we must reckon with the fact that available data are sparse: arrays of observed frequencies will typically contain many cells containing tiny numbers, and even more cells containing zeros. Natural language is like that. Think of the example of recording incidence in a corpus of the various wordforms listed as entries in a dictionary. I have already discussed the case of our probabilistic dictionary; but, even if the language were not English, and even if the dictionary were smaller than the one we have derived from CUVOALD while the corpus used as a data source were several times larger than Brown and LOB together, anyone familiar with the general nature of human language would surely predict that the frequency counts would show a small number of very high-frequency words, many words occurring once, twice, or a handful of times, and plenty of words listed in the dictionary but not found at all in the corpus.

Vocabulary is an extreme case even in natural language of the way in which categories tend to be both very unequal in frequency and numerous relative to the size of data-sets that can practically be assembled; but the pattern runs through many areas of language structure. Even the highly simplified Mk 2 annotation scheme, for instance, recognized more than two hundred distinct grammatical categories, some of which were extremely frequent and others vanishingly rare.

Probabilistic work in an area of this kind has to be rather subtle in its use of statistical concepts, in a way that past work by computational linguists (myself included) has not always been. In particular, it is important to understand that dividing observed frequency of examples of a category by total observed examples of all categories is *not* the best way to estimate the probability of the category.

This comes as a shock to many people. Suppose that we would like to know the probability that a word chosen at random from some body of English text not yet examined will be the word *lamp*, and we have access to a million-word sample of English text among which it turns out that twenty word-tokens are instances of the form *lamp*. (That is in fact the frequency of this wordform in the LOB Corpus.) Then, while many people might suggest that the available evidence is not enough to make any estimate very reliable, many would also suppose that *on the available evidence* the best possible estimate for the probability of *lamp* is twenty in a million, $p = 0.00002$. That is wrong. The figure $p = 0.00002$ is the probability which, if it were in fact the probability of *lamp*, would make twenty the frequency most likely to be observed in a million-word sample. That is not the same as saying that an observation of twenty instances in a million makes $p = 0.00002$ the best estimate for the probability of *lamp*. Just by looking at the statistics of the million-word sample, without extra evidence, we can produce a better probability estimate than this; and for research of the APRIL kind it is rather desirable that we should do so.

The fallacy identified in the preceding paragraph becomes plainer if one considers observed frequencies of zero. Suppose we want to estimate the probability of *bluebell*, and our million-word sample contains no instance of *bluebell* (the word does not occur in LOB). Is it reasonable to infer that the best estimate for $p(bluebell)$ is zero in a million or 0.0, meaning that *bluebell* never occurs in English (or, what amounts to more or less the same thing, that there is no English word *bluebell*)? Surely not. The reasonable inference seems to be that *bluebell* has some positive probability which is quite low. It is less obvious, but nevertheless true, that the evidence available gives us a way of putting a specific figure on that positive probability.

NLP researchers typically have not inferred zero probability estimates from zero sample frequencies. Because the usual reason for estimating probabilities of simple phenomena is to multiply estimates together in order to arrive at probabilities for interesting compound phenomena, zero estimates are very bad news: they propagate through multiplications, ensuring that any compound phenomenon in which just one factor has such an estimate is as a whole predicted to be impossible, even if all the other factors have high probabilities. Research on statistics-based NLP has tended to get round this problem by adding some small quantity to all the cells of an observed frequency array, so that even cases where the true observed frequency is zero are assigned a positive frequency before probabilities are estimated by dividing by the total of the numbers in all the cells.

We saw in ch. 3 that my pilot annealing system did this, by adding 0.1 to the observed frequency of each MD_1D_2 figure to deal with the many daughter transitions that did not occur in the data. Likewise the CLAWS word-tagging system discussed in ch. 2, which depended on statistics about pairwise transition frequencies between the wordtags of the 132-member LOB tagset, added a small quantity to each cell of the matrix of transition frequencies (Marshall 1987: 54) in order to guard against the danger that a path containing an unobserved transition between, say, tag p and tag q would automatically be eliminated from consideration, even if the choice of these tags for the relevant words implied an immediately preceding transition from tag n to tag p, and an immediately following transition from tag q to tag r, which were both of unusually high frequency.

Since CLAWS worked well, this way of compensating for zero observed frequencies, which looked like common sense to many of us, was evidently harmless in this particular application. But that may have been a lucky chance, because it has subsequently become clear that, in general, adding a small quantity to the cells of a frequency array is an extremely poor way of avoiding zero probability estimates. It does produce positive estimates, but often they are wildly wrong (Gale & Church 1994 cite standard applications in which estimates produced in this way are out by factors of up to several thousand). I do not believe that APRIL can afford to use this kind of probability estimation.

A far more appropriate estimation method has been in the public domain for several decades, having been developed by Alan Turing and his then statistical assistant (now emeritus professor of statistics at the Virginia Polytechnic Institute), I. J. Good, during their work at Bletchley Park in the Second World War. Bletchley Park in Buckinghamshire was the site of the main Allied codebreaking effort, where machines such as Colossus, one of the chief precursors of the digital computer, were developed in order partially to automate the task of cracking enemy ciphers including that produced by the German Enigma machine.[3] The Bletchley Park work depended heavily on formalizing statistical measures such as 'weight of evidence' in a linguistic context, and one by-product was a theoretically-respectable technique – the classic publication was Good 1953 – for deriving probability estimates from frequency distributions of the general type described above as characteristic for natural language.

I became aware of the Good-Turing technique when I began work on parsing by simulated annealing in the 1980s. However, at that time it seemed impractical to use it. The variants of the Good-Turing technique discussed in Good's 1953 paper were mathematically very demanding; the effort needed to use them could have been disproportionate to any benefit gained. (For that matter, other statistical techniques exist to achieve essentially the same goal but are, if anything, even more mathematically cumbersome.) More recently, however, William Gale of AT&T Bell Laboratories has developed a much less daunting variant, the *Simple Good-Turing* estimator, which has proved to yield very satisfactory probability estimates for natural language data and is highly suitable for APRIL use (and, I believe, for use in many other NLP applications).

I shall limit myself to an outline description of the Simple Good-Turing estimator here, since Gale and I have published elsewhere a full account, including a minimally technical step-by-step recipe for applying it as well as an explanation of its theoretical rationale (Gale & Sampson 1996).[4]

Any variant of the Good-Turing estimation technique revolves round tables of *frequencies of frequencies*. Consider, for instance, the frequencies of various wordforms in a corpus. If the corpus is English, the most frequent wordforms (counting punctuation marks as words) will be *the*, comma, full stop, *of*, and *and*, which in LOB occur with the following frequencies:

the	68,351
comma	54,548
full stop	50,323
of	35,745
and	27,873

No other word has the same frequency as *the*, so for LOB the *frequency of frequency 68,351* is 1 – we write that for $r = 68,351$, $n_r = 1$. Many high-frequency wordforms have unique frequencies. But as one moves to lower frequencies, frequencies of frequencies rise: for LOB, if $r = 313$, $n_r = 3$, because *among*, *really*, and *group* are each represented by 313 instances. For $r = 14$, $n_r = 78$; for $r = 10$, $n_r = 451$; and so forth. One can plot r against n_r graphically; although for any real data-set the points of such a plot will naturally show a certain amount of irregular scatter, if the plot uses logarithmic scales on both axes then the points for lower frequencies, where n_r is greater than 1, will fall close to a straight line, with frequency-of-frequency rising as frequency falls.

If this line were projected into the high-frequency side of the plot it would give fractional frequencies-of-frequencies, which are clearly impossible – n_r may be 1 or 0 but cannot be anything in between. In the LOB case n_{35745} is 1, for the word *of*, but many neighbouring n_r values are 0 – the nearest nonzero n_r values are $n_{50323} = 1$ for full stop on one side, and n_{27873} for *and* on the other. In order to grasp the underlying relationship between the r and n_r numbers, though, one can think of the isolated nonzero values that occur in the n_r column between runs of zero values as smeared out over the parts of those runs which are closer to that nonzero figure than to the next higher and lower frequencies which have nonzero n_r values. That is, for $r = 35,745$ we can replace 1 in the n_r column by $1 \div \frac{1}{2}(50,323 - 27,873) = 0.0000891$.

Using these replacement values, the points of the r versus n_r plot will be log-linear across the whole frequency range. Let us write 'S_r' for the line of best fit to the points of this plot: that is, for any value of r, S_r will be a value close to n_r but with the irregularities of the observed n_r values smoothed out (and averaged with neighbouring zero values, if the r value is high and therefore surrounded by stretches of unrepresented frequencies).

Now (neglecting some special considerations about low frequencies which are important for applying the Simple Good-Turing technique and are fully discussed in Gale & Sampson (1996), but would complicate the present exposition unnecessarily), it can be shown that for nonzero frequencies a good estimate of p_r is:

$$\frac{(r+1)S_{r+1}}{NS_r}$$

– where N is the total number of items in the sample: in the case of LOB, a little over one million. This formula will yield a figure for p_r that will normally be somewhat lower than r/N, which is what we would expect: since some English words, such as *bluebell*, are not found in the sample at all, the estimated probability for words that do occur should be a little lower than their observed frequency, to leave some probability over for the unobserved words.

And a corollary of the theorem which yields the above formula gives us an estimate for P_0, the joint probability of all the unobserved items: this is n_1/N, that is, the number of *hapax legomena* (words that occur just once each) divided by the total number of word-tokens. LOB contains 1,157,319 word-tokens of which 22,441 are hapaxes, so the P_0 estimate for LOB is 0.0194 – this is the estimated probability that, if a word-token is chosen at random from a text that is not in LOB but is typical of the same kind of material from which LOB was selected, that token will represent some wordform (such as *bluebell*) not found in LOB.[5]

An Example of the Good-Turing Technique

As a fuller example, consider the issue discussed on pp. 130–2 above of transition probabilities between root daughters. Because paragraphs consist of indefinitely long sequences of typographic sentences separated by punctuation marks, rather than postulating prototype structures for O nodes we have decided that APRIL3 will assess a root node by reference to the conditional probabilities of the various nonterminal labels in the root-daughter sequence, given the immediately following punctuation marks. To calculate these conditional probabilities we need estimates for the probabilities of the various pairs of tags co-occurring.

In the simplified SUSANNE scheme, 25 distinct labels occur on nonterminal root daughters – the overwhelming majority are classified as S, 'declarative main clause', but for instance adverbial clauses, Fa, and noun phrase, N, also sometimes occur as independent typographic sentences. It may well be that, in English in general, other tagmatags apart from the 25 in our data can occur as root daughters, but in order to avoid undue expansion of the solution space APRIL3 limits its guesses at root-daughter labels to those labels which actually occur in this position in our data.

We distinguish four categories of following item: full stop, question mark, exclamation mark, and 'other'. (The 'other' category covers, for instance: ellipsis mark; a case of a sentence immediately following another without intervening punctuation; a word such as an interjection which is treated typographically as part of the preceding sentence but is not part of

tagmatag	full stop	?	!	other
Fa	19	0	0	0
Ff	1	0	0	0
Fr	1	0	0	0
J	1	0	0	0
J!	0	0	1	0
L	22	0	0	1
L?	0	2	0	0
L?+	0	2	0	0
N	15	3	0	1
N!	1	0	0	0
N"	0	1	0	0
N+	1	0	0	0
Q	257	56	27	20
R!	0	0	0	1
S	5411	14	10	23
S!	1	0	0	0
S!+	0	0	1	0
S*	15	0	0	1
S*+	4	0	0	0
S+	164	3	0	2
S?	1	65	0	1
S?+	0	7	0	0
Tb?	0	1	0	0
Tg	2	0	0	0
Z	1	0	0	0
totals	5917	154	39	50

Figure 7.4 Incidence of punctuation with grammatical category of typographic sentence

it grammatically; and so forth.) We expect, for instance, that the categories S and S? (declarative and interrogative main clause) are more likely to precede full stop and question mark, respectively, than *vice versa* (and the figures bear this out). The observed frequencies for the 100 possible pairings of tagmatag with following item are shown in Fig. 7.4. The total of all frequencies, that is the number of nonterminal root daughters in the data, is 6160 – in what follows the symbol N always refers to this number. The table of frequencies and frequencies-of-frequencies is as follows:

r	n_r
1	17
2	4
3	2
4	1
7	1
10	1
14	1
15	2
19	1
20	1
22	1
23	1
27	1
56	1
65	1
164	1
257	1
5411	1

Since there are 17 unique pairs, the P_0 estimate is $17/N = 0.00276$. The Simple Good-Turing calculations specify how much to reduce the probability estimates for the tag-pairs which are observed, in order to make room for this positive probability for unobserved pairs. Thus, if the probability of a unique pair such as relative clause (Fr) before full stop were estimated naively as $1/N$, this would give 0.000162; but Simple Good-Turing corrects this to 0.000125. The estimated probability for a twice-observed pair is corrected from $2/N = 0.000325$ to 0.000278. And at the other end of the frequency scale, the estimated probability of S before full stop is corrected from $5411/N = 0.8784$ to 0.8776 – implying that if our 6160 observations had been truly representative of the population, they would have contained not 5411 but only 5406 examples of this tag-pair.

These probabilities of co-occurrence allow us to calculate the conditional probabilities we need, using the formula $p(a|b) = p(a\&b) \div p(b)$. The probabilities for the root-daughter categories full stop, question mark, exclamation mark, and other can be calculated from their relative observed frequencies as respectively 0.961, 0.0250, 0.00633, and 0.00812. Therefore, for example, the estimated probability of exclamatory adjective phrase (J!) given exclamation mark (a combination observed once) is $0.000125 \div 0.00633 = 0.020$; while the probability of S given full stop is $0.8776 \div 0.961 = 0.91$.

In view of the limitations of our data, two significant figures are probably as many as it is reasonable to give in these estimates; and this means that, in this example, the Good-Turing corrections to the estimated probabilities for the commoner tag-pairs are of little importance (the correction quoted above for S before full stop only affected the fourth significant figure). But the corrections for less-common observed tag-pairs are highly relevant; and so is the estimate for P_0. It remains now to discuss the issue of estimating probabilities for the 61 individual tag-pairs which have a zero observed frequency, and whose joint probability we have estimated as 0.00276. We might share this figure equally among the 61 cases, giving a probability of 0.000045 for each unattested tag-pair. But we can do better than that.

In general, the best way to share out the P_0 figure given by an application of Good-Turing methods is to find some way of breaking down the unobserved phenomena into complexes of simpler phenomena for which positive observed frequencies are available, and to share out the P_0 figure in proportion to the combined frequencies of the simple phenomena that contribute to the respective complexes. For instance, if one were to apply the Good-Turing method to a body of phonemically transcribed material in order to estimate the probabilities of different English syllables, one might estimate the probabilities of any phonologically-possible syllables that are missing from the data as proportional to the products of the probabilities of the respective consonants or consonant-clusters and vowels or diphthongs which make them up.

Admittedly, this involves an assumption about independence of the probabilities of the component elements that will usually not be altogether true. In the phonological example, for instance, the /b/ and /g/ sounds are characteristically rare after diphthongs, despite the occurrence of a few exceptions as in the words *astrolabe*, *Doig*; so, if P_0 is shared among the unattested syllables in proportion to (probability of initial consonant(s) × probability of medial vowel or diphthong × probability of final consonant(s)), syllables containing diphthongs followed by /b/ or /g/ will be assigned too large a share. Nevertheless, estimates calculated in this fashion are likely to be very much more accurate on balance than those produced by simply dividing P_0 equally between all the unattested cases (which involves an assumption about equiprobability that will usually be quite false).

In our case the elements sharing the P_0 figure are pairs of tagmatag and following punctuation category, so we could share P_0 proportionately to the product of tagmatag frequency and punctuation-category frequency. However, that would not be the best way to do the breakdown in this case. The reason why we are interested in probabilities for tagmatags before different punctuation marks is that we expect to find correlations between particular punctuation marks and particular broad classes of tagma; for instance, the question mark is likely to be common after any interrogative tagma, whether interrogative main clause (S?), interrogative verbless clause (L?), or another interrogative category. The relevant broad tagma classes are marked by particular characters within the tagmatags: ? for *interrogative* tagmas, ! for *exclamatory* tagmas, * for *imperative* tagmas, " for *vocative* tagmas, and absence of these symbols in the case of declarative or otherwise *neutral* tagmas: let us call these *mood classes*. In order to break the tag-pairs down into simpler elements for which the assumption of independent probabilities may be at least approximately true, it will be best to split the tag-pairs into *mood class and following punctuation mark*, on the one hand, versus *remainder of tagmatag* (omitting mood-class marker) on the other. For instance, the unattested tag-pair J! before full stop would be treated as a combination of 'exclamatory tagma followed by full stop', and J.

The observed frequencies in root-daughter position of tagmatags without mood markers are:

Fa	19
Ff	1
Fr	1
J	2
L	25
L+	2
N	21
N+	1
Q	360
R	1
S	5542
S+	184
Tb	1
Tg	2
Z	1

These figures can be turned into estimated probabilities simply by dividing by their total, 6160.

The observed frequencies in root-daughter position of the various combinations of mood marker and punctuation-mark category are:

interrogative tagma + full stop	1
interrogative tagma + ?	77
interrogative tagma + !	0
interrogative tagma + other	1
exclamatory tagma + full stop	2
exclamatory tagma + ?	0
exclamatory tagma + !	2
exclamatory tagma + other	1
imperative tagma + full stop	19
imperative tagma + ?	0
imperative tagma + !	0
imperative tagma + other	1
vocative tagma + full stop	0
vocative tagma + ?	1
vocative tagma + !	0
vocative tagma + other	0
neutral tagma + full stop	5895
neutral tagma + ?	76
neutral tagma + !	37
neutral tagma + other	47

Unfortunately, this list itself contains a number of zeros. In principle we might apply the Good-Turing technique a second time to these numbers, but (in view of the use to be made of them) the resulting corrections to the nonzero figures would be even less significant than in the case of the tag-pair figures; here, the most it is worth doing is to note that five combinations in the list have frequency 1, so that P_0 for this data-set can be estimated as $5/N$, and to share this quantity equally between the seven unattested combinations. Estimated probabilities corresponding to the nonzero frequencies will then be produced by multiplying the frequencies by $(1-5/N)/N$.

We now have a basis for producing differential probability estimates for the various zero-frequency cases in Fig. 7.4. Consider, for instance, the two cases L (neutral verbless clause) before question mark, and Tb? (complementizerless subordinate clause marked as interrogative) before exclamation mark. The former breaks down into:

The Current System: Language Model   145

neutral tagma before *?*: frequency 76, estimated probability $76(1-5/N)/N$
L: frequency 25, estimated probability $25/N$

The latter breaks down into:

interrogative tagma before *!*: frequency 0, estimated probability $(5/7)/N$
Tb: frequency 1, estimated probability $1/N$

Thus estimated probabilities for L before question mark and Tb? before exclamation mark will be produced by multiplying the pairs of estimated probabilities just shown, dividing each of the resulting products by the total of the 61 such products for the various unattested tag-pairs, and multiplying them by $P_0 = 17/N$. Without carrying out the latter operations (which are the same for the two cases, and for all other unattested tag-pairs), it is easy to see that the estimated probability for L before question mark will be approximately 2658 times larger than that for Tb? before exclamation mark – despite the fact that in both cases the observed frequency of the tag-pair was zero.

What we actually need for the APRIL language model are estimates of the conditional probabilities of (in these cases) L given following question mark, and Tb? given following exclamation mark — which can be calculated from the estimated probabilities of the combinations by dividing them by the probabilities for the punctuation marks. From Fig. 7.4 we see that there are 154 question marks and 39 exclamation marks in root-daughter position, in other words the former is about four times commoner than the latter. This will somewhat reduce the differential between the absolute probabilities; but the estimated conditional probability for L given question mark will still be about 700 times larger than than for Tb? given exclamation mark.

This is a large difference. It may be worthwhile for the system to propose the label L for a nonterminal node before a question mark, and (depending on the material below the node) such a configuration might turn out to be part of the optimal solution; whereas it could well be that the corresponding figure for Tb? before exclamation mark is so low that such a proposed node label is never retained in an annealing run. (It might even be advantageous to arrange that labelling proposals with such low probabilities are not generated.) Thus the use of Good-Turing methods, in place of the naive assumption that all unattested phenomena are equiprobable, is not a mere theoretical nicety: it has significant consequences for the working of the system in practice.

There are numerous areas in the APRIL language model where probability estimates have to be derived for phenomena, many of which have zero observed frequencies. APRIL3 standardly uses the Simple Good-Turing technique in such cases.

Prototype Optimization

We have seen that the heart of the APRIL language model is a set of 'prototype' daughter-label sequences for each nonterminal label, chosen in such a way that the various daughter-sequences found below a given nonterminal in correct analyses of real-life language samples are similar to one or another of the prototypes for the nonterminal. If one has a sample of analysed texts (with the analyses expressed in terms of the symbols to be used in the language model, for instance in our case using simplified tags rather than fully-detailed SUSANNE tags), then, once a set of one or more prototype sequences for each nonterminal has been settled on, the language model is almost fully determined and can be created essentially automatically. (The only additional decisions that need to be taken relate to issues discussed earlier such as how to group intruder loops for purposes of recording intruder probabilities, and how if at all to divide single tagmas between multiple skip-and-loop networks, for instance by separating closing conjuncts from what precedes them.)

Choosing sets of prototype sequences is a very large task, however. Even simplifying the tags as we currently do, our working treebank contains a total of 11,955 distinct productions and 317 distinct nonterminals – thus on average about 38 distinct expansions of each nonterminal, but far more for the common nonterminals: there are 2077 distinct expansions of S, for instance. Considering that whenever the annealing parser evaluates a node it must compare the daughter-label sequence with each prototype sequence for the respective mother label (and that this process will occur many thousands of times in the analysis of a single sentence), reasonably efficient parsing requires that prototypes should be far less numerous than this. We have seen that the effort of trying manually to reduce many observed productions to few prototypes became a very serious research bottleneck in the work on parsing by annealing previous to APRIL3.

It seems that a good prototype-set for a nonterminal will represent a compromise between the need to search the solution space rapidly, which requires few prototypes per nonterminal, and the need for any observed daughter-sequence to be similar to some prototype sequence, which is best served by increasing the number of prototypes (perfect matching would be achieved if each observed production were included as a prototype, though even then the matching would be perfect only with respect to the data sample from which the prototypes were derived – new analysed samples would still contain productions different in detail from any of the prototypes).

Thus different desiderata pull the ideal size of a prototype-set in opposite directions. Furthermore, in a smallish prototype-set, to make any limited modification (such as substituting one label for another in some particular sequence, or shortening a sequence by eliminating one of its labels) is very likely to make the prototype-set a better fit to some observed productions but a worse fit to others. These are just the characteristics of a problem domain that suggest that optimization by simulated annealing may be a suitable way to deal with the domain, and the APRIL3 language model has been developed by this means.

Our software includes a *language-model annealer*, quite distinct from the parse annealer discussed earlier: the role of the language-model annealer is to derive an optimal prototype-set from an observed set of productions, with specified frequencies for individual productions, for a given mother label.[6] This aspect of our current research is already complete in a first version at the time of writing: we now have a set of prototype sequences for our simplified version of the SUSANNE annotation scheme, and properties of this prototype-set will be discussed in what follows.

I shall first explain our approach to prototype annealing in abstract terms. Suppose the set of observed productions for some mother label M, with their observed frequencies, is as shown in Fig. 7.5. (Seven distinct productions is unrealistically few, but the example will serve to explain how the method works.) If prototypes must be similar to observed productions, then it is reasonable to suggest that any worthwhile prototype will be either identical to one of the observed productions or derivable from some observed production by omitting one or more of the elements of the latter. (This is not axiomatic – thus, since each observed production in Fig. 7.5 includes Z, W, or Q, it might conceivably be that a prototype including all three symbols would give good results even though no observed production includes more than one of the three. But our language-model annealer would not consider this possibility.) The solution space in annealing a prototype-set for a set of observed productions will be the class of mappings from the elements of an array such as Fig. 7.5 into the Boolean set {On, Off}. One solution for Fig. 7.5 is shown in Fig. 7.6. Boxes containing symbols are On, empty boxes are Off. The prototype-set of Fig. 7.6 contains five prototypes: there is no prototype corresponding to the production M → P C Y Z in Fig. 7.5 because each of the four daughters has been assigned the value Off, and there is no prototype corresponding to M → Q R S T U because, although several of the daughters are On, the mother is Off. The first prototype is identical to the first observed sequence (each daughter is On); the second observed sequence X A B Y Z has yielded the prototype X B Y, the other daughters being Off; and so forth.

The permissible moves for random walks through this type of solution

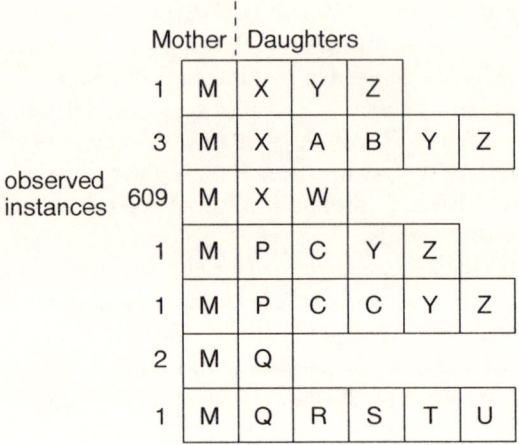

Figure 7.5 Observed productions for a hypothetical nonterminal symbol

space are defined very simply: a randomly-chosen element is switched from On to Off or *vice versa*.[7]

The cost function for prototype-sets is defined in two stages: we first specify a cost for an individual prototype sequence relative to an individual observed production, and then use this measure to define the cost of a set of prototypes relative to a frequency distribution over a set of observed productions.

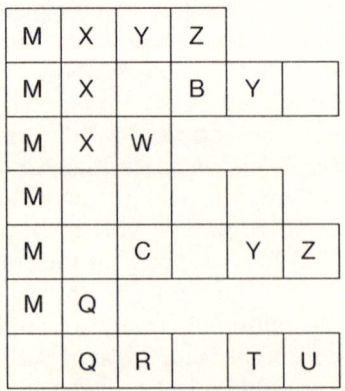

Figure 7.6 A sample element of the solution space for the data of Figure 7.5

The Current System: Language Model 149

The cost of a prototype sequence relative to an observed production is defined by counting the arcs of various categories traversed when the production is driven over the skip-and-loop network for that prototype. In terms of the state-numbering of Fig. 7.1, each traversal of a loop arc or a skip arc (a jump between two odd-numbered states) counts two, each traversal of a spinal arc labelled with a prototype element counts one, and each traversal of a spinal jump arc from an even- to an odd-numbered state is costless. Thus a prototype sequence has a higher cost, the less similar it is to the observed sequence, but there is a positive cost even if the sequences are identical (since we want the prototype-set to be small as well as representative of the observed data).

In order to avoid figures for long (observed and/or prototype) sequences swamping those for short sequences in our prototype-set evaluation function, we normalize the arc traversal cost as just defined by dividing it by the summed lengths of prototype and observed sequences. The resulting quantity is then raised to a power greater than 1. This last step is a response to the need to make prototype-sequence cost increase more than linearly with increasing dissimilarity between the respective symbol strings. The choice of exponent is made empirically; with larger exponents, the resulting prototype-sets contain more numerous prototype sequences for each mother label, and the average number of elements in prototype sequences is greater. We have found 4 to be a suitable choice of exponent. (This and other aspects of the cost function for language-model annealing discussed in this section are the outcome of experimentation with alternatives, and we certainly cannot claim that our experiments have been exhaustive enough to ensure that our current cost function is the best possible.)

To illustrate the foregoing with an example: consider the prototype sequence A B C D, whose skip-and-loop network is shown in Fig. 7.1, relative to an observed sequence L B M C D N – the symbols L, M, and N are 'intruders' accepted on the loops attached to states 0, 4, and 8, prototype element A is skipped via the jump arc from state 1 to state 3. The arc traversal total is 11 (three loops, one skip arc, three spinal arcs); consequently the cost of the prototype A B C D relative to the observed production L B M C D N is $\left(11 \div (4 + 5)\right)^4 = 2.232$.

I now define the cost of a set of prototypes relative to a frequency distribution over a set of observed sequences. For each observed sequence, we take its 'cheapest' prototype sequence, and multiply its cost by the frequency of the observed sequence. These figures are summed over the observed sequences, and the sum is multiplied by the number of sequences in the prototype-set which are the cheapest sequence with respect to at least one observed sequence.

It is this product which the language-model annealer seeks to minimize during an annealing run; and, on termination of the run, the set of prototypes output is limited to just those sequences whose cost contributed to the value of the solution at freezing, omitting 'useless' prototypes which contain some On daughters but which are not the cheapest prototype relative to any observed sequence.

Because optimization by simulated annealing is such a processing-intensive technique, readers may be interested in an indication of the sort of times needed for automatic language-model generation by this method. The language-model annealer code has been carefully designed to minimize the amount of recalculation required, but creating a prototype set is nevertheless a lengthy business. Using the annealing schedule we have settled on as offering a satisfactory balance of thorough searching against speed, it takes about 36 hours on a single-processor Sun Sparc 10 to produce sets of prototypes for the range of 317 nonterminals recognized by our current parsing scheme; fourteen hours of this time are accounted for by the single mother label S, main clause, which is the label for which our data give the largest solution space (there are just over 10,000 daughters which can be On or Off, hence a space of more than 2^{10000} solutions to be searched).

Results from the Language-Model Annealer

At the time of writing, we have developed two complete alternative sets of prototype daughter-sequences for each nonterminal, expressed in terms of the simplified SUSANNE annotation scheme – one set using the value 2 and the other the value 4 for the exponent discussed above. Both of these sets of prototype sequences look sensible, although we believe that the set produced with exponent 4 probably strikes a better balance between the need for prototypes to be few and the need for observed sequences to resemble prototypes closely. Of course, it remains to be seen how successful the language model derived from these prototypes will be in practice at preferring correct to incorrect analyses of input texts; it may be that early results from the APRIL3 parse annealer will lead us to modify the language model, either by making changes to its current output, or by altering the evaluation function or other aspects of the language-model annealer and rerunning it to generate a further set of prototype sequences. (The current version of the language-model annealer does not include a deterministic neighbourhood search phase – cf. p. 35 – after attainment of the freezing criterion; we are committed to incorporating this in an improved version.) But almost all the prototypes in the current sets seem intuitively reasonable, and, where an occasional sequence appears clearly unsuitable for inclusion in the language model, normally it belongs to a class that could be mechanically identified – for instance, one-element sequences consisting just of a punctuation mark.

In principle, we are not committed to full automation of the language-model generation process. Our parse annealer is fully automatic because that is the purpose of the research project; if APRIL3 delivered analyses of its inputs which required manual postediting, this would amount to failure to achieve project goals. In the case of language-model generation, on the other hand, automatic development of prototype-sets is just a device we have opted to use in order to advance the work of the project, and if it turned out that we can improve our language model by manual postediting the output of the language-model annealer, there would be no objection to this. Initial impressions are, however, that manual intervention may possibly not be necessary.

The nature of the prototype-sets generated is not entirely similar to what was envisaged in advance. But that tends to be so when problems are addressed by stochastic optimization, and in such cases one has to consider whether optimizing parameters need to be adjusted in order to yield solutions closer to those expected, or whether rather the optimizing system may be showing that one's prior expectations were short-sighted. (If it is easy to work out what the optimal solution in some problem domain will be like, there probably will be little point in applying stochastic optimization in that domain.)

Some individual prototype sequences are intuitively strange, but strange in interesting ways. One of the prototypes for the mother category 'noun phrase', for instance, translated out of SUSANNE symbols into words, runs:

article + noun + comma + comma

Two commas will never occur without something inserted between them, and a human analyst would be far more likely to think of including the intervening element in a prototype than of including the commas and leaving what separates them to be treated as an 'intruder'. Yet it is true that English noun postmodifiers include many diverse grammatical categories – relative clauses, appositional noun phrases, prepositional phrases, and other items, all of which have distinct labels even in the simplified version of the annotation scheme – but that elements of any of these different types will often be surrounded by commas. It may indeed be that in practice the commas are a better cue to the nature of the construction than is the identity of the intervening element.

Another daughter-sequence for the noun-phrase mother category where the language-model annealer may be exhibiting more 'wisdom' than a human is the one-member sequence JB, the wordtag for 'attributive-only adjective' (e.g. *former*). At first sight, it seems quite undesirable to give good marks to a parsetree in which an adjective is categorized as a noun phrase – if a single adjective is categorized as a phrase at all, under the SUSANNE scheme it would normally be an adjective phrase, symbolized J. But the rules of the SUSANNE scheme (Sampson 1995: 176) insert adjective-phrase nodes above single adjectives only in predicative position, which is precisely where a word like *former* cannot occur. And, although *former* alone is unlikely to function as a noun phrase, a phrase such as *the former* acting as subject, object, etc. will indeed be labelled as a noun phrase with understood noun. So again the prototype may serve its purpose well although to a human it initially looks misleading.

In order to give a clearer impression of the nature of the observed data used by the system and of the relationship between input to the language-model annealer and its output, I now give details of input and output for one nonterminal category, SUSANNE category J, 'adjective phrase'. Fig. 7.7 shows the 165 daughter-label sequences found below the mother label J in our data; the leftmost column gives the number of instances of each production in the data. The language-model annealer (using exponent 4) reduced these to the following sixteen prototype sequences:

```
DA JJ
FB YH
J
JA
JB
JJ
JJ Ti
JJ P
JJ YH JJ
MD
P
RG JJ
RR JJ
Tg
Tn
YH FA
```

The meanings of the symbols in the Figure and in the above prototype-set are fully defined in Sampson 1995, and it would be inappropriate to take the space to give complete and detailed definitions here; but the following list gives brief definitions of a number of them, including all those appearing in the prototype sequences:

2	AT	DA	JJ			24	JJ	YH	JJ			
1	AT	DA	Tn			2	JJ	YH	P			
2	AT	JJ	P			1	JJ	YP	JJ	YP		
2	AT	JJ				1	JJ	YP	RE			
1	D	JA	P	Fc		800	JJ					
3	D	JJ	Fc			1	LE	FB	YH	ZZ1		
1	D	JJ	J+	P		1	LE	JB				
1	D	JJ	P	R	Fc	9	LE	JJ				
2	D	JJ	P			2	LE	MD				
8	D	JJ				1	MC	YH	FA			
1	D	YH	JJ			1	MC	YH	JJ			
1	DA	FB	YH	Tn		3	MC	YH	MD			
5	DA	JJ	Fc			2	MD	JJ				
2	DA	JJ	P	P		1	MD	P				
20	DA	JJ	P			1	MD	YH	P			
1	DA	JJ	Ti	Fc		5	MD					
2	DA	JJ	Ti			1	N	JA				
74	DA	JJ				5	N	JJ	P			
1	DA	RR	JJ	P		20	N	JJ				
1	DA	Tg	P	P		1	N	ND1	P			
1	DA	Tg	P			1	N	RG	JJ			
3	DA	Tg				1	N	YH	FA			
1	DA	Tn	Fc			9	N	YH	JJ			
5	DA	Tn				4	ND1	JJ				
1	DA	YH	JJ			1	NN	YH	FA			
1	DA1	JJ	Fc			1	NN	YH	JJ			
6	DA1	JJ	P			13	NN1	JJ				
6	DA1	JJ				6	NN1	YH	FA			
1	DD	DA	JJ	P	Fc	29	NN1	YH	JJ			
2	DD	JJ				1	R	DA	JJ			
1	DD1	JJ	P			1	R	JJ	Fc			
6	DD1	JJ				2	R	JJ	P			
1	FB	YH	FA			1	R	JJ	Tf			
3	FB	YH	JB			2	R	JJ	Ti	Fc		
21	FB	YH	JJ			1	R	JJ	YC	R	YC	Fc
3	FB	YH	N			6	R	JJ				
5	FB	YH	NN1			1	R	Tn	Fc			
1	FB	YH	Tn			1	RG	JB	Tg			
3	FB	YH	ZZ1			1	RG	JB				
1	FB					1	RG	JJ	Fc	P		
3	FO	YH	FA			17	RG	JJ	Fc			
1	Fc	AT	DA	JJ		2	RG	JJ	Fn?			
1	Fc	YC	AT	DA	Tn	1	RG	JJ	P	Fc		
1	Fc	YC	AT	JJ		30	RG	JJ	P			
1	J	JJ				1	RG	JJ	RG			
1	J	YH	J			1	RG	JJ	RR			
4	J					2	RG	JJ	Tf			
1	JA	P	P			1	RG	JJ	Ti			
6	JA	P				103	RG	JJ				
9	JA	Ti				1	RG	RG	JJ	Fc		
15	JA					1	RG	Tg	Fc			
1	JB	YH	P			1	RG	Tg	P			
5	JB					1	RG	Tg				
6	JJ	Fc				3	RG	Tn	Fc			
18	JJ	Fn				1	RG	Tn	J+	P		
1	JJ	Fn?				1	RG	Tn	P	Fc		
1	JJ	J+	Ti			2	RG	Tn	Ti			
2	JJ	JJ	JJ			1	RG	Tn				
1	JJ	JJ				1	RG	YH	JJ			
24	JJ	JJ				1	RR	IC	Tg			
3	JJ	P	Fc			1	RR	J				
5	JJ	P	P			1	RR	JA	P			
1	JJ	P	Ti			2	RR	JA				
222	JJ	P				1	RR	JJ	Fc			
10	JJ	R				3	RR	JJ	Fn			
1	JJ	RG				1	RR	JJ	P	P		
2	JJ	RR	P			1	RR	JJ	P	YC	Fa	
2	JJ	RR				27	RR	JJ	P			
2	JJ	Tf				1	RR	JJ	R			
1	JJ	Ti	Fc			2	RR	JJ	Ti			
64	JJ	Ti				1	RR	JJ	YC	R		
1	JJ	Tn+	Ti			197	RR	JJ				
1	JJ	YC	A			1	RR	RG	JJ	P		
1	JJ	YC	J-	YC	J+	P	1	RR	RG	Tn	JJ	P	Fc
1	JJ	YC	J-	YC	P	1	RR	RR	JJ			
1	JJ	YC	J-	YC	RR	2	RR	Tn				
1	JJ	YC	J-	YC	Ti	1	RR	YH	JB			
1	JJ	YC	R	YC		4	RR	YH	JJ			
1	JJ	YC	R			1	Tn	JJ				
1	JJ	YC	Tg			2	XX	JJ				
1	JJ	YD	J+	YQ	YD	1	XX	RR	JJ			
1	JJ	YD	RR			1	XX	YH	RR	YH	JJ	
1	JJ	YH	FA									
1	JJ	YH	IO									

Figure 7.7 SUSANNE productions for the category 'adjective phrase'

AT	article
D	determiner phrase, e.g. *so many*
DA	determiner capable of following article, e.g. *more*
FA	suffix
FB	prefix
Fc	comparative clause, e.g. *than we have*
JA	predicative adjective, e.g. *alone*
JB	attributive adjective, e.g. *former*
JJ	general adjective
MD	ordinal numeral
N	noun phrase
ND1	direction, e.g. *south*
NN1	singular common noun
P	prepositional phrase
R	adverb phrase
RG	qualifier, e.g. *very*
RR	general adverb
Tg	present-participle clause, often one-word, e.g. *depressing*
Ti	infinitival clause, e.g. *to do the job*
Tn	past-participle clause, e.g. *beaten*
XX	*not*
YH	hyphen

Most of the prototypes are clearly reasonable. For instance (as seen in Fig. 7.7), the SUSANNE scheme regularly classifies constructions headed by present-participle or past-participle clauses (Tg and Tn) as adjective phrases, when modifier elements are added to the clauses to create larger constructions requiring separate labelled nodes: the phrase *thoroughly depressing*, say, would be analysed as a one-word Tg clause *depressing* post-modified by an adverb to make a two-word J phrase. The APRIL language-model annealer has retained the head elements in its prototype-set, leaving the various possible modifiers to be accepted on intruder loops.

In the case of hyphenated adjectival compounds made by adding a prefix or a suffix to an independent word, e.g. *pro-Western* or *bullet-proof*, the language model treats the hyphen and the affix as core elements of the construction and the other word as an 'intruder'. This looks rather unnatural, but it could well be a suitable strategy for evaluating analyses in practice: English allows a diversity of wordtypes to be hyphenated with affixes, though the resulting compounds very commonly function adjectivally.

The only one of the sixteen J prototypes listed above which it is very difficult to see as potentially valuable is the single-daughter prototype P. It is extremely common for a J to consist of an adjective postmodified by a prepositional phrase, but JJ P is included as a separate prototype. There are very few productions in Fig. 7.7 which include a P label and which do not match one of the other prototypes better than they match the one-element sequence P.[8]

However, even if this prototype is non-optimal, that does not necessarily imply that a language model derived from the current prototype-set will perform badly. The very fact that so few productions in Fig. 7.7 have P as their closest prototype means that the routine which adds probabilities to the language model, by driving the observed productions over the arcs of networks structured as in Fig. 4.7 on p. 80, will assign a low probability to the arc leading from the start state for mother-label J to the skip-and-loop subnetwork for prototype P. Thus the inclusion of this prototype in the set does *not* imply that APRIL will give good scores to implausible structural analyses containing singular-branching J nodes above P nodes. There is a certain robustness in the relationship between prototype-sets and language-model performance: it may be that the latter will be able to tolerate a degree of imperfection in the former, inevitable when the prototypes are created automatically.

The language model is not yet integrated into a functioning parse annealer, so one cannot yet be more specific. As we have seen, if it turns out that the prototype-sets delivered by the first version of the language-model annealer are unsatisfactory in practice, we have several methods in mind, both automatic and manual, for improving them. The prototypes yielded by our current language-model annealer do, however, look good enough to serve as the basis for a first working version of APRIL3 as they stand.

Notes

1. An alternative, which might be preferable, would assign to a production the sum of the scores for all the prototypes associated with the mother label. This would allow different prototypes to contribute to the score of a production by matching different parts of it; it would require a language model that had been optimized rather differently from the manner described later in this chapter.
2. The phrase 'major word' refers to the fact that, for instance, the system will not penalize an analysis that treats *the Archbishop of Canterbury* as a proper name, although *the* and *of* are not capitalized.
3. Activities at Bletchley Park are now widely agreed to have been one of the chief factors in the Allied victory in the war, but they remained highly secret long after its end (it came as quite a surprise to me, when the policy of secrecy was recently dropped, to discover how many of those who had taught me at the Universities of Cambridge and Oxford in the 1960s had originally developed their involvement with formal approaches to natural language as members of the Bletchley Park 'faculty'). However, detailed accounts of the work are now available (e.g. in Hodges 1983, Hinsley & Stripp 1993) – and cf. Robert Hams' best-selling novel (Hams 1995).

4. We drafted this publication in June 1994; if I may be permitted a personal reflection, it was a rare pleasure while England was caught up in commemorating the fiftieth anniversary of D-Day to be working, in my study overlooking the coast from which that crusade was launched, on a paper which created a link (however tenuous and distant) with some of the remarkable feats that allowed the war to be won.
5. The calculation of P_0 is much easier than that of p_r (for nonzero r), because it does not depend on the smoothing line S_r. One might imagine that S_r can be dispensed with altogether because, if we know P_0, we ought to be able to equate p_r with $(1 - P_0)r/N$. This is a mistake: the ratio between p_r and r is not constant for different values of r, rather r/N approximates p_r better when r is high than when r is low. (The ratio of tokens of *the* to all words in LOB is likely to be quite an accurate estimate of the probability of *the*, but the corresponding ratio for some word that occurs just once or twice will be a poor guide to the probability of that word.)
6. The language-model annealer software is not included among the 'deliverables' which we expect to make available to other sites after the conclusion of the project, and consequently documentation for it is not available in the same finished state as for the deliverable parts of the system. On current plans, what we shall distribute will include a particular language model of English, rather than software for language-model creation.
7. As implemented in the current version of the system, the random choice of element to toggle between On and Off is governed by a fixed ratio between moves applying to mother elements (which turn entire prototype sequences On or Off) and moves applying to individual daughter elements within a prototype (three out of ten moves generated are of the former type, seven out of ten of the latter); and, for reasons similar to those discussed on p. 126, a move applying to a daughter element whose mother is Off is not legal.
8. One example is the production J → N ND1 P, of which there is a single case. I believe this reflects the fact that the data for the language model are taken from a slightly out-of-date release of the SUSANNE analysed corpus, in which some sequence such as *15 miles south of here* must have been misanalysed as a J tagma (it should be labelled R, cf. Sampson 1995: 220).

8 Parallel Tree Optimization

The Need for Speed

Even if stochastic optimization is a good way of finding correct analyses for realistically messy input language, there is a large practical problem: simulated annealing (and any other stochastic optimization technique) is very slow. It is inevitable that a method which finds its way towards good solutions, in any problem domain, by blind trial and error must take a great deal longer than a 'clever' algorithm which heads towards the right answer systematically. It is only because of the vast aeons of time through which modern geology shows the world to have existed that biological evolution has had the chance to populate the world with complex, well-adapted living species. There was no possibility of a Darwin promulgating evolution theory in the days when people believed that the world was just a few thousand years old, as the Bible seemed to say.

When evolutionary processes are simulated on a computer, the length of a 'generation' is counted in microseconds rather than in days or years, as in the natural world; so solutions are attained far quicker. Nevertheless, if annealing runs typically last for hundreds of thousands, or millions, of steps, then the time taken to process an input is a serious problem even with equipment that operates as fast as a computer. Annealing runs with APRIL at present typically take minutes or hours to attain the freezing criterion. A 1987 experiment with an early version of the system gave an average time of 12 minutes per annealing run on a 16-word input sentence, for instance. Since our method of evaluating solutions has subsequently become far subtler, and thus computationally more expensive, there is little doubt that with the same annealing schedule the corresponding figure would now be higher (though we are now using faster equipment).

We do not routinely carry out time trials, which are fairly meaningless for a number of reasons. Beyond a certain point, optimizing our code for speed would obscure its logic and make it hard to modify (we have striven to make the code as efficient as possible while remaining conceptually clear, but clarity is more important at this stage than speed); we have devoted little attention to finding ideal annealing schedules (choice of an unnecessarily high intial temperature can easily change runs lasting minutes into runs lasting days, with scarcely measurable improvements in average output marks); and we have not exploited various devices discussed in the literature that could accelerate the algorithm. Tovey (1989), for instance, examines a number of devices (following Simon (1976) he calls them 'swindles') whereby optimization algorithms can be constructed which appear to execute simulated annealing runs, and do deliver virtually equivalent performance, but do not actually do all the work entailed by true simulated annealing. (For instance, in cases where the true function for evaluating solutions is expensive to calculate, the 'Surrogate Function Swindle' finds some simple approximate function and uses that most of the time; a proportion of moves are evaluated by both functions and the resulting information about the inaccuracy of the surrogate function is exploited in order to compensate for the use of that function on most moves.) Tovey finds that some 'swindles' are effective (they 'can reduce cpu time by an order of magnitude or two, without detracting much from [the] good characteristics [of simulated annealing]') .

Undoubtedly there is speed to be gained via tricks like Tovey's, as well as in the areas of annealing-schedule optimization and coding efficiency. Even when all of these possibilities are exploited, however, an annealing parser might still be too slow for use in speed-critical domains such as speech processing. This problem could melt away eventually as advances in computer hardware technology make processor speed ever faster; but I believe it is very desirable to investigate the possibility of accelerating the technique in a different manner, by exploiting the potential of parallel computing. The body of the present chapter describes an experiment along these lines.

For readers unfamiliar with the concept, I begin by explaining what parallel computing is. (Johnson & Durham 1986 offer an authoritative and readable survey of the field.)

Parallel Processing

Computers are machines which execute well-defined operations very fast; if it were not for the fact that computers work so much faster than people, it might scarcely have been worth automating many of the tasks for which computers are used nowadays. Computers began as fast machines and became much faster as the years went by, and users are constantly pressing for yet more speed; with each quantum increase, new applications become feasible. However, the great majority of computers – until the 1980s, all commercially available computers – share a design feature which severely limits the rate at which they can work: they are *sequential* machines. A computer will contain many thousands, or millions, of places that can store a piece of information (a data item, or an instruction), but it will normally have just one place where an instruction can be applied to a data item. For the machine to achieve anything, its program must cause instructions and data items to be moved one after another into the unique processor location, executed, and the results shifted back into the memory.

Thus the single processor in a conventional computer represents a bottleneck limiting the machine's work rate. The time for executing an instruction is short and growing shorter, but this progress cannot be maintained indefinitely; the laws of physics mean that it must always take an irreducible minimum of time. It seems *prima facie* obvious that a good way to get more work out of computers per unit of time should be to build machines containing numerous processors, so that many calculations can be executed at once.

In principle this was appreciated very early in the history of computing; it is remarkable that the very first article in the inaugural number of the journal of the UK professional society for computing, the British Computer Society, was on 'parallel programming' (Gill 1958). In practice, though, manufacturers kept to the single-processor principle (often called 'von Neumann architecture') for many years. But multiprocessor or *parallel computers* began to be made in the 1970s, and became commercially successful in the 1980s; by the middle 1980s, research on parallel computing had become one of the hottest topics in computer science. It is probably fair to say that in the 1990s the spotlight has drifted a little away from this area, partly because of recent hardware developments – it happens that sequential processing hardware has achieved impressive new increments of speed at a time when there have been delays in developing a new, faster generation of parallel-processing hardware. But any reduction of interest in this topic is likely to be only a passing phase. The laws of physics are still lying in wait to bring the acceleration of sequential machines to a halt, even if technology succeeds in pushing closer to that ultimate boundary than might once have seemed likely; and however fast sequential machines become, logically it would seem that parallel machines with n processors should be able to work n times faster.

There is a large difficulty, however; the gradual realization of just how large this difficulty is has probably been a factor in cooling the initial excitement about parallel processing. It is no use having a machine which can carry out n times more calculations per second than the fastest available sequential machine, unless we can harness that power so that the tasks required for an application are completed n times faster (or at least considerably faster) than the sequential machine can complete them. The software problems involved in getting multiple processors to co-operate so as to carry out useful functions efficiently have proved very challenging.

Some tasks can easily be decomposed into numerous subtasks which do not interact. Companies marketing parallel computers often demonstrate their power via a graphics program that plots the Mandelbrot set (see e.g. Gleick 1988: 221ff.). Establishing whether any given point in the complex number plane is in or out of the Mandelbrot set requires many repetitive calculations; and the set is visually an immensely intricate and beautiful object, giving the demonstration a natural impact. But the calculations for any one point do not affect those for any other, so it is straightforward to divide up the set of points in the two-dimensional display between as many processors as are available.

By no means all computing tasks can be decomposed into independent subtasks in this fashion, though. Very often, subtasks need information about one another before they can be completed, so that information must be exchanged among the processors of a parallel machine while a complex computation is being executed. In this situation it is by no means inevitable that dividing an overall task between multiple processors will give a speed advantage over running it entirely on one processor. Just the opposite can easily happen. Situations can arise in which processor A is waiting for information from processor B before proceeding, but processor B is likewise waiting for information from processor A; *deadlock* in this sense is a new way in which computer software can fail, additional to problems such as endless loops which are already familiar with sequential machines. And even if deadlocks are avoided and a program running on parallel equipment does succeed in producing the desired output, it often turns out that the program exploits the available processor power inefficiently, so that the time taken is as long as or longer than would be needed by a single processor of comparable performance. A central concern of parallel-processing research is to find efficient algorithms for parallelizing tasks which do not inherently consist of numerous wholly independent subtasks.

This chapter defines a method of parallelizing the tree-optimization task, and describes a series of experiments to assess the efficiency of this algorithm. It will be obvious from earlier chapters that, if parsing by stochastic optimization proves to be a useful technique, the very long random walks it requires make it highly desirable to find ways of parallelizing it. Furthermore, tree structures are so ubiquitous in computer science – Donald Knuth (1968: 305) has described trees as 'the most important non-linear structures arising in computer algorithms' – that finding efficient ways of optimizing them is an issue whose significance extends far beyond the APRIL project. Johnson & Durham (1986: 80–1) identified cognition-related applications, such as natural language processing and vision, as among the most central eventual beneficiaries of parallel computing; and tree structures are crucial throughout the cognitive domain. (For the relevance of tree structures in vision, see e.g. Miclet 1986.)

On the other hand, optimizing a tree is not a task like plotting the Mandelbrot set which can be decomposed in an obvious way into independent subtasks. A tree structure divides naturally into nodes, but the APRIL tree-optimization function cannot be addressed by sharing the nodes of a tree between processors. Alternative trees over a string in general have different numbers of nodes, and even as between two trees with the same number of nonterminal nodes there is in general no natural identity relationship between the nodes of one tree and those of the other. If individual tree nodes are items that are constantly created and destroyed during an annealing run, it seems that division of the task between multiple processors must be done on some other basis.

Furthermore, despite its significance the tree-optimization problem has not yet become a standard issue in the parallel-processing research literature. Various writers have discussed parallelizing the calculation of functions defined on tree-shaped data structures (e.g. JáJá 1992: 108ff., various chapters in Reif 1993), but in these cases the tree structure is fixed and the problem is about efficiently combining data contained at various points in it. Gibbons & Rytter (1988: ch. 4) discuss parallelization of context-free parsing, but this is parsing of the compilation kind, which aims to recover the unique tree by virtue of which an input is a 'legal' string: comparison of alternative tree analyses is not involved. None of these writers considers the question of seeking tree analyses for inputs which maximize a statistical measure of merit. Consequently the experiment discussed below, while limited in scope, may be worthwhile as launching a potentially significant new research topic.

An Algorithm for Optimizing Trees

My tree-optimizing algorithm can be defined as follows. For an input string of length v, consider the set of all continuous segments of the string whose length is at least two. Define a *tree-state* as an assignment to each such segment of a nonterminal label, and a partitioning of the segment into two or more subsegments each of length one or more. For instance, the segment (3,8) – that is, the segment stretching from the third to the eighth element of the string – might be assigned the label N and the partition (3,5)(6)(7,8). A tree-state defines a labelled tree. The label assigned to the segment $(1,v)$, representing the whole string, is the label of the root node, while the partition assigned to that segment shows which segments give information about the daughters of the root node, and so on recursively; a length-one partition element shows that the respective daughter is a leaf node.

As a simple example, the tree-state for a five-word string shown in

162 Evolutionary Language Understanding

Fig. 8.1 determines the tree shown in Fig. 8.2. Note that most of the information in Fig. 8.1 is redundant, playing no part in determining the shape of the tree; only the lines printed in bold actually contribute towards defining the structure of Fig. 8.2. The information in line (1,4), for instance, would be relevant if the partition of the root line had been (1,4)(5), but as it stands line (1,4) makes no difference to the tree.

The tree-optimizing task is parallelized by sharing the segments of an input among the processors of a parallel computing system; unlike the nodes of alternative trees over an input string, the set of input segments is fixed and can thus be shared once for all between the processors available. Each processor executes a random walk through the space of alternative

segment	label	partition
1,5	S	(1)(2,5)
1,4	F	(1,2)(3)(4)
1,3	L	(1,2)(3)
1,2	S	(1)(2)
2,5	P	(2,3)(4,5)
2,4	N	(2)(3,4)
2,3	Q	(2)(3)
3,5	P	(3)(4)(5)
3,4	T	(3)(4)
4,5	R	(4)(5)

Figure 8.1 A tree-state for a five-word string

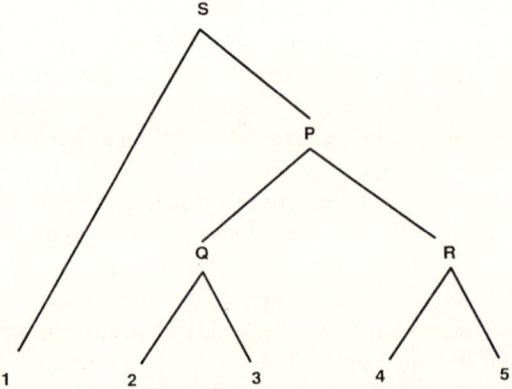

Figure 8.2 The tree defined by the tree-state of Figure 8.1

label/partition assignments available for its segments, and the set of processors as a whole thereby explores the space of alternative labelled trees. In order to evaluate the consequences of a change in one of its segments for the value of the tree, each processor maintains a model of the entire tree-state, which is periodically updated with information transmitted from other processors about the current state of their own segments.

For move-evaluation to be accurate, it seems *prima facie* that no processor could be allowed to make a move until it had received information about the latest moves made by all other processors. This would lead, if not to deadlock, then at best to loss of any speed advantage from parallel processing. But the simulated annealing technique is founded on the insight that it does not matter for individual moves in an optimizing process to be adverse, provided there is an increasing bias towards favourable moves. The hope motivating my parallel tree-optimizing algorithm is that, analogously, it will not matter for individual moves to be decided on inaccurate information, provided there is an increasing tendency for move-evaluation to be accurate. Thus, individual processors should be allowed to make decisions about accepting or rejecting changes to their own segments using information about other processors' segments which is somewhat out of date, given that progressive lowering of the annealing temperature causes a lower proportion of generated moves to be accepted and hence reduces the likelihood that any particular feature of another processor's tree-model will actually have changed over a given time period.

The aim of my experiments was to discover whether splitting the tree-optimization task between separate processors each running continuously, without waiting to ensure accuracy of information about other processors' current tree-states, is in fact compatible with achieving good end-results. (Aarts & Korst (1989: 110) report different degrees of success by researchers who have tried this general approach with other simulated-annealing applications.)

Implementation of the Algorithm

My implementation of this algorithm used Occam, which is arguably the only available programming language that has been created in response to a theoretically well-worked-out conception of parallel computing, rather than being developed as an extension of an existing sequential language. Accordingly Occam offers a good vehicle for examining the soundness of fundamental algorithms, without the risk that apparently poor results might be a consequence of the awkward process of parallelizing a language whose core was designed with no thought of parallel processing.[1] The Occam language was developed as a realization of Tony Hoare's theory of parallel processing as 'communicating sequential processes' (Hoare 1978, 1985). It is named after

William of Ockham, the fourteenth-century philosopher known for the maxim *Entia non sunt multiplicanda praeter necessitatem*: Occam is indeed a strikingly 'small' language, which may make for limitations in its use in complex practical computing applications but is a clear virtue for testing fundamental algorithms. In turn, the concepts underlying the Occam language have been translated into hardware through the *transputer* developed by Inmos Ltd.

The experiments reported below ran on a Meiko M40 Computing Surface, a system containing sixty-four T414-20 Inmos transputers, each of which is a device possessing a 2Mb memory and four external connections, which can be linked to one another in any desired configuration under software control. My software was written in Occam 2 (Burns 1988).

It is relevant to explain that these experiments were conducted during a few months of sabbatical leave spent as a Visiting Fellow at the Research Initiative in Pattern Recognition, RSRE Malvern; I had no access at my then home institution to parallel-processing equipment. The bulk of the available time was spent in coming to terms with a (to me) very exotic computing environment, and in software development, leaving only a short period for running experiments with the finished software. It will be quite apparent to the reader from the description which follows that my parallel parsing experiments were a far smaller and more amateurish enterprise than the APRIL project described in the body of this book. However, the results achieved, while limited in scope, are interesting and suggestive.

In my experiments, varying numbers of transputers were always connected in a ring pattern, with one transputer running a master program and the others running a common slave program (see Fig. 8.3). The ring is seen as an effective approach to parallelization of problems in which changes to one element of the data space depend on current states of many other elements (Wadsworth 1992: 47).[2]

A run begins with the master reading from a file and circulating to the slaves the statistics about English grammar used for evaluating analyses; these were fixed throughout my experiments, and will be discussed later. There follow one or more cycles each comprising the following sequence of activities:

- the user manually enters an input string in the form of a sequence of word-class codes, together with values for the various parameters determining an annealing schedule;
- all of these items are circulated to all processors;
- the system conducts a sequence of ten annealing runs on the input string using the given schedule, beginning each run with a different seed for the random-number generator;
- various statistics on the group of runs are computed, printed to screen, and manually recorded.

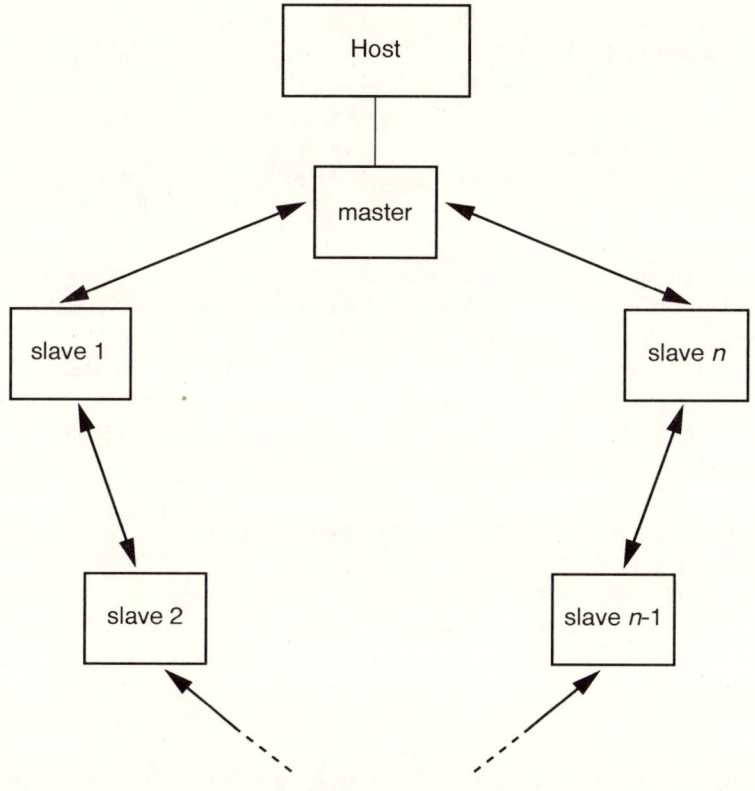

Figure 8.3 Configuration of processors for the parallel parsing experiments

The tree-evaluation function and annealing-schedule parameters used will be discussed shortly. First, let me explain how master and slaves interact during an annealing run.

Master and slaves each maintain a model of the current tree in the form of a tree-state as defined above. The partition assigned to a length-i segment is coded as a length-i bit-vector (that is, sequence of 1s and 0s) in which the initial position and at least one other position is filled by a 1, representing the beginning of a subsegment; thus the earlier example of the partition (3,5)(6)(7,8) for the segment (3,8) would be coded 100110. At the beginning of an annealing run master and slaves all start with an arbitrary initial tree-state in which each segment is assigned the label S ('sentence') and a bit-vector containing all 1s. Ownership of the segments is determined by partitioning the set of segments between the slaves in such a way as to approximately equalize the total 'load' (in a sense to be discussed) of the sets of segments assigned to different slaves. No segments are assigned to the master. The decision about which slave is assigned which segments is made by a principle intended to achieve a situation in which pairs of segments that are relatively likely to correspond to pairs of nodes in an immediate-domination relationship in the tree, and are hence highly relevant for the evaluation of one another's state-changes, are relatively likely to be assigned either to the same slave or to slaves near one another in the ring, so that delays in information transmission are minimized (but I believe there is room for improvement in this aspect of the algorithm).

The concept of segment 'load', which is also used to determine the relative proportions of its time which an individual slave devotes to working on the various segments assigned to it, was initially defined in terms of the number of alternative states available for a segment (i.e. roughly as $2^i H$, where i is segment length and H is the size of the nonterminal vocabulary from which the label is drawn).[3] Intuitively this seemed to be the appropriate way to ensure that the logical space of alternative labelled trees is searched 'fairly'. However, because this definition gave very large load differences between long and short segments, in practice it led to annealing runs in which processors failed to do any work at all on their shortest segments; therefore in the experiments reported I used a different definition of 'load' in terms of the number of alternative immediate changes of state available to a segment – since a move involves changing the label and one bit of the partition vector, the load of a length-i segment becomes roughly iH.[4]

After these initialization processes are complete, the master records the time and repeats the following cycle of actions until attaining a freezing criterion:

- it pauses for a fixed delay (the length of which was input as one of the annealing parameters);

- after the delay it transmits its current tree-state to slave n;
- it waits until slave 1 transmits to it slave 1's current tree-state, which it uses to replace its own tree-state;
- it evaluates its tree-state and checks for attainment of the freezing criterion.

If the criterion is not attained, the master begins another cycle by pausing for the fixed delay. If the freezing criterion is attained, the master transmits to slave n a termination signal, waits to receive a copy of this signal from slave 1, records the time lapse since the beginning of the run, and delivers its current tree-state as the output from the run.[5]

Turning to the slave processors: they operate in two modes, choice between which is governed by an Occam PRI ALT construction: that is, one type of action is executed whenever an appropriate message is waiting on an inward channel, otherwise the other action is executed.

If the channel from the next-higher-numbered slave (in the case of slave n, from the master) contains a tree-state, the slave copies into its own tree-state the lines representing segments it does not own, ignoring the information about its own segments (for which its own tree-state is authoritative), and it then transmits its entire tree-state to the next-lower-numbered slave (in the case of slave 1, to the master). Thus information about all segments circulates in due course to all processors. If the same incoming channel contains the termination signal, the slave passes this on. Whenever neither type of signal is waiting, the slave repeatedly executes annealing steps.

An annealing step is carried out as follows. The slave selects one of its 'own' segments randomly with a probability proportional to segment load. It selects a label randomly with equal probabilities from the nonterminal vocabulary (provided the selected segment is not the root, whose label is never changed), and selects one place randomly with equal probabilities from the set of places in the segment's bit-vector where change is allowable (the first bit must always be 1, and each bit-vector must contain at least two 1s – thus no bit may be changed in a two-word segment). The value of the tree that would result from making the change is compared with the value of the current tree, by reference to the slave's current tree-state. In the usual simulated-annealing manner, if the change would improve or leave unaltered the tree-value, it is adopted, whereas if it would worsen the tree-value by a quantity d, then it is adopted with probability $\exp\left(\frac{-d}{T}\right)$.

The annealing schedule specifies:

- the delay, r, between the master's completion of one communication cycle and initiation of the next (see above);
- an initial temperature, T_0, at which each slave begins an annealing run;

168   Evolutionary Language Understanding

- a cooling factor, c ($0 \ll c < 1$): a slave reduces its current temperature T by multiplying by c after each v annealing steps, where v is the length of the input;
- a freezing criterion, f (a large integer): the master terminates an annealing run after f consecutive occasions when an updating of its tree-state received from slave 1 fails to alter tree-value.

An aspect of the algorithm which I altered in the light of experience relates to changes to segments that do not contribute to the tree defined by a slave's current tree-state (cf. the non-bold lines in Fig. 8.1 above). Originally slaves chose segments to change without reference to whether or not the segments were currently 'in the tree': any change to a segment not in the tree would naturally leave tree-value unaffected and hence would automatically be accepted. I took this to be a useful way of encouraging wide-ranging exploration of the solution space. But, in practice, it had an undesirable effect: with a reasonably long input, such a low proportion of segments are 'in the tree' at any given time, and hence such a small proportion of potential tree-changes have a chance of being rejected, that lowering annealing temperature has only a minimal effect on the rate at which the tree changes.

To cure this problem, I modified the algorithm so that, when generating a move, a slave selects among only those of its segments currently contributing to the tree (according to the information in its own tree-state), unless it has no such segments, in which case it chooses among all its segments. This cured the problem just mentioned, and seemed *prima facie* to work well. I suspect, however, that this version of the algorithm may involve problems whose effects are less obvious. Note for instance that the root segment is always 'in the tree', so the slave which owns that segment will never change any of its other segments unless they happen also to be in the tree – this may well entail undesirable biases in the pattern of exploration of the solution space.[6]

The experimental arrangement described here is clearly not an ideal way of harnessing multiple processors to the tree-optimization task. Most obviously, the division of labour between master and slaves is illogical. For much of the duration of an annealing run the master is idle, coming into action only periodically to initiate updating cycles and monitor progress; there is no reason why the master should not be assigned a share of segments and play its own part in the random-walk process. But this is of little importance for my central goal of discovering whether dividing knowledge about tree-structure up between separate processors degrades optimization performance. (In the experiments discussed here I was interested in comparing only *relative* speed of solution-optimization as between single-processor and multi-processor configurations. I made no attempt to maximize absolute speed, and the coding undoubtedly contains many serious inefficiencies.) Probably more significant is the fact that updating information travels only in one direction – this may well make the multi-processor configurations less efficient than they need be relative to the single-processor configuration. Originally I had intended information to travel in both directions round the ring, with slaves selecting which direction to send information about a particular segment in a manner intended to ensure that each slave is most up-to-date about segments most likely to be relevant for its own annealing decisions. Because this plan involved some programming complexities, notably in connection with simultaneous arrival at a processor of information from two directions, I simplified things by adopting the crude system of clockwise-only circulation; the anticlockwise direction was used only for a trivial purpose in the setting-up stage of program runs, before annealing begins.

Again, it should be possible to improve performance by arranging for slaves to transmit information simultaneously rather than sequentially, and not to stop annealing while they respond to communications. In these and other ways the experiment described here seems with hindsight rather poorly designed. One might feel, though, that if even this experiment succeeds in delivering interesting results, the outlook is that much more promising for improved future implementations of the algorithm.

If my experimental design was crude, the same is even more true of the grammatical analysis scheme and analysis-evaluation function used in the experiments. These were essentially the same as in the pilot annealing parser discussed in ch. 3 above, so that the analytic scheme reduced the subtleties of the Treebank annotation to 30 terminal and 14 nonterminal symbols. A tree was evaluated by multiplying together (not averaging) the conditional probabilities of its various non-root node labels given their preceding-sister and mother labels, with unobserved transitions replaced by an arbitrary low positive probability (the resulting analysis value being expressed as a negative logarithm). Clearly, although this crude evaluation function does sometimes succeed in preferring the correct analysis of an input to all rival analyses, a parser based on it can be no more than a toy; the time constraints on my research made it quite impractical to use a more realistic metric.

Nevertheless, as a testbed for exploring the parallel tree-optimizing algorithm I believe this crude scheme is not worthless. Finding the lowest-valued labelled tree for an input string can be seen as a computational exercise in its own right (and one which, as we have seen, is likely to have applications in areas other than natural language grammatical analysis); we can ask how successfully that exercise is carried out by configurations of different numbers of processors, without considering the question whether the lowest-valued analyses coincide with analyses that are linguistically correct. Furthermore, while the evaluation function used is quite inadequate, it surely bears at least a distant family resemblance to the kinds of evaluation function needed in serious natural language parsers, and if so one may hope that favourable results from the simple function offer a hint, at least, that good results may be available from an implementation incorporating a more complex and adequate function.

Before leaving the issue of the analytic scheme, one special point must be mentioned, about singular nodes. The system of representing trees by assignments of labels and partitions to segments cannot handle singular nodes, which would require contradictory label assignments for a single segment. We have seen that, in the Treebank scheme, most singular nodes occur immediately above terminal nodes, and in this position their occurrence and labelling (in terms of the crude label-set used in these experiments) is fully predictable from the labels of the nodes above and below; for instance, if a leaf node labelled 'plural noun' is a constituent of a node labelled 'finite clause', there must be an intermediate singular node labelled 'noun phrase'. In the algorithm under discussion, the space of alternative labelled trees explored by the random-walk mechanism includes no trees with singular nodes. Whenever a tree reached in the random walk is evaluated, it is first translated into a format which permits singular nodes to be represented, and predictable singular nodes immediately above leaves are inserted; when the tree is then evaluated, the value of these nodes is derived from a table of frequencies of mother-label/unique-daughter-label pairings, rather than in terms of conditional transition frequencies. The random walk then continues from the tree in segment-assignment format, without singular nodes. As in the case of APRIL Mk 2, the residual problem of singular nodes that do not immediately dominate terminal nodes, which are relatively infrequent in the Treebank scheme but are not straightforwardly predictable, was ignored: I avoided submitting to the system any input whose correct analysis included such a node. (This applied to 11 of a random sample of 100 sentences from the LOB Corpus.)

Experimental Results

In order to compare the results of distributing knowledge about the current tree among varying numbers of processors, I used rings containing respectively one, four, and sixteen slave transputers in addition to the master transputer. With one slave, full knowledge of current tree structure resides on a single processor, and the master has no function other than to determine when the freezing criterion is attained. For comparative purposes it was clearly important for one of the experimental conditions to be a single-slave configuration (in which knowledge was not split up among separate processors), but it happened that the smallest domain available to me contained three rather than two transputers; rather than cutting one of the processors out of the ring it was simpler to include all three and arrange for slave 1 to own all the segments, with slave 2's activity confined to immediately relaying any communication transmitted between master and slave 1, and this is what I did. I do not believe this will have significantly affected the experimental results, though the possibility should be borne in mind.

In comparing the processing power available in the various experimental conditions, below, I have counted just the active slaves, and treated the resources available in the three conditions as related by the ratio 1:4:16. This seems to me appropriate, since the master transputers do none of the work; but, if the reader queries this way of comparing performance, I would point out that it is a conservative approach, since it implies that multi-processor configurations are efficient only if they exceed the performance of a single-processor configuration by a larger factor than would be required if resources were seen as related in the ratio 2:5:17 or 3:5:17.

We have seen that an annealing schedule is defined by four parameters: initial temperature T_0, cooling factor c, freezing criterion f, and the delay r between the master's receipt of an updating report from slave 1 and transmission of a report to slave n. Normally with simulated annealing there is little interest in varying T_0 (provided this is high enough to allow the full solution space to be explored, raising it higher merely incurs extra processing to no purpose); and in experiments with early versions of this system varying r did not seem to yield interesting results. For my experiments with the final version, therefore, I always used the fixed values of 50.0 for T_0 and 1000 ticks of the low-priority transputer timer for r (one tick = 64 microseconds), and concentrated on varying c and f in order to get five schedules which would cause given inputs to be processed with diverse degrees of thoroughness. The values $f = 300$ and $c = 0.975$ (i.e. $1 - 0.025^{1.0}$) seemed to give reasonable results, so I used these values for the 'middle' schedule and took the values $f = 225$, $c = 0.93713$ $(1 - 0.025^{0.75})$, and $f = 150$, $c = 0.842$ $(1 - 0.025^{0.5})$, to give less intensive annealing schedules, and the values $f = 450$, $c = 0.99006$ $(1 - 0.025^{1.5})$, and $f = 600$, $c = 0.99605$ $(1 - 0.025^{2.0})$, to give more intensive schedules.

Thus a full set of experimental data-points for any input string required a total of 150 annealing runs (3 processor configurations × 5 schedules × 10 runs with different random seeds); depending on input length and annealing schedule, an individual run lasted between 20 seconds and 90 minutes. I was able to collect complete sets of results for only four input sentences of diverse lengths, though I also have partial data on several other inputs.

(With hindsight I believe it might have been better to use a wider spread of c and f values, and to have tried higher values for T_0, but either of these decisions would have meant completing fewer runs in the time available.) All of the four inputs came from 'Press' sections of the LOB Corpus; in my work they were identified as Inputs 1, 3, 7, and 9. They ran as follows (omitting two pairs of inverted commas occurring in the original texts – cf. ch. 4, note 8):

Input 1: *Thus it becomes an offence punishable with imprisonment for anyone who publishes a report likely to cause alarm or prejudicial to public safety.* (LOB A02.083; 24 words.)

Input 3: *He covered his face with his free hand when the charge was read.* (LOB A12.205; 14 words.)

Input 7: *Mr. W. J. Daniel (Worcester) urged that it was vitally necessary to have longer breaks from work because_of the stress and strain of working 50 weeks in the year.* (LOB A27.021; 32 words. Our scheme treats *because_of* as an idiom equivalent to a single word.)

Input 9: *If, however, the Soviet Government seems determined to swallow up West Berlin then there is little for the West to do except stand firm.* (LOB B02.051; 27 words.)

The first question I was interested in, whether splitting up-to-date knowledge about current tree-state between separate processors would destroy the tendency of the annealing process to move towards better analyses, was soon answered in the negative. Indeed, for a given input and annealing schedule the result at freezing from the four-slave configuration was commonly better than that from the single-slave configuration, and the result from the sixteen-slave configuration better still. (With the annealing schedules I used, a run did not normally locate the global optimum, although sometimes that did happen. For my purpose of comparing the performance of different numbers of processors it was not desirable that runs should usually reach the global optimum, since this would have offered no basis for measuring comparative success. As it was, I could measure how close a given run came to the optimum.)

The tendency of the system to reach better outputs with more processors was not as surprising as it sounds, because a run over a given input with given annealing-schedule settings usually lasted longer with more processors – it was rather as if splitting knowledge about the current solution between processors acted like a constant increment to the annealing temperature.[7] An ordinary single-processor annealing system is expected to find better analyses with more processing. So, in order to compare the performance of multi-processor and single-processor configurations in a meaningful way, I had to develop a method of measuring the trade-offs between processing time and output values so as to determine whether or not the extra resources of the multi-processor configurations were being efficiently exploited.[8]

Here I met an unforeseen snag relating to the way output values were counted. Since simulated annealing in general gives different results starting from different random seeds for the same input and annealing schedule, it seemed essential to look at *mean* output values for sets of runs with different seeds, rather than to assume that the result from a single run was representative; originally my program simply recorded the arithmetic mean of the values of the outputs from each set of ten runs. But this figure is not very significant when one considers that the task of approaching the global minimum becomes harder as one gets closer. Variance among the set of ten figures tended to be considerably higher in experimental conditions involving more processors; taken together with the 'diminishing returns' aspect of the optimizing process, just referred to, this had the consequence that mean output values were misleadingly poor for multi-processor configurations. The scores to be averaged ought not to be raw tree-values but should be points on a logarithmic scale of closeness to the minimum, so that proper credit could be given for tiny improvements in value from a point that is already close to the minimum, where even small improvements are hard to find.

But there were two difficulties with this. One was that some runs did reach the minimum. The situation is not analogous to dart-playing, where the surface of the target is continuous and even the best-aimed dart will diverge to some finite extent from the mathematical centre. Differences between labelled trees are discrete; if a run reaches the global optimum, its distance from the optimum is zero and the logarithm of zero is an infinite quantity that cannot be averaged with other numbers.

And perhaps a greater problem was that I did not in general know what the optimal analysis of an input, or its value, was. I knew the correct analyses of the inputs, and their values, but we have seen that – because of the crudity of the evaluation function used – an input would often have an incorrect analysis whose value was lower (sometimes substantially lower) than the value assigned to the correct analysis. For input 1, for instance, the correct analysis had the value 100.6, but experiments with early versions of the system threw up incorrect analyses valued at 84.2 and 88.7. There was no way I could systematically discover the lowest-valued analysis for a given input (if there existed a method to do this, it would not be sensible to use stochastic optimization in this domain). Thus it seemed necessary to measure performance in terms of distance from an unknowable position.

The solution I adopted to both these problems was extremely *ad hoc*; but it allowed me to express relative performance of configurations with different numbers of processors in a fashion that seems meaningful. Before I ran the final experiments reported here, I had already made many annealing runs with earlier versions of the system over each example used as an input to the final version, and I had recorded the best analysis-values found for each input. For each input I thus had a 'best known value' which was either the lowest value achieved on earlier runs, or the value of the correct analysis, whichever was lower. I then defined a notional 'ideal' value for each input to be 5% below its best known value, allowing for the possibility of analyses better than the best known. For the runs analysed below, I recorded the output of a run as:

$$\log_{10}\left(\frac{\text{value achieved at freezing} - \text{ideal value}}{\text{ideal value}}\right)$$

and I took the mean of ten such figures as representing the performance of a given processor configuration on an input with a given annealing schedule.

Figure 8.4 displays the set of performance figures for three processor configurations and five annealing schedules on one sentence, input 1, which is close to the average length for the Treebank. Each point represents a set of ten runs with one processor configuration (denoted by the shape of the point) and schedule; the vertical scale represents mean output value calculated as just explained, and the horizontal scale shows the logarithm of the mean run duration, in ticks.[9]

Whichever of the three processor configurations one looks at, the corresponding set of five points in Fig. 8.4 fall on a broadly northwest-to-southeast trend: in other words, annealing runs which last longer are tending to produce better results, as they should. But furthermore, the line to which the four-slave points approximate is somewhat below that for the single-slave points, and the sixteen-slave points are well below the four-slave points. So, adding processors improves results.

Fig. 8.5 re-presents the information of Fig. 8.4, replacing the logarithmic time scale of that Figure with a logarithmic scale of ticks × slaves, in other words it measures the total quantity of processing done on a run. This suggests, very remarkably, that sixteen-slave runs tend to be *more* successful, relative to runs with fewer processors, than one could predict from the amount of extra processing done: it seems that dividing the task among sixteen processors has yielded an advantage over and above the fact that each part of the tree receives sixteen times as much work.

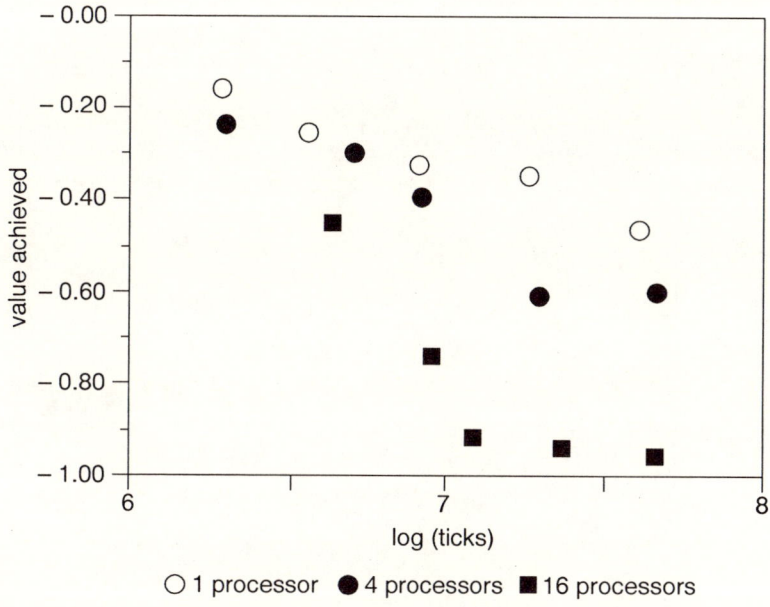

Figure 8.4 Input 1, value against time

I should say at once that this outcome on input 1 involved a measure of beginner's luck. For contrast, Figs 8.6 and 8.7 give plots on the same basis as Figs 8.4 and 8.5 respectively for input 3. The points for the single-processor configuration show little tendency to group round a northwest-to-southeast axis, and the sixteen-slave points even show a reverse trend. Input 7 gave results as unsuccessful as those for input 3; input 9 gave good results, though not as dramatically good as in the case of input 1. Rather than continuing to display results in graphic form, in what follows I shall represent the results for all four inputs in precise numerical form.

For each of the four inputs, I used regression analysis to find the line of best fit for the five points representing single-slave runs over that input. Regression analysis yields a linear equation of the form $a + bt = C$, where t is (in this case) the logarithm of mean run-duration and C is mean output value calculated as discussed above; and it gives a correlation coefficient r showing how well individual points are predicted by the equation – if the points all fall close to a straight line, r is close to either 1 or −1 (the latter in our case, because value *falls* as run-duration *rises*), while if r is close to zero

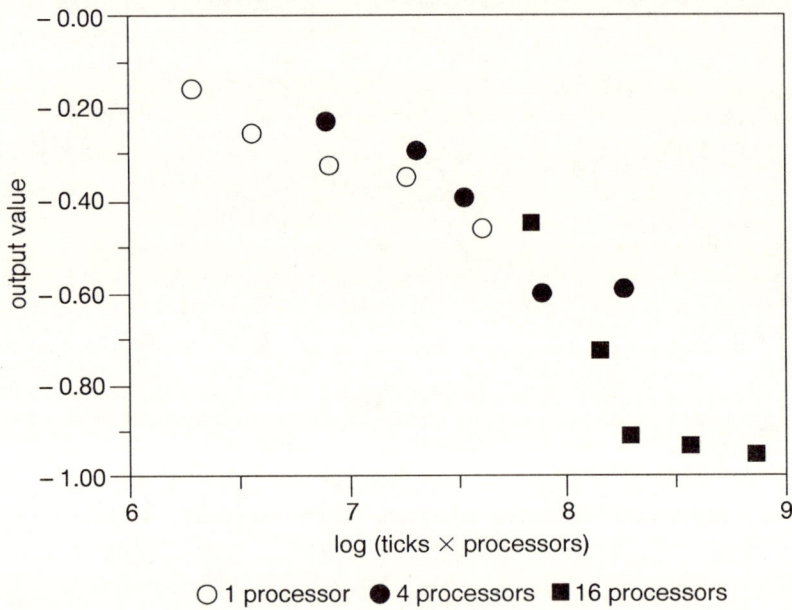

Figure 8.5 Input 1, value against processing

then the points are not close to a straight line, so that the values of *a* and *b* are fairly meaningless. For our purposes the constant term *a* is of little interest, but the regression coefficient *b* is important as representing the slope of the line which fits the points: if *b* is close to zero the line is nearly horizontal, meaning that increasing the quantity of processing in an annealing run is failing to improve the results achieved, while a large negative *b* represents a steep gradient showing that analysis-value improves greatly with additional processing.

The values of *a*, *b*, and *r* for my four inputs are:

	length in words	a	b	r
Input 1	24	1.14	−0.21	−0.98
Input 3	14	0.79	−0.08	−0.61
Input 7	32	0.64	−0.10	−0.97
Input 9	27	1.02	−0.20	−0.98

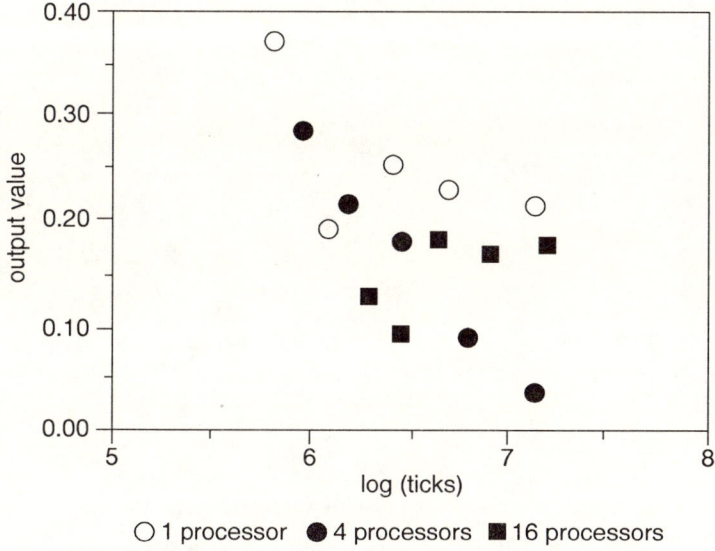

Figure 8.6 Input 3, value against time

With the shortest input, r is relatively close to zero, corresponding to the fact that the single-slave points in Fig. 8.6 are scattered in a non-linear fashion; in so far as there is a linear tendency, it is close to the horizontal. In other words, the strategy of optimization by annealing gives largely random results with input 3, a fact which I suspect has to do with its shortness – the idea that an annealing parser is likely to be most successful with long inputs was already discussed on p. 39 above, and the crudity of the tree-evaluation metric used in the present experiments may well exaggerate the disadvantage suffered by short inputs. Each of the other three inputs has r close to -1, but for the longest input the slope is again close to the horizontal: in other words, increasing the annealing effort yields only small improvements in analysis value, probably because successful analysis of this particular input depends heavily on sophistications omitted from the crude evaluation function used. Inputs 1 and 9 on the other hand have healthily large negative b, and r close to -1.

It seems, then, that 1 and 9 are inputs with which the single-slave version of my annealing system can deal relatively successfully despite its crudity, while inputs 3 and 7 are relatively intractable for one reason or another. Bearing this in mind, let us now try to be precise about how far

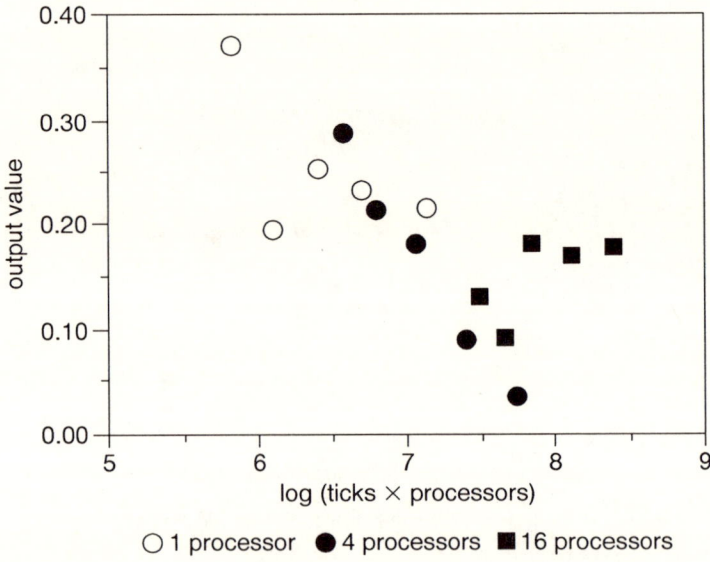

Figure 8.7 Input 3, value against processing

the multi-slave configurations succeeded in exploiting the extra processing power at their disposal.

The term *linearity* is used for the extent to which multiple processors yield a proportional reduction in time needed to complete a task on a single processor. A perfectly linear n-processor implementation of an algorithm takes $1/n$th as long to execute a given task as a single-processor algorithm would take (assuming all processors are alike). We can use the lines of best fit for the single-slave configuration to produce a numerical measure of linearity. If an n-slave run ($n > 1$) over an input on a given schedule has a mean duration t_n and yields an analysis with value C, we can compare t_n with the expected duration t_1 to achieve an analysis with the same value C using a single slave, as predicted by the line of best fit for the input. Then we may define the degree of linearity of the n-slave configuration with respect to the input as $\log_n \left(\frac{t_1}{T_n} \right)$.

A perfectly linear implementation will thus have degree of linearity 1, while an implementation in which processing takes the same time with n slaves as with one slave will have linearity 0. An implementation can have negative linearity, if adding processors causes a task to take longer than is needed with a single processor; and linearity can be greater than 1 if moving from one to n processors increases speed by a greater factor than n. This last would normally, I think, be seen as an abstract mathematical possibility unlikely to be realized, but we have seen that just this does seem to have happened in the case of the sixteen-slave implementation with input 1.

I computed linearity figures for each of the five data-points for the four-slave and sixteen-slave configurations with respect to the four inputs. The means of the various sets of five linearity figures are:

input	slaves	mean linearity
1	4	0.80
1	16	1.73★
3	4	1.74
3	16	0.83
7	4	0.07
7	16	−0.49
9	4	0.26
9	16	0.35

The linearity figures for input 7 are very bad. For input 3 they look extremely good; but we have seen that the correlation coefficient is so small in the case of input 3 that the line of best fit is more or less meaningless, and it follows that the linearity figures, which are derived from that line, are equally meaningless. I would not pretend that the linearity figures quoted for input 3 tell us anything at all. On the other hand, the figures for the two 'tractable' inputs, 1 and 9, are all positive; remarkably, for each of these inputs the sixteen-slave figure is considerably higher than the four-slave figure, and more remarkably still, as we saw earlier, the sixteen-slave figure for input 1 is far above 1.

A Provisional Conclusion

My tentative conclusion is a cautiously optimistic one. When a task is resistant to single-processor annealing it is surely unsurprising and unworrying that parallelizing the task fails to help. It is well known that successful annealing requires an evaluation function and move-generating function which induce a favourable geometry in the solution space; I knew in advance that the evaluation function used in the experiments reported here was not much good, and I guess that the particular properties of inputs 3 and 7 happen to interact particularly unfavourably with this crude function. It is to avoid these problems that the (sequential) APRIL3 project has developed a far more sophisticated evaluation function. (APRIL practice also suggests ways in which the move-generating function used in the present experiments could be improved.) What I did not know before doing the present experiments was that, in cases where single-processor annealing does succeed, parallel annealing works better, and in some cases considerably better.

Clearly the results reported here, which are distilled from just 600 annealing runs in all, can offer no more than a hint about the potential of parsing by parallel tree-optimization. To assess the technique seriously it will be necessary to anneal a much wider range of inputs, using sophisticated evaluation and move-generating functions and more intensive annealing schedules which vary r and T_0 as well as c and f; and other changes will also be appropriate in the experimental arrangements: notably, rather than comparing multiple-processor performance with an implementation of the same algorithm on a single processor, it should be compared with an implementation on the single processor of an annealing algorithm designed to be efficient as a sequential system without regard to the demands of parallel processing. The present findings do, however, offer a basis for thinking that larger-scale research of this kind is worth trying.

Notes

1. On inherently parallel languages v. parallel extensions of sequential languages, see e.g. Wadsworth 1992: 45–6. A competitor to Occam as a language incorporating parallelism from the start is Ada, but even Ada can be described as fundamentally a sequential language with somewhat complex provisions to allow concurrency; on Occam v. Ada see e.g. Burns 1988: ch. 11.
2. I suspect that it might ultimately be preferable to connect the processors in a pattern more closely related to the tree structures with which the computation is concerned, but the limited time available for experimentation meant that many subtleties had to be sacrificed to simplicity of programming.
3. More exactly, $(2^{i-1})H$ for a non-root segment, since the first and at least one other bit must be 1, and 2^{i-1} for the root segment, whose label is always S.
4. More exactly, $(i-1)$ – for a non-root segment and $i-1$ for the root segment.
5. As it stands the circulation of a termination signal serves no purpose (but I am describing the experiments I actually ran rather than the perfectly logical experiments I might have run). At one stage I had planned to arrange for the output to incorporate segment-changes made by slaves between their last previous transmission and receipt of the termination signal.
6. Chris Booth has suggested a modification whereby slaves decide at each step to

choose either an 'in-tree' or an 'out-of-tree' segment by reference to a probability which would be input as an additional annealing-schedule parameter. With more time I should have liked to implement this idea.
7. Interestingly, this effect whereby more processors gave longer annealing runs was much weaker for annealing schedules towards the more intensive than towards the less intensive end of the range of schedules used.
8. Strictly, there was an alternative way forward. I could have abandoned the system of freezing after f changeless updates and used elapsed time itself as the freezing criterion, forcing runs on different processor configurations to last for identical durations. But this approach seems alien to the essence of simulated annealing; it could cut processing off while a high proportion of moves were still being accepted, or immediately after an adverse move had happened to be accepted when few moves were being made. I did not consider it seriously.
9. The first set of ten runs with the sixteen-processor configuration at the most intensive annealing schedule gave a point (7.652, −0.696). Because this seemed anomalous and the experimental arrangements involved a great deal of manual intervention creating the possibility of errors (for instance, the input string had to be typed in full for each set of ten runs), I ran this set of runs again and got the point shown at the lower right of Fig. 8.4, namely (7.654, −0.952); and since this was compatible with the general trend I discarded the earlier point. However, the random-number seeds will have differed on the two sets of ten runs, and it is possible that the large difference in mean output values is attributable to this rather than to manual error.

*If the discarded point discussed in footnote 9 were used rather than its replacement, this figure would fall to 1.53.

9 Epilogue

The preceding chapters have offered a snapshot of a continuing research programme that at the time of writing has some while to run before the present project terminates. It would be premature at this point to state a 'conclusion' in the sense of a final assessment of the value of the technique of parsing by annealing. The APRIL3 project is an ambitious one, being the first time we have attempted to make our probabilistic system carry out the full task of moving from 'raw' written text to grammatical analysis (and to execute the analysis using an automatically generated language model). I cannot surmise at this point how successful the finished system is destined to be; I certainly do not expect it to solve all the problems of natural language parsing.

But it is possible to make suggestions about where APRIL-like systems are likely to be useful, and where classical compiler-like techniques may be more appropriate. When we began work in the 1980s, the NLP field was characterized by a rather unhealthy dogmatism. Some proponents of classical approaches would not hear of corpus-based or statistical techniques having anything to contribute, and we corpus linguists for our part had to defend our minority position fairly vigorously for fear of being shouldered aside altogether. A decade later, the situation is far more relaxed. Probably everyone now recognizes that both styles of work are needed. (Gazdar 1995 offers a survey of the way the two approaches to NLP have been growing together.) Although compiler-like natural language analysis systems continue to 'fall over' on many inputs, some of them are beginning to deliver remarkable results on those inputs which they can handle. While working as a consultant on assessment of NLP products I have been particularly impressed, for instance, by SRI International's Core Language Engine (Alshawi 1992); although this does require its inputs to consist of careful, polished prose, it has proved capable of delivering analyses for a fair proportion of such inputs (including moderately complex sentences) that contain quite subtle representations of their logic, of a kind that go well beyond anything likely to be delivered by a statistics-based system in the foreseeable future.

On the other hand, compiler-like analysis systems remain fragile with respect to 'messy' language. If inputs are not guaranteed to consist of perfectly well-formed sentences, and particularly where the application requires surface, but not necessarily deeper, logical analysis, then probabilistic techniques are likely to be specially useful. Where parsing is applied in order to constrain the output of a speech-recognition system, for instance, so that word-hypotheses which are satisfactory in terms of the relationship between speech wave and dictionary information are nevertheless eliminated when they cannot be fitted into a plausible grammatical structure, it seems quite unlikely that a compiler-like system would be suitable.

It is ironic that our APRIL research even now is based entirely on written English, because it is in speech applications that our kind of system is likely to come into its own; and speech applications are almost certainly the most important area of NLP in terms of potential economic value. The reason why APRIL research has not yet been able to work with spoken language relates to an outstanding gap in the range of research resources available internationally: we have very little material allowing us to study patterns of usage in spoken language. Whereas the Brown Corpus of written English has been available since the 1960s, the first machine-readable corpus of spoken English, the electronic version of the London-Lund Corpus, was published only in 1980; for American English, plans to develop a speech corpus were announced as recently as 1991 (Chafe *et al.* 1991). And although the London-Lund Corpus includes remarkably complete information about phonological details, neither London-Lund nor most other spoken-language corpora available to date have included any annotation at all relating to grammatical properties of words or sentence structures. (One exception is the Polytechnic of Wales Corpus, cf. Fawcett 1980, though this is very specialized, containing only the speech of young children in a single locality, annotated in terms of a rather unusual scheme of grammatical analysis.)

The problem is not merely that people have not produced collections of analysed samples of adult speech. There are no generally recognized standards in terms of which such analyses might be done. When linguists set out to record the grammatical structure of written language, individuals will differ in various details of the annotations they produce, but there is considerable consensus about the grouping of words into tagmas and the chief categories of word and tagma that ought to be distinguished. But when it comes to the distinctive structural features of informal spoken language, such as speech repairs or hesitation phenomena, there is no tradition giving even vague guidance about how to integrate these things into representations of the grammatical structures of utterances. My group has developed some initial proposals in this area (Sampson 1995: ch. 6), and has produced small quantities of analyses in conformity with these proposals, but what we have done is no more than a beginning.

Until we have sizeable samples of spoken language, structurally annotated in accordance with standards that cover these distinctive speech phenomena as well as the ordinary grammatical considerations shared by both linguistic modes, there is no possibility of extracting the statistics needed to apply probabilistic techniques to spoken inputs. But then, development of structurally-annotated speech corpora is a priority need for many other purposes too. I think my suggestion, above, that the richest prizes to be gained from NLP technology will accrue from applications dealing with the spoken mode is not seriously controversial. But it is very difficult for the research community to begin to develop such applications while it has no adequate source of hard information about just what actually happens in speech. Probably everyone who thinks about it suspects that the editing phenomena of informal speech – the fact that people frequently change tack or substitute one form of wording for another in mid-utterance – are likely to create special difficulties for applications which need to analyse the logic of utterances; but we need to discover how large those difficulties are, whether they fall into predictable patterns or are wholly diverse, how their incidence varies with speech situation, and so forth.

When such data resources become available, I expect parsing by stochastic optimization to become most attractive for spoken inputs. There are two reasons to say that. The fact that this technique is relatively robust in face of messy structures is one. The other is that, in my experience, spoken language seems to contain much less than written language of another phenomenon which, when it does occur, is always likely to be better handled by compiler-like than by optimizing parsers: namely, structures which are statistically unusual but in terms of grammatical rules are nevertheless legal.

In the years when linguistic theory was most heavily dominated by the compilation paradigm, its writings were sometimes preoccupied by structures of this kind. Students were often puzzled to understand why even elementary linguistics courses spent a great deal of time on examples such as:

John kept himself from expecting himself to prevent himself from believing himself to be proud of himself.

That for Icarus to fly is unnatural is obvious.

Galileo and adolescents scanned the skies and scorned the schools respectively.

(taken from a student textbook on transformational grammar (Jacobs & Rosenbaum 1968: 241, 245, 255)). Newcomers to the subject often felt that examples like these represented a false extrapolation from straightforward, plausible forms of words to other forms of words that share certain abstract logical properties with them, but are not thereby entitled to be treated as genuinely part of the language. Theoretical linguists suggested that conformance with grammatical rules was the only significant criterion for membership of a language, and the only criterion with which a scientific account of a language could realistically hope to deal; but others felt that grammaticality was not enough – that users of a language in practice do not press the rules of its grammar to their limits, and that a natural language (as opposed to a formal language-like system) should be seen as a system governed partly by grammaticality considerations but partly by other regularities that are equally significant in human terms and equally open to analysis.

Let me give a concrete example. In terms of logical rules of grammar, the subject slot in an English clause can be filled by a noun phrase; and wording that realizes the category 'noun phrase' can be either definite or indefinite. In practice, indefinite noun phrases rarely function as subjects (which is one reason for the oddity of the *Galileo and adolescents* example above – *adolescents* is indefinite); but this is not a rigid grammatical rule: it is a statistical regularity of usage, and a proportion of normal, acceptable real-life clauses will violate it.

Some of the examples quoted as 'well-formed' in the theoretical linguistics literature have seemed implausible with respect to either language mode. But in so far as language users do sometimes press rules of grammar to their logical but unnatural conclusion, this happens, I believe, much more in writing than in speech. That suggests that it is in the automatic analysis of written text that there is the greatest need for compiler-like parsers, which analyse purely in terms of grammatical rules but are capable of detecting subtle, rarely encountered implications of those rules; whereas statistical optimizing techniques may be more useful for spoken-language analysis, where usage is more consistently limited to high-frequency patterns but the patterns relate to diverse considerations, not just to grammatical rules.

Ideally, one would like to find ways of exploiting the strengths of both optimizing and compiler-like techniques within one system – though at present it is easier to express that ideal than to formulate concrete proposals about how such a hybrid system would operate.[1] Researchers have spent several decades discovering how much it is possible to achieve using automatic parsers of the 'pure' compiler type, and they have some impressive results to show. Parsing by statistical optimization is a far newer technique, so at this stage I believe our strategy of seeing how far one can get with a pure version of this approach, using a system that knows nothing about the rules of English grammar, is an appropriate one. Once we know more about what each approach can and cannot do, we may be better placed to see how to combine them.

I said earlier (p. 39) that spoken language analysis seems ultimately to require systems that can run continuously and accept an indefinitely lengthy stream of input, discovering any structural boundaries in the stream, including those of the largest units to be recognized, as part of its analytic activity. To this end I believe that, if the APRIL technique is taken further than will be possible during our current project, a high priority for future development should be to move from the present 'batch processing' of separate sentences to the kind of 'continuous flow annealing' outlined on p. 58–9. Those of us involved in the APRIL programme have believed more or less from the start that this is the direction we ought to move in, and we suspect (because of considerations about natural language structure discussed by Marcus (1980) and those who have developed Marcus's ideas) that continuous-flow processing might even be easier for an annealing parser than the current technique of processing all the words of a large unit simultaneously.

With hindsight, it is not entirely clear why we have not yet tried it. Information technology research projects are like liners that cannot make large changes of direction quickly. Whether or not the performance of a continuous-flow annealing parser would be superior, conceptually the batch-processing system is simplest – so we began with that, and our work built up a momentum of its own. On the APRIL3 project the highest priorities have been to include the problem of resolving character-strings into tagged words, and, rather than developing a radically novel system, to implement the batch-processing type of system we have already explored in the form of a suite of software well enough engineered to be fit to distribute outside our group.

Once that is achieved, others may have their own ideas about how the technique can be exploited and improved. I hope they will.

Note

1. For recent moves in this direction, see e.g. papers in Carrasco & Oncina 1994, Voutilainen 1994.

References

Place of publication of books is given only when the publisher does not list a London office. Conference proceedings are cited in accordance with the format of the British Library *Index of Conference Proceedings*.

Aarts, E. & J. Korst 1989 *Simulated Annealing and Boltzmann Machines: A Stochastic Approach to Combinatorial Optimization and Neural Computing*. Wiley (Chichester).
Aarts, J. & T. van den Heuvel 1985 'Computational tools for the syntactic analysis of corpora'. *Linguistics* 23.303–35.
Aho, A. V. *et al.*, eds. 1974 *The Design and Analysis of Computer Algorithms*. Addison-Wesley.
Allwood, J. *et al.* 1990 'Speech management – on the non-written life of speech'. *Nordic Journal of Linguistics* 13.3–48.
Alshawi, H., ed. 1992 *The Core Language Engine*. MIT Press.
Altenberg, B. 1990 'Spoken English and the dictionary'. In Svartvik 1990.

Baker, J. K. 1979 'Trainable grammars for speech recognition'. In *Speech Communication – Sessions – 97th Meeting – Selected Preprints – Acoustical Society of America*. Cambridge (Mass.), June 1979.
Barnard, S. T. 1987 'Stereo matching by hierarchical, microcanonical annealing'. In *IJCAI 87 – 10th international joint conference on artificial intelligence – Papers – International Joint Conferences on Artificial Intelligence Inc.*, 2 vols. Milan, August 1987.
Basu, A. & L. N. Frazer 1990 'Rapid determination of the critical temperature in simulated annealing inversion'. *Science* 249.1409–12.
Black, E. *et al.* 1993 *Statistically-Driven Computer Grammars of English: The IBM/Lancaster Approach*. Rodopi (Amsterdam).
Bloomfield, L. 1933 *Language*. Holt.
Boehm, B. W. 1981 *Software Engineering Economics*. Prentice-Hall (Englewood Cliffs, N.J.).
Bounds, D. G. 1987 'New optimization methods from physics and biology'. *Nature* 329.215–19.
Bridle, J. S. & R. K. Moore 1984 'Boltzmann machines for speech pattern processing'. *Proceedings of the Institute of Acoustics* 6.315–22.
Briscoe, E. J. & J. Carroll 1996 'A probalistic LR parser of part-of-speech and punctuation labels'. In Jenny Thomas & M. H. Short, eds., *Using Corpora for Language Research*. Longman.
Burns, A. 1988 *Programming in Occam 2*. Addison-Wesley (Wokingham, Berks.).

Carrasco, R. C. & J. Oncina, eds. 1994 *Grammatical Inference and Applications*. Springer.
Černý, V. 1985 'Thermodynamical approach to the traveling salesman problem: an efficient simulation algorithm'. *Journal of Optimization Theory and Applications* 45.41–51.

Chafe, W. L. *et al.* 1991 'Towards a new corpus of spoken American English'. In Karin Aijmer & B. Altenberg, eds., *English Corpus Linguistics: Studies in Honour of Jan Svartvik*. Longman.
Chomsky, A. N. 1957 *Syntactic Structures*. Mouton ('s-Gravenhage).
Chomsky, A. N. 1963 'Formal properties of grammars'. In R. D. Luce, R. R. Bush, & E. Galanter, eds., *Handbook of Mathematical Psychology*, vol. 2. Wiley.
Chomsky, A. N. 1965 *Aspects of the Theory of Syntax*. MIT Press (Cambridge, Mass.).
Chomsky, A. N. 1980 *Rules and Representations*. Blackwell (Oxford).
Cox, D. R. & H. D. Miller 1965 *The Theory of Stochastic Processes*. Chapman & Hall.
Creutz, M. 1983 'Microcanonical Monte Carlo simulation'. *Physical Review Letters* 50.1411–14.

Davis, L., ed. 1987 *Genetic Algorithms and Simulated Annealing*. Pitman.

Ellegård, A. 1978 *The Syntactic Structure of English Texts*. Gothenburg Studies in English, 43.
Engelien, B. & R. McBryde 1991 *Natural Language Markets: Commercial Strategies*. Ovum Ltd.

Fawcett, R. P. 1980 'Language development in children 6–12: interim report'. *Linguistics* 18.953–8.
Fillmore, C. J. 1968 'The case for case'. In E. Bach & R.T. Harms, eds., *Universals in Linguistic Theory*. Holt, Rinehart and Winston.
Fillmore, C. J. *et al.* 1988 'Regularity and idiomaticity in grammatical constructions'. *Language* 64.501–38.
Fujisaki, T. 1984 'A stochastic approach to sentence parsing'. In *Computational linguistics – 10th International conference – Papers and programme – Association for Computational Linguistics* [Held in conjunction with the 22nd Annual Meeting of the Association for Computational Linguistics]. Stanford (Calif.), July 1984.

Gale, W. A. & K. W. Church 1994 'What is wrong with adding one?' In Nelleke Oostdijk & P. de Haan, eds., *Corpus-Based Research Into Language*, Rodopi (Amsterdam).
Gale, W. A. & G. R. Sampson 1996 'Good-Turing frequency estimation without tears'. To be in *Journal of Quantitative Linguistics*.
Garside, R. G. & F. A. Leech 1987 'The UCREL probabilistic parsing scheme'. In Garside *et al.* (1987).
Garside, R. G. *et al.*, eds. 1987 *The Computational Analysis of English: A Corpus-Based Approach*. Longman.
Gazdar, G. 1996 'Paradigm merger in natural language processing'. In R. Milner & I. Wand, eds., *Research Directions in Computer Science*. Cambridge University Press (Cambridge).
Gazdar, G. & C. Mellish 1989 *Natural Language Processing in Pop-11: An Introduction to Computational Linguistics*. Addison-Wesley (Wokingham, Berks.).
Geman, S. & D. Geman 1984 'Stochastic relaxation, Gibbs distributions, and the Bayesian restoration of images'. *IEEE Transactions on Pattern Analysis and Machine Intelligence*, PAMI-6.721–41.
Gibbons, A. & W. Rytter 1988 *Efficient Parallel Algorithms*. Cambridge University Press (Cambridge).
Gibbs, W. W. 1994 'Software's chronic crisis'. *Scientific American* September, 1994,

pp. 72–81.
Gill, S. 1958 'Parallel programming'. *The Computer Journal* 1.2–8.
Gleick, J. 1988 *Chaos: Making a New Science*. Sphere Books.
Goldfarb, C. F. 1990 *The SGML Handbook*. Clarendon Press (Oxford).
Good, I. J. 1953 'The population frequencies of species and the estimation of population parameters'. *Biometrika* 40.237–64.
Greene, J. & K. Supowit 1986 'Simulated annealing without rejected moves'. *IEEE Transactions on Computer-Aided Design*, CAD-5.221–8.
Grune, D. & C. J. H. Jacobs 1990 *Parsing Techniques: A Practical Guide*. Ellis Horwood (New York).

Hagège, C. 1976 *La grammaire générative: réflexions critiques*. Presses Universitaires de France (n.p.).
Hajek, B. 1988 'Cooling schedules for optimal annealing'. *Mathematics of Operations Research* 13.311–29.
Harris, R. 1995 *Enigma*. Hutchinson.
van Herwijnen, E. 1990 *Practical SGML*. Kluwer.
Higman, B. 1967 *A Comparative Study of Programming Languages*. Macdonald.
Hinsley, F. H. & A. Stripp, eds. 1993 *Codebreakers: The Inside Story of Bletchley Park*. Oxford University Press.
Hinton, G. E. & T. J. Sejnowski 1983 'Optimal perceptual inference'. In *Computer Vision and Pattern Recognition* – Conference – Papers – IEEE, Computer Society. Washington, D.C., June 1983.
Hoare, C. A. R. 1978 'Communicating sequential processes'. *Communications of the ACM* 21.666–77; reprinted in N. Gehani & A. D. McGettrick, eds., *Concurrent Programming*, Addison-Wesley (Wokingham, Berks.), 1988.
Hoare, C. A. R. 1985 *Communicating Sequential Processes*. Prentice-Hall International.
Hodges, A. 1983 *Alan Turing: The Enigma of Intelligence*. Burnett Books.
Holland, J. H. 1992 *Adaptation in Natural and Artificial Systems: An Introductory Analysis with Applications to Biology, Control, and Artificial Intelligence* (2nd ed.). MIT Press.
Holmes, J. N. 1988 *Speech Synthesis and Recognition*. Van Nostrand Reinhold (UK) Co. (Wokingham, Berks.).
Hornby, A. S. 1975 *A Guide to Patterns and Usage in English* (2nd ed.). Oxford University Press.
Howell, P. & K. Young 1991 'The use of prosody in highlighting alterations in repairs from unrestricted speech'. *Quarterly Journal of Experimental Psychology* 43A.733–58.
Huang, M. D. *et al.* 1987 'An efficient general cooling schedule for simulated annealing'. In *ICCAD 87* – 5th International conference on computer aided design – Selected papers – Institute of Electrical and Electronics Engineers, Circuits and Systems Society – Institute of Electrical and Electronics Engineers, Computer Society. Santa Clara (Calif.), November 1987.
Hutchins, W. J. & H. L. Somers 1992 *An Introduction to Machine Translation*. Academic Press.

Jacobs, R. A. & P. S. Rosenbaum 1968 *English Transformational Grammar*. Blaisdell Publishing Co.
JáJá, J. 1992 *An Introduction to Parallel Algorithms*. Addison-Wesley (Reading,

Mass.).

Johansson, S. 1986 *The Tagged LOB Corpus: Users' Manual*. Norwegian Computing Centre for the Humanities (Bergen).

Johansson, S. *et al.* 1991 'Working paper on spoken texts'. Report to Text Encoding Initiative working meeting, Myrdal, Norway, November 1991.

Johnson, M. E., ed. 1989 *Simulated Annealing (SA) & Optimization: Modern Algorithms with VLSI, Optimal Design, and Missile Defense Applications*. American Sciences Press (Columbus, Ohio); dated 1988 but published 1989.

Johnson, T. 1985 *Natural Language Computing: The Commercial Applications*. Ovum Ltd.

Johnson, T. & T. Durham 1986 *Parallel Processing: The Challenge of New Computer Architectures*. Ovum Ltd.

Katz, J. J. 1971 *The Underlying Reality of Language and Its Philosophical Import*. Harper & Row.

Kirkpatrick, S. *et al.* 1983 'Optimization by simulated annealing'. *Science* 220.671–80.

Knowles, G. & L. Lawrence 1987 'Automatic intonation assignment'. In Garside *et al.* 1987.

Knuth, D. E. 1968 *The Art of Computer Programming*, vol. 1. Addison-Wesley (Reading, Mass.).

van Laarhoven, P. J. M. & E. H. L. Aarts 1987 *Simulated Annealing: Theory and Applications*. Reidel (Dordrecht).

Labov, W. 1975 'Empirical foundations of linguistic theory'. In R. Austerlitz, ed., *The Scope of American Linguistics*. Peter de Ridder Press (Lisse).

Lakatos, I. 1976 *Proofs and Refutations: The Logic of Mathematical Discovery*. Cambridge University Press.

Leeds, H. D. & G. M. Weinberg 1961 *Computer Programming Fundamentals*. McGraw-Hill.

Levelt, W. J. M. 1983 'Monitoring and self-repair in speech'. *Cognition* 14.41–104.

Lundy, M. & A. Mees 1986 'Convergence of an annealing algorithm'. *Mathematical Programming* 34.111–24.

McInnes, F. R. *et al.* 1989 'Enhancement and optimisation of a speech recognition front end based on Hidden Markov Models'. In *Eurospeech 89* – 1st European biennial conference on speech communication and technology – Papers – European Speech Communication Association. Paris, September 1989.

Maegaard, Bente 1989 'EUROTRA: the machine translation project of the European Communities'. In J. A. Campbell & J. Cuena, eds., *Perspectives in Artificial Intelligence*, vol. 2. Ellis Horwood.

Marcus, M.P. 1980 *A Theory of Syntactic Recognition for Natural Language*. MIT Press.

Marcus, M. P. *et al.* 1993 'Building a large annotated corpus of English: the Penn Treebank'. *Computational Linguistics* 19.313–30.

Marshall, I. 1987 'Tag selection using probabilistic methods'. In Garside *et al.* 1987.

Metropolis, N. C. *et al.* 1953 'Equations of state calculations by fast computing machines'. *Journal of Chemical Physics* 21.1087–92.

Miclet, L. 1986 *Structural Methods in Pattern Recognition*. North Oxford Academic.

Mitton, R. 1986 'A partial dictionary of English in computer-usable form'. *Literary and Linguistic Computing* 1.214–15.

Moore, R. K. 1992 'User needs in speech research'. Unpublished paper delivered at the Workshop on European Textual Corpora, Pisa, January 1992.

Myers, G. 1991 'Politeness and certainty: the language of collaboration in an AI project'. *Social Studies of Science* 21.37–73.

Nunberg, G. 1990 *The Linguistics of Punctuation.* Center for the Study of Language and Information (Stanford, Calif.).

Obermeier, K. K. 1989 *Natural Language Processing Technologies in Artificial Intelligence: The Science and Industry Perspective.* Ellis Horwood (Chichester).

Pierce, J. R. 1969 'Whither speech recognition?' *Journal of the Acoustical Society of America* 46.1049–51.

Pinker, S. 1994 *The Language Instinct: The New Science of Language and Mind.* Allen Lane.

Pullum, G. K. 1991 *The Great Eskimo Vocabulary Hoax.* University of Chicago Press.

Quirk, R. *et al.* 1985 *A Comprehensive Grammar of the English Language.* Longman.

Reif, J. H., ed. 1993 *Synthesis of Parallel Algorithms.* Morgan Kaufmann (San Mateo, Calif.).

Reyle, U. & C. Rohrer 1988 *Natural Language Parsing and Linguistic Theories.* Kluwer.

Rumelhart, D. E. *et al.* 1986 *Parallel Distributed Processing: Explorations in the Microstructures of Cognition,* 2 vols. MIT Press.

Sampson, G. R. 1980a *Making Sense.* Oxford University Press (Oxford).

Sampson, G. R. 1980b *Schools of Linguistics: Competition and Evolution.* Hutchinson.

Sampson, G. R. 1987a 'Evidence against the "grammatical"/"ungrammatical" distinction'. In W. Meijs, ed., *Corpus Linguistics and Beyond.* Rodopi (Amsterdam).

Sampson, G. R. 1987b 'MT: a nonconformist's view of the state of the art'. In Margaret King, ed., *Machine Translation Today: The State of the Art.* Edinburgh University Press.

Sampson, G. R. 1987c Review article on Rumelhart *et al.* 1986. *Language* 63.871–86.

Sampson, G. R. 1989a 'How fully does a machine-usable dictionary cover English text?' *Literary and Linguistic Computing* 4.29–35.

Sampson, G. R. 1989b 'Language acquisition: growth or learning?' *Philosophical Papers* 18.203–40.

Sampson, G. R. 1989c 'Simulated annealing as a parsing technique'. In N. E. Sharkey, ed., *Models of Cognition: A Review of Cognitive Science,* vol. 1. Ablex (Norwood, N. J.).

Sampson, G.R. 1992 'Probabilistic parsing'. In J. Svartvik, ed., *Directions in Corpus Linguistics: Proceedings of Nobel Symposium 82.* Mouton de Gruyter.

Sampson, G. R. 1993 'Notes and queries' contribution. *Speakeasy* 28.10–11.

Sampson, G. R. 1995 *English for the Computer: The SUSANNE Corpus and Analytic Scheme.* Clarendon Press (Oxford).

Sampson, G. R. 1996 'Depth in English grammar'. To be in *Journal of Linguistics.*

Selman, B. & G. Hirst 1985 'A rule-based connectionist parsing system'. In *7th Annual conference* – Papers and programme – Cognitive Science Society. Irvine

(Calif.), August 1985.
Selman, B. & G. Hirst 1987 'Parsing as an energy minimization problem'. In Davis 1987.
Simon, G. 1976 'Computer simulation swindles, with applications to estimates of location and dispersion'. *Applied Statistics* 25.266–74.
Sommerville, I. 1992 *Software Engineering* (4th ed.). Addison-Wesley (Wokingham, Berks.).
Sontag, E. D. & H. J. Sussman 1985 'Image restoration and segmentation using the annealing algorithm'. In *Decision and control* – 24th Conference – Papers – IEEE, Control Systems Society – Society for Industrial and Applied Mathematics – ORSA. Fort Lauderdale (Fla.), December 1985.
Speech and natural language – 1st Joint workshop – Papers – Defense Advanced Research Projects Agency – Information Science and Technology Office. Philadelphia, February 1989.
Sperberg-McQueen, C. M. & L. Burnard, eds. 1994 *Guidelines for Electronic Text Encoding and Exchange (TEI P3)*. Association for Computers and the Humanities/Association for Computational Linguistics/Association for Literary and Linguistic Computing (Chicago and Oxford).
Stenström, A-B 1990 'Lexical items peculiar to spoken discourse'. In Svartvik 1990.
Svartvik, J., ed. 1990 *The London-Lund Corpus of Spoken English*. Lund University Press (Lund).
Szu, H. H. & R. Hartley 1987 'Fast simulated annealing'. *Physics Letters A* 122.157–62.

Taylor, L. *et al.* 1989 'The syntactic regularity of English noun phrases'. In *4th Conference* – Papers, abstracts and programme – Association for Computational Linguistics, European Chapter. n.p. [in fact Manchester], April 1989.
Toulouse, G. 1977 'Theory of the frustration effect in spin glasses: I'. *Communications on Physics* 2.115–19.
Tovey, C. A. 1989 'Simulated simulated annealing'. In Johnson 1989.

Unicode Consortium 1991–2 *The Unicode Standard: Worldwide Character Encoding* (Version 1.0), 2 vols. Addison-Wesley (Reading, Mass.).

Vecchi, M. P. & S. Kirkpatrick 1983 'Global wiring by simulated annealing'. *IEEE Transactions on Computer-Aided Design* CAD-2.215–22.
Voutilainen, A. 1994 *Three Studies of Grammar-Based Surface Parsing of Unrestricted English Texts*. Publication no. 24, Department of General Linguistics, University of Helsinki (Helsinki).

Wadsworth, C. 1992 'Who should think parallel?' In R. H. Perrott, ed., *Software for Parallel Computers*, Chapman & Hall.
Wilks, Y. A. 1978 'Making preferences more active'. *Artificial Intelligence* 11.197–223.
Winograd, T. 1983 *Language as a Cognitive Process, vol. 1: Syntax*. Addison-Wesley.

Yngve, V. H. 1960 'A model and an hypothesis for language structure'. *Proceedings of the American Philosophical Society* 104.444–66.

Index

Technical terms are indexed only for passages which define them.

Aarts, E. 35–6, 59, 163
Aarts, J. 20
Ada 180 n.1
Aho, A.V. 54
Allwood, J. 95
Alshawi, H. 182
Altenberg, B. 95
ambiguity 24, 29 n.3, 40
American/British flag 128 n.7
annealing schedule 37, 44
announcement system *see* text-to-speech system
APRIL dictionary 112
assembly code 11–12
Augmented Transition Network 98

Baker, J.K. 54
Barnard, S.T. 38
Basu, A. 52 n.1
Bayes's Theorem 116–18
Biber, D. 101 n.7
Black, E. 21
Boehm, B.W. 87
Boltzmann machine 28, 31
Booth, C. 180 n.6
boundary marker 67
Bounds, D.G. 31
Bridle, J.S. 82 n.4
Briscoe, E.J. 82 n.7
Brown Corpus 20 *and passim*
Burnard, L. 99
Burns, A. 164, 180 n.1

Carrasco, R.C. 186 n.1
Carroll, J. 82 n.7
case theory 98
Černý, V. 35
Chafe, W.L. 183
chip design 38–40
Chomsky, A.N. 15–17, 20, 22, 24–5, 80
Chomsky normal form 54
Church, K.W. 137
CLAWS word-tagger 24–5, 57, 101 n.8, 137
closed move-set 33, 47
co-ordination 132–3; *see also* wordlevel co-ordination
Coding Guidelines 89
Colossus 137
competence 20–2, 80–1, 94–5
compiler, compilation paradigm 11ff., 182–5
compiler-compiler 13, 19, 21
constituent 29 n.1
context-free 16–17, 54–5, 115, 130, 161
continuous flow annealing 58–9, 186
Core Language Engine 182
corpus linguistics 19ff.
CorrecText 7
Cox, D.R. 24, 33
Creutz, M. 38
currently-following node 120
CUVOALD dictionary 107–8, 135

Darwin, C.R. 30, 157
database interface 5
Davis, L. 31, 35
deadlock 160, 163
deep grammar *see* logical grammar
default tagging rules 106, 113, 117–18
Dennis, M.D. 56
depth 36–7
deterministic neighbourhood search 35, 68, 126–7, 150
deviant language 19
DragonDictate 5
Durham, T. 158, 160
dynamic programming 27, 54, 130

Engelien, B. 5
Enigma 137
entry batch indicator 128 n.7
ergodic move-set *see* closed move-set
error trapping 88
EUROTRA 98
evaluation metric 33–4, 44–6

Fawcett, R.P. 183
Fillmore, C.J. 96, 98
flat tree 46, 120–1
Francis, W.N. 20
Frazer, L.N. 52 n.1
freezing criterion 35–7
frequency of frequency 139
frustration 36
Fujisaki, T. 82 n.10

Gale, W.A. 137–9
Garside, R.G. 27, 29 n.5, 41, 58, 92, 97
Gazdar, G. 17, 182
Geman, S. & D. 39
generative grammar 15–17, 22–3, 25, 83 n.12
genetic algorithm 31
ghost elements 101, 119
Gibbons, A. 161
Gibbs, W.W. 101 n.3
Gill, S. 159
Gleick, J. 160

global minimum 32
Goldfarb, C.F. 99
Good, I.J. 137
Good-Turing technique 137–46
grammar checker 7–8, 23, 92
Grammar Evaluation Interest Group 82 n.7
grammatical idiom 82 n.9, 105–7, 110, 172
Grammatik 7
Greene, J. 37
Grune, D. 11

Hagège, C. 55
Haigh, R. 56
Hajek, B. 36
Harris, R. 155 n.3
Hartley, R. 38
head and modifiers 60–1
heraldry 111
van Herwijnen, E. 99
hesitation 95
van den Heuvel, T. 20
Higman, B. 14
Hinsley, F.H. 155 n.3
Hinton, G.E. 28
Hirst, G. 83 n.12
Hoare, C.A.R. 163
Hodges, A. 155 n.3
Holland, J.H. 31
Holmes, J.N. 54
Hornby, A.S. 128 n.7
Howell, P. 95
Huang, M.D. 35, 52 n.1
Hutchins, W.J. 4

idiom *see* grammatical idiom
inflexion pattern 128 n.7
initial symbol 14, 17
Intellect 5
International Phonetic Association alphabet 99
intonation 7
intruder, intruder loop 78, 129, 131, 134–5, 146, 149, 151, 154

Index

Jacobs, C.J.H. 11
Jacobs, R.A. 184
JáJá, J. 161
Johansson, S. 96, 101 n.7
Johnson, M.E. 35
Johnson, T. 5, 158, 160
jump arc 78

Katz, J.J. 94
Kirkpatrick, S. 35, 39
Knowles, G.K. 40
Knuth, D.E. 160
Korst, J. 35–6, 59, 163
Kučera, H. 20

van Laarhoven, P.J.M. 35
Labov, W. 20
Lakatos, I. 2
Lancaster-Leeds Treebank 26 *and passim*
language-model annealer 147–50
lattice 127 n.1;
 and see word-hypothesis lattice
Lawrence, L. 40
Leech, G.N. 20, 27
Leeds, H.D. 29 n.2
left-branching structure 121
Levelt, W.J.M. 95
linear processing 39, 68, 71
linearity 178–9
Linnaeus, C. 92, 94
load 166-7
LOB Corpus 20 *and passim*
local minimum 32
logical grammar 10–11, 57, 74–5, 85, 95–8, 100–1
logical word 104, 110, 119
London-Lund Corpus 183
loop arc 78
Lovell, M. 101 n.4
Lundy, M. 35

machine code 11–12
machine translation 4, 6, 98
Maegaard, B. 98

Mandelbrot set 160–1
Marcus, M.P. 58, 100, 186
Markov process 24
Marshall, I. 24, 137
maximally left-branching tree 121
McBryde, R. 5
McInnes, F.R. 116
Mees, A. 35
Mellish, C. 17
message understanding 5
metallurgy 35
Metropolis, N.C. 35
Miclet, L. 161
microlattice 104–7, 112–13
Miller, H.D. 24, 33
Mitton, R. 107, 128 n.7
modifier 60–1
mood class 143
Moore, R.K. 82 n.4, 95
Myers, G. 3, 65

neighbourhood relationship 33–4, 38, 59
von Neumann architecture 159
neural network 31
Nunberg, G. 101 n.6

Obermeier, K.K. 8
Occam 163–4
office-management system 5
Oncina, J. 186 n.1

Paley, W. 30
parallel processing 157–81
parser-generator *see* compiler-compiler
Pathswitch 122–5
Pennsylvania Treebank 100, 118
performance 20–2, 81, 94
Pierce, J.R. 54
Pinker, S. 16
Polytechnic of Wales Corpus 183
portability 88
prior probability 79
probabilistic dictionary 107–13, 117
production system 13–14, 16

pronunciation field 128 n.7
prototype production 78 *and passim*
Pullum, G.K. 17

Quality Plan 89–90
Quirk, R. 95

regression analysis 175–6
Reif, J.H. 161
report generation 5
Requirements Definition 88
Requirements Specification 88–9
Reyle, U. 11
Rohrer, C. 11
Rosenbaum, P.S. 184
Rumelhart, D.E. 31
Russell, B. 19–21
Rytter, W. 161

SAMPA code 128 n.7
Schützenberger, M.P. 16
secondary orthographic details 108, 110, 114
Segal, G. 29 n.6
Segmenter 106, 112
Sejnowski, T.J. 28
Selman, B. 83 n.12
sentence boundary 39, 58, 67, 91, 186
SGML 99
Simon, G. 158
Simple Good-Turing estimator 138–46
Simple, Peter 56
simulated annealing 28ff.
singular branching 26–7, 42–3, 75–6, 119–20, 125, 170
skip-and-loop network 78ff.
Software Specification 89
solution space 33, 44
Somers, H.L. 4
Sommerville, I. 87
Sontag, E.D. 39
speech repair 95
speech-to-text system 5, 22
spelling checker 7

Sperberg-McQueen, C.M. 99
spinal arc 78
Stenström, A.-B. 95
stochastic optimization 28ff.
Stripp, A. 155 n.3
Subject-Auxiliary Inversion 55, 60
Supowit, K. 37
surface grammar 10–11, 57, 74–5, 85, 95–7, 100
Surrogate Function Swindle 158
SUSANNE Corpus and analytic scheme 10, 26, 57, 59, 92 *and passim*
Sussman, H.J. 39
swindle 158
Szu, H.H. 38

tagged-word distribution 110–11
tagged-word frequency 110
tagma 29 n.1
tagmatag 10–11, 41
talkwriter *see* speech-to-text system
Taylor, L. 94
temperature 35ff.
Test Plan 89
Text Encoding Initiative 99, 101 n.7
text-to-speech system 5–7, 40, 97
Toulouse, G. 36
Tovey, C.A. 38, 59, 158
transformational grammar/rule 17, 46, 96
transputer 164
travelling salesman 33
tree size correction 65–6
tree-state 161–3
Turing, A.M. 4, 137
typographic word 104, 110

Unicode 99
universals of grammar 15
useless prototype 150
User's Guide 89

valency code 128 n.7
Vecchi, M.P. 39

vision 39, 160–1
Vodis 5
Voutilainen, A. 186 n.1

Wadsworth, C. 164, 180 n.1
Weinberg, G.M. 29 n.2
Wharton, M. 56
Wilks, Y.A. 74
William of Ockham 164
Winograd, T. 98
word-ancestor assessment 66–8, 127

word-hypothesis lattice 7, 85–6, 88, 102–7, 119–20
Word-Hypothesis Lattice Builder 106–7
word processing 5–8, 91
Word Tagger 106–15
wordlevel co-ordination 107
wordtag 10–11, 41

Yngve, V.H. 55, 121
Young, K. 95